NORMAN MAILER AT 100

ALSO BY
ROBERT J. BEGIEBING

CRITICISM

Acts of Regeneration: Allegory and Archetype
in the Work of Norman Mailer

Toward a New Synthesis: John Fowles,
John Gardner, and Norman Mailer

The Literature of Nature:
The British and American Traditions
(a critical anthology with V. Owen Grumbling)

NONFICTION

A Berkshire Boyhood: Confessions and
Reflections of a Baby Boomer

The Territory Around Us: Collected Literary
and Political Journalism, 1982-2015

NOVELS

The Strange Death of Mistress Coffin

The Adventures of Allegra Fullerton

Rebecca Wentworth's Distraction

The Turner Erotica

Conversations | *Correlations* | *Confrontations*

NORMAN MAILER AT 100

ROBERT J. BEGIEBING

Louisiana State University Press

Baton Rouge

Published with the assistance of the V. Ray Cardozier Fund

Published by Louisiana State University Press
lsupress.org

Manufactured in the United States of America
First printing

DESIGNER: Michelle A. Neustrom
TYPEFACE: MillerText
PRINTER AND BINDER: Sheridan Books, Inc.

Jacket photograph by William Coupon.

Library of Congress Cataloging-in-Publication Data
are available at the Library of Congress.

ISBN 978-0-8071-7813-3 (cloth) | ISBN 978-0-8071-7896-6 (pdf) |
ISBN 978-0-8071-7895-9 (epub)

For Linda
Whose constancy made the books possible.

CONTENTS

PREFACE

I intend this book to acknowledge and celebrate the 100th anniversary in 2023 of the birth of Norman Mailer. That year also happens to be the 75th anniversary of the publication of his first novel *The Naked and the Dead,* the book that launched him as if "shot out of a cannon," as he put it, into literary celebrity. On Mailer's significance, perhaps novelist William Kennedy, in a tribute to Mailer at the 2008 meeting at the Academy of Arts and Letters, said it best: "He was the ubiquitous radical moralist, historian, and public scourge, his readers were legion, as were his enemies, and he was a singular mind, the literary phenomenon of his generation." My hope is that the contents of the book taken together demonstrate that in 2023 Mailer is still a provocative presence in American letters; that he is part of our larger American literary landscape from the debates of our founders, to the traditions of Western Romanticism, and to the whole juggernaut of twentieth-century modernism; that he is, moreover, prescient in his social and political criticisms of American society and therefore still speaks to us today, if we are willing to listen.

Norman Mailer at 100 is a hybrid collection of critical essays, a dramatic dialogue, an imaginary interview, and my interview with Mailer for *Harvard Magazine* on his Brooklyn boyhood, his Harvard years, and the composition of *Ancient Evenings.* Ralph Waldo Emerson, Walt Whitman, Carl Jung, Ernest Hemingway (twice), Kate Millett, Joan Didion, and historian Joseph Ellis are the seven figures I connect with Mailer through eight chapters. The authors listed are some of those who influenced Mailer, with whom he discovered literary empathy, or whose themes and social/political critiques correlate with Mailer's or spark debate. They are also authors who help us open a way into Mailer's life and work when we yoke them with Mailer through an essay or conversation. This book is not without literary analysis but is largely contextual: highlighting Mailer's responses to literary influences, global and American politics, contemporary societies, economic inequity, and war. It is this contextual (and intertextual) nature of the book that I hope will provoke fresh interest in Mailer not only for scholars but also for that "legion" of educated readers to which Kennedy referred.

D oes Mailer matter? He is obviously a controversial figure. But one might as well ask whether any major American author from the past matters to us in our distracted twenty-first century. In Mailer's case we should consider a few basic facts of his life and work. Although he was often in conflict with the American literary establishment and spoke out about its failings, he was, nonetheless, also richly honored by that establishment. Anyone who has achieved two Pulitzer Prizes, a National Book Award, the National Book Foundation Medal for Distinguished Contribution to American Letters, the Presidency of PEN America, the Harvard University Signet Medal for Achievement in the Arts (twice), the Emerson-Thoreau Medal from the American Academy of Arts and Sciences, the cofounding of *The Village Voice*, some forty books of fiction and nonfiction, uncountable essays and speeches and interviews, and four produced films has to matter to the literary culture.

Moreover, the Mailer archives held in the University of Texas Harry Ransom Center demonstrate Mailer's decades-long involvement with numerous writers of all levels of achievement, with important periodicals and publishers, with universities, and with other organizations that contribute to our literary culture. He was a public figure for so long, with his flawed humanity so often on display that—sometimes his own worst enemy—he has given the gatekeepers of academic anthologies, among others, ample material to choose from when arguing for his insignificance to us, when removing and embargoing him from anthologies of American literature. But as Toni Morrison put it in introducing Mailer at the National Book Award Lifetime Achievement dinner in 2005 (after noting, not without some justification, his "obtuseness regarding women"), Mailer is such a "carnivorous intelligence accompanied by huge and provocative talent" that the "history of American literature in the 20th and early 21st century would be both depleted and inaccurate, minus the inclusion of the work of Norman Mailer."

One thing the gatekeepers seem not to understand is that Mailer continually revises and reshapes his ideas, reinventing himself and his works. He is on a journey. Any work or public appearance is a stop along the way. Critics, especially academics, too often approach a book or public appearance as merely a concretized artifact, rather than part of an author's larger, evolving process. Any ideological flaws they detect condemn a work or its author and ignore the authorial quest, the untidy journey of a committed life. No major American writer has been at once so prolific and so misunderstood. As Joan Didion pointed out, with typical acerbity, in her 1979 review of *The Executioner's Song* in the *New York Times:* "It is one of those testimonies to self-regard in the literary life that large numbers of people remain persuaded that Norman Mailer is no better than *their* reading of him."

Mailer matters as well to our broader culture. The sheer number of his often-controversial television appearances as a public intellectual, trickster-provocateur, and latter-day Jeremiah alone should claim for him an impact on American society and popular culture from the middle twentieth through the early twenty-first centuries. *Advertisements for Myself* (1959) is *the* transitional text in his corpus and in retrospect feels prophetic. He anticipated in that book the looming world of the sixties: the countercultures, the sexual revolution, the obsession with politics, the antiwar movement, and the new immersive and personal forms of nonfiction and fiction. He spoke out about or was fully engaged with the civil rights movement, civil disobedience against the war in Vietnam, the 1970s flowering of the women's liberation movement, the space program, political conventions, and the big prize fights. In his keynote address celebrating the inauguration of the Mailer archives at the Ransom Center, Morris Dickstein said, "You could no doubt write a history of the age through Mailer's idiosyncratic involvement in it." From *Advertisements* on through his political reporting and such collections as *The Presidential Papers, Cannibals and Christians, The Time of Our Time, Why Are We at War?* to *The Big Empty* in 2006, Mailer has written through his original vision and protean styles about the celebrities and the political, economic, and social issues of our time. He was a central innovator in the participatory and New Journalism of the sixties and seventies, opening forever boundaries between genres and demonstrating that writing itself is a medium of intimate discovery in our postmodern reality. (Mailer's working sense of the fluidity among genres has encouraged me to offer a mix of genres in this book about him, to place "face-to-face" dialogues, real and invented, beside essays that reflect more the dialogic nature of those internal exchanges, familiar to any writer, with one's distant literary forbears and contemporaries). There are also a half-dozen Mailer biographies and there are his fat FBI file and his 160 weeks total on the *New York Times* Best Seller Lists over fifty-nine years. David Remnick once referred to Mailer as "the American Balzac." Arthur Schlesinger Jr., in his citation during Mailer's induction into the American Academy of Arts and Letters in 1984, said of Mailer: "In a career of living dangerously, he has shown qualities of passion, imagination, literary power and psychological subtlety that will surely make posterity regard him as one of the giants—if at times a wounded giant—of our age."

Mailer's works and remarks, I would add, can seem at once timely and timeless; that is, they carry both popular and historical interest; they have the potential to stand the test of time that other more commonly acceptable insights expressed in our mass media by commentators inhaling heavily off the popular zeitgeist do not. Like some Old Testament prophet (our Hosea, Micah, Amos, or Jeremiah?), he saw the "creative rage" of "Almighty prose" as "God's Broadsword." As Houston Smith reminds us in *The World's Religions*: "The great writing prophets could sense God's disapproval of injustices that . . . were perpetrated not by individuals . . . but that were concealed in the social fabric. . . . The Writing Prophets challenged corruptions in the social order and oppressive institutions." One might make a case that this prophetic tradition is the Jewish root of Mailer's life and antinomian work.

To suggest just one recommendation for encountering Mailer's prophetic broadsword of almighty prose, we might read, or read again, his intimate reporting on the 1968 presidential conventions in *Miami and the Siege of Chicago*. Mailer in his orotund style does not so much convince readers as sweep them along, beyond agreement/disagreement—like some latter-day Melville or Ruskin—in cataracts of prose. Lengthy catalogues of detail, quick-changing sequences of metaphor, startling aperçu, quick and revelatory character sketches, and sonorous rhythms are on full display, as they are in the better-known *Armies of the Night*. Out of such stylistic energy and detail, the reader finds, ultimately, an analysis that is of continuing pertinence to us today. Our current political factions, follies, and foibles—our nation at war with itself—look familiar in that political coverage from a half-century ago, reminding us how high a mountain we too will have to climb if we hope to reclaim vibrant democracy in America.

Some chapters more obviously than others reveal their connections between Mailer and us today—whether on women's rights, on democracy in the twenty-first century, or on the necessity of authors to maintain a dissident distance from their cultures, whether they live in Russia, China, America, or any other country. But my chapters connecting Mailer with canonical authors are also pertinent for us today, beyond the obvious fact that those authors are canonical because they still resonate if we attend to them. Emerson helps us understand Mailer's sense of the need for dissent and self-reliance against the pressures of mass society; Whitman helps us understand better Mailer's fears and hopes for democracy; and Hemingway throws into relief Mailer's own young man's experience of war as an essentially criminal act, whether the year is 1916, 1944, or 2020. Even reading my 1983 interview with Mailer in *Harvard Magazine* as he talks about his theories regarding the social and environmental evils of plastics (theories he's held since the early sixties), we see but one example of his enduring pertinence and prescience. Moreover, the interview covers Mailer's entire life and career up to the early eighties—his boyhood, the Harvard years, the Army, and the ten-year composition of his novel in progress, *Ancient Evenings*. As a celebration of the author's 100th birthday, the interview (my own "conversation" with Mailer) is the only chapter that adds such a dimension of expansive biographical coverage to this collection celebrating that centenary.

Each reader of Mailer no doubt has a story to tell about how Mailer became of significance to her or him. In my case, I was in my twenties when I started reading him, not only *The Naked and the Dead* but *Advertisements for Myself, The Presidential Papers*, and *Cannibals and Christians*. Those books became my way in. I recall thinking after reading them that I had the same reaction my father (an engineer and musician who didn't read much literature) had upon first reading the copy of *Walden* I had given him for Christmas. "Jesus, Bob," my father said in a telephone call thanking me. "Somebody finally went and said it!" Mailer, too, I later discovered, unlike the mass of his postwar contemporaries, finally went and said it!

ACKNOWLEDGMENTS

Most of the essays and dialogues in this book were published in earlier versions in periodicals, most notably in *The Mailer Review*, edited by Professor Phillip Sipiora of the University of South Florida. I am indebted to Professor Sipiora for his advice, encouragement, and editorial imagination and eye. Mailer's authorized biographer and archivist, J. Michael Lennon, read all but one piece in an early draft and offered commentary that added substantially to the quality of the final document. Moreover, Professor Lennon's generosity with unpublished and other archival materials fostered whatever originality this book might lay claim to. This book, therefore, owes much of whatever distinction it has achieved to these two scholars.

Along the way, colleagues and friends have read an essay or dialogue and saved me from myself by their insightful commentary and suggestions. Among these, I owe special thanks to Merle Drown, Owen Grumbling, Diane LesBecquets, Gerald Lucas, Wes McNair, Erik Nakjavani, and Paul Sweeney. My interview with Mailer for *Harvard Magazine* was much improved by the legendary skills of former editor John Bethell. Many colleagues in the Norman Mailer Society over the years have inspired me with their essays and conference papers, discussions and debates, and convivial exchange of ideas. To one and all, my heartfelt thank you.

NORMAN MAILER AT 100

1

MAILER AND HEMINGWAY

Epistolary Backgrounds to Their Generational War Novels

> I was one of the few writers of my generation who was concerned with
> living in Hemingway's discipline . . . that probably I could not become a
> very good writer unless I learned first how to keep my nerve, and what is
> more difficult, learned how to find more of it.
>
> —NORMAN MAILER, *Advertisements for Myself* (265)

Norman Mailer and Ernest Hemingway spoke for their respective generations (as if for fathers and sons) with war novels that catapulted two young authors to best-seller celebrity. They wrote of two different world wars in two different theaters, focused their novels differently through their point-of-view techniques, and told either a love story (Hemingway's *A Farewell to Arms*, 1929) or a story of repressed lusts (Mailer's *The Naked and the Dead*, 1948). Hemingway was already a published novelist; Mailer, though published, was not. (Mailer referred to *The Naked and the Dead* as "a best-seller that was the work of an amateur" in his introduction to the Henry Holt 50th anniversary edition [xi]). Yet both authors were writing during their twenties about the disillusionments and the absurdities of war, and about the competency of a few and the incompetency of the many trapped in battle zones together. Both authors divide their narratives into a clear dramatic structure (five acts for Hemingway, four acts for Mailer). Both authors owe a substantial debt to the European and American literary naturalists who came before them; both embrace twentieth-century literary modernism as well. In the aftermath of success, both commit to live fully engaged lives that inspire their work rather than to suppress their lives in service to their literary work (to live more like Stephen Crane than Henry James). Both discover in the writing of their war novels a durable theme—the dissenting "criticism of society," as Michael Reynolds, quoting Edmund Wilson, so aptly argued for Hemingway (282).

Comparing the letters of each author over similar issues can feel at times like a sort of scripted dialogue, even though the other author is absent but potentially present (or even imagined). The dialogic nature of compared letters between two correspondents not writing to one another may feel at times, as well, like what occurs when we carry on our internal dialogues or dialogues with distant others. But internal and distant dialogues are some of the ways we make sense of the world and our place in it. Such comparing of authors' letters, moreover, can help us arrive at a more nuanced understanding of their published work as well.

I suspect that yet another close analysis of either novel would not reveal much that feels new. But after reading the first four volumes of the *Letters of Ernest Hemingway* from Cambridge University Press (2011–2018) and the *Selected Letters of Norman Mailer* from Random House (2014), I noticed some resonant correlations among the instigating forces behind the two novels and between the two authors' experiences of publication and the aftermath of success. Hemingway's focus is on the common humanity of a man and woman in love amidst the chaos of war; Mailer's focus is on the humanity of the common man at war. The letters, offering us a look behind the scenes, reveal not only both authors' personal travails and triumphs but their common humanity as well.

First, let's grant the most significant difference between the two war stories. Hemingway's is as much a love story (and in letters to Max Perkins, his editor, he was insistent on selling the novel as such) as it is a war story. Mailer is writing in a more expansive and naturalistic tradition of men at war, men without women beyond male memories and repressed longings (id and eros over atrophied agape, so to speak). But that difference comes out of each man's experience at the time of deployment, Mailer as a conscripted infantry grunt in the Pacific Islands, Hemingway as an American Red Cross volunteer ambulance corps driver with the honorary or assimilated rank of second lieutenant, attached to the Italian Army. Hemingway was young and single and had fallen in love with the woman who nursed his battlefield wounds, Agnes von Kurowsky; Mailer was a newlywed, in love with his wife Bea. More important from a scholarly perspective, Mailer's letters to Bea served as his writer's notebook from which he drew his material—characters, settings, incidents, themes. Neither Mailer nor the male characters in his novel were immersed in both combat *and* courtship, as Hemingway and his protagonist were. One result is that Hemingway's naturalistic themes—lost illusions, the role of Fate in our lives, the biological trap connected to that Fate, an uncaring or absent God, the animality of wounded bodies in combat or in childbirth, the violence and irrationality and existential absurdity brought forth in war, the coarse expressions of male lust, and so on—are temporarily ameliorated by an intervention, the intervention of that most "unnaturalistic" experience of love, of love's authentic commitments, of the lovers' search for the "good place" or the "home" to nurture that love as a stay against the predatory world. If you cannot escape Fate, you can experience something like self-transcendence for a time through love. Something akin to religious feeling, as the priest and Count Greffi remind Lieutenant Henry. The shits may kill you, all right, but they cannot own your deeper, hard-earned, independent (loving) self.

In Mailer's novel, no such intervention in the naturalistic themes occurs. Indeed, Mailer was feeling too locked in to the naturalistic tradition of his first published novel (he wrote two apprentice novels earlier, both already showing Hemingway's influence) as he worked on his second. He acknowledged this problem in a letter to Warren Allen Smith of *The Humanist* on 20 February 1951. He had been looking back on *The Naked and the Dead* during the writing of *Barbary Shore* and transitioning to the stranger, more "visionary," more political and allegorical writing of his second published novel.

> In the past my writing has always been influenced by the naturalists but I am coming more and more to feel a certain uneasiness, a certain doubt, as to how fruitful this tradition will continue to be. The problem which confronts the serious novelist today . . . is to enlarge his consciousness to the limit of his ability, and in the process so much is accumulated that the old comfortable forms of naturalism can no longer express his intent. . . . [T]he personal problem I feel is to surmount the

creative hurdles which Marx and Freud present, rather than substituting a reactionary and static set of premises. (*Selected Letters* 103)

EPISTOLARY RESOURCES OF THE NOVELS

We now know that Mailer intentionally wrote to Bea not only to express his love but to request that she save the letters to document his experiences of men, combat, tactics, landscapes, and ideas as resources in helping him compose his war novel once he returned home. "Hello, again, baby,—I'm going to send my notes like this—it's better than keeping them in a book," he writes to Bea in October of 1945 (*Selected Letters* 43). Stationed in Japan that March, and after months of sending descriptive letters to Bea, he asks again: "Darling, as a little project, will you separate all my letters that have things in them written about this novel. . . . I think I first conceived it back in Ord in October [1944]" (54). The novel, then, was conceived before he shipped out and experienced the combatant's life depicted in the novel. And once he did ship on the USS *Sea Barb* at the end of 1944, the epistolary "notebook" began, even at sea heading to the Philippines. While at sea Mailer witnessed a Pacific sunset: magical islands appearing miragelike and existing "only in mankind's dream" in the glow of many hues "compressed by the overcast into a band of brilliant striations" (21–23). He later refers to the sunset again and tells Bea he will get the sunset/island/the jungle/mountain vision into the book as a symbol of "the birth struggle" the men will be going through, "suggesting the deeper meaning of their lives most men never see" (49). Rather than using that sunset as it happened en route to the Philippines, Mailer will save that now symbolic vision until late in the novel, as the men huddling off-shore by the back of Anopopei Island in a surreptitious landing craft are about to start out on their "birth struggle"—that long, climactic patrol to Mount Anaka in search of a passage behind enemy lines: "The men stared and stared. The island hovered before them like an Oriental monarch's conception of heaven, and they responded to it with an acute and terrible longing" (*Naked* 453–54).

Some of the men Mailer finds in the various units he joins are the most translatable element from epistle to novel. In Mailer's letters, Croft, Wilson, Martinez, Red, and Ridges are, in varying degrees of detail, first described or "booked" into his epistolary notebook.

Croft is unusual not only because of the detail devoted to him in letters and novel (more than any other character) but because he was based on platoon sergeant Donald Mann, under whom Mailer trained at Fort Bragg *before* he was deployed. "A man of medium height who held himself so erectly he appeared tall. His narrow, triangular face was utterly without expression. . . . He hated weakness and he loved practically nothing," rarely conscious of "the crude unformed vision in his soul," as Mailer translates Croft into *Naked* (156). Sergeant Mann is also a recognizable Army type, an uncannily similar character in appearance and language to the platoon sergeant I had during my own basic training at Fort Devens, a generation later. But in the novel, Croft will take on a central, Melvillian role, as the one driven mad by his obsessions and by those obsessions driving the others under his command through a hell of their own on Mount Anaka. Descriptions of Croft in the novel are frequent, including a long Time Machine episode, but as Mailer tells Bea, his "vision sergeant" is the very center of the novel as "an archetype of all the dark, bitter, inarticulate, capable & brooding men that America spawns," another American "demoniac . . . like Ahab in *Moby Dick*" (*Selected Letters* 50). There are other parallels between the Croft of the novel and the Mann of the letters. But since Mailer wishes his incidents to arise out of character (not character out of plot, as he tells Bea), the situations he places Croft in, as with the others who are described in the letters, are what make the characters come alive (47). And the situations are sometimes described in the letters as well before they occur in the novel.

One of the foundational incidents defining Croft's character is based on a story Mailer heard from another soldier who was alone with a sergeant "noted for his cruelty" at an outpost where they had captured a Japanese soldier. Mailer's epistolary account of the incident is replicated in Croft's speech and actions in part 2, chapter 7, of the novel; Croft had treated the prisoner with water, food, and a smoke as if he were being friendly, only to put a bullet in the prisoner's head immediately thereafter (*Selected Letters* 48). The sadistic incident (which Mailer tells Bea about twice) is all the more senseless because as sergeant of a Recon platoon it's Croft's *job* to bring back all incidental captives and their documentary evidence to Headquarters Intelligence (G-2) for interrogation and analysis. The exception would be when Recon is sent specifically on a search-and-destroy mission, as they are at another point described in Mailer's letters (29–34).

———

In the sadistic episode, however, Croft is in part purging his moment of uncharacteristic weakness as he sat alone in a machine-gun foxhole on guard duty. This moment in the novel is in turn based on two things that appear in the letters to Bea. First, another story Mailer heard regarding a GI on guard alone facing across the Driniumor River in New Guinea a much larger force of Japanese soldiers crying out, "Yank . . . Yank . . . we're coming to get you Yank" (*Letters* 51). Croft's experience of terror, of uncharacteristic weakness, inspires not only his rage for revenge on the lone prisoner but his obsession for conquest against the mountain that is blocking the platoon's final patrol from accomplishing its mission.

Secondly, Croft's terror is based on one of Mailer's earliest combat experiences, even before joining the reconnaissance platoon, as he too sat alone guarding a stretch of river with a machine gun. In this second source, the physiological and psychological reaction to the enormous pressure of imminent attack and death that Mailer details in his letters are transplanted to his description of Croft's own moment of terror in the novel (*Naked* 146–55), just as those physiological details of combat fear will be to other men, such as Roth, also on guard alone at a machine-gun emplacement (113–16) and Martinez on a solo recon mission during the final patrol to the Mountain, armed only with his trench knife (586–98). Mailer described his own intensification of physical responses to combat in a letter to Bea in April of 1945: a "sensation of not exactly fear. . . . But awareness so acute that it approached pain and fear. . . . a tension like hot steel from collar bone to collar bone that seemed to lock my throat. . . . I was sweating tremendously." The unreal amplification and focus of one's senses is also an important part of the physical response. On that patrol Mailer ended up guarding alone a section of creek when "the pressure against my throat seemed completely constricting" (*Selected Letters* 26–27).

A month later, Mailer is writing to Bea another memory note "to purge" another intensification of body and mind while on a search-and-destroy mountain patrol. Mailer was weak from "grippe," stepped on a Japanese corpse that exhaled grotesque odors, and ascended the mountain with agonies of exertion. "That hill became alive," he reports; "I hated it with more fervor than I could possibly any human being. . . . I was discovering that you can never plumb the last agony of exertion" (30–34). It was on this patrol also that the platoon stepped into a hornet's nest, an incident that will figure during the climactic ascent of Mount Anaka and the first of two final turns of combat absurdity. In a comic scene following upon agonies and deaths, the hornets will disband the debilitated remainder of Croft's deadly patrol, a patrol that was futile anyway because, in the final turn of combat futility and absurdity, the campaign for the island is already won. As Polack puts it, "And we broke our ass for nothin'" (*Naked* 700–705). The final turn happens when Major Dalleson is left in charge of operations at Division Headquarters while General Cummings is away seeking naval support to enhance a tactical invasion to break up the Japanese line of defenses. Slowly muddling and blundering his way in operational planning, Dalleson isn't even aware that the enemy has been ground down, their leadership killed, their medical facilities exhausted, their ammunition and supply dumps blown. A reality "the official history of the campaign" will ignore (647–57, 705).

We see from the letters, then, how Mailer's own suffering on guard and on patrol will be shared later by the characters in his novel. As J. Michael Lennon points out in his endnote to Mailer's letter to Bea, once he was transferred to Recon Platoon, Mailer went on about twenty-five patrols, including some skirmishes and firefights and could not have written the last third of the novel without such experience (748). As Mailer will tell Bea in an unpublished letter: "Moments of combat were the only positive thing I ever got out of the army," referring to the tension, utter absorption, and release of combat (ms. 14 September 1945). Lennon, with typical generosity, supplied me with twenty-two as yet *unpublished* letters from Mailer's time in the Army; future citations from those manuscript epistles will appear as above (ms. [i.e., manuscript] and date).

Two other characters are worthy examples of their first appearance in Mailer's letters. Wilson is based on two G.I. friends, Amerson (a man afflicted with venereal disease and other ailments in contrast to "his former robustness") and another soldier who would become Mailer's lifelong friend, Francis Gwaltney ("a Welshman by way of Arkansas"), with his "magnificent tongue," as he tells Bea. Wilson will become the source of much of the GI humor throughout the novel and the source of much revelation of other characters during their greatest extremity of labor and fear on the long trek back to the boat from the platoon's debacle on Mt. Anaka. Mailer planned this episode as a means to switch viewpoints back and forth

7

"from bearer to bearer to wounded man" while Wilson lies dying and while his comrades suffer. In an obvious reference to *As I Lay Dying*, Mailer tells Bea he "wants it [the bearing of Wilson's wounded and then dead body] to be Faulknerian" (*Selected Letters* 37, 43, 55).

Another major character gets substantial mention in the letters before he appears in the novel. "There's a character I want to get into the jungle novel," Mailer writes to Bea from Choshi, Japan, in October of 1945. "He was my section sergeant in Recon back on Luzon . . . Ysidro Martinez. A Mexican, soft-spoken, shy, deceitful like an animal in the brush, and he demonstrated more courage than any man I've ever known. Not bravery, for he was not brave, and after the campaigns & 30 months overseas he was very scared. . . . obsessed by the feeling that his number was up." Before a patrol he was nervous and moody; on guard he often had the shakes–"And yet, he always picked himself to lead the most dangerous patrols." He was "a complex man" (41–42). Martinez demonstrates "courage," which Mailer defines earlier for Bea as "the triumph of the body for it is the mind that plays the coward and the body that surmounts its agony and keeps the muscles moving. . . . It is an illumination of the greatness in man but is lost in all the brutality and slaughter" (35). He will demonstrate further planning of Martinez's character in a letter to Bea from Japan about trying to capture "the wonderful complexity of the man" (ms. 9 February 1946). In a later letter to his parents Mailer develops the idea of courage further: "I've learned in the Army about physical courage and mental courage. . . . some of the more obscure and frightening reaches of men's souls. . . . These are ordinary men asked to perform an extraordinary job. . . . I think I can set up a little epic" (*Selected Letters* 52). He must be aware of echoing here Melvillian and Whitmanesque epics of the common man. The best fictional development of the kind of courage he described, even if futile, Mailer depicts in that final solo reconnaissance Martinez carries out.

Some major characters, such as Lieutenant Hearn and Red receive relatively brief mention in the letters, despite their large presence in the novel. Red is a good example. Red Matthiesen is the guy, Mailer writes to Bea, who says, "If there is a god, he must be a sonofabitch." And adds that "there isn't anything special about the animal that can smell as bad as a dead man" (44). As he moves through the novel, Red Valsen is like an olfactory organ detailing the smell and physical condition of the many corpses the platoon encounters, decaying corpses who also appear at moments among Mailer's letters to Bea. And through his long biographical Time Machine episode, we come to see Red as the quintessential working-class man on the road during the Depression, as Mailer describes him first to Bea: "A Norwegian from Montana about thirty . . . utterly unsentimental" but "very intelligent and quite sensitive," under "the hardness" (*Selected Letters* 222–35; ms. 19 August 1945). Red, who became Mailer's taciturn but respected friend, was a short-timer—one who had been in the Pacific theater much longer and getting due for rotation out—who had the suppressed "nightmare" short-timers carry with them after months of brutal experience: the feeling that their number is up, as Mailer explains to Bea (ms. 6 April 1946). This nightmarish fear Mailer encapsulates in an episode, first described to Bea, where Red's tommy gun jams as he is about to shoot for the hell of it into a "dead" Japanese soldier, who then rises for a bayonet charge at Red, who in turn is saved only by a bullet into the soldier from Croft.

Deeper by the day into the planning of his novel while stationed in Japan, Mailer tells Bea in November of 1945 that he is making a list of all the men he can recall clearly, a dozen or so, and working out their relations to the other men and to the mountain, the central obstacle, danger, and symbol of his novel. Out of that list the characters will come "a few as themselves and a half dozen more as synthetics of several." Especially important, he tells Bea, will be each man's "view toward the mountain," which views should "generate story business" (47). How the men look at the mountain will be, Mailer writes to Bea, "an effective way to anchor the symbol of the mountain range to the story and the emotions of the men in it" (ms. 19 August 1945). Through the device of Ahab's doubloon nailed to the mast in the "Doubloon" chapter in *Moby Dick*, each mariner reveres the doubloon as the white whale's talisman, while viewing it expresses something of his character, motivation, and fate. So too in Mailer's novel: each soldier's view of Mailer's organizing symbol, Mount Anaka, informs the reader of something essential about the soldier's individual character, his motivations, and his fate in the platoon's climactic moments of the novel. For Croft the mountain is a taunt or challenge that inflames him, a hunger, an ecstasy connected to his murder of the prisoner. It beckons him, "held an answer to something he wanted," but Lieutenant Hearn was balking him from challenging the mountain. As the patrol wears on, the mountain seems, as the whale to Ahab, more like "a personal affront." To Gallagher it is terrifying in its size but also an absorbing beauty, all that he found unobtainable in his life. To Red, the cynical realist, it is a vague harassment, a gloom, but also an indifference. To Lieutenant Hearn, who wrote *A Study of the Cosmic Urge in Herman Melville* as his thesis at Harvard, the mountain is troubling, awesome, fearsome, too immense, too powerful, the emblem of a titanic struggle between ocean and mountainous land. The slopes of Anaka, as it will turn out, are the locus of Hearn's own death. To General Cummings, the mountain is "the axis of the island, its keystone," like the General himself, "bleak and alone commanding the heights," but also the potential path to his defeat of the Japanese Army (*Naked* 447–48, 497, 527, 563). We see once again that a good deal of the material of composition for the novel has been worked out in Mailer's mind and letters before he returns home to Brooklyn to begin composing the manuscript.

I recall from my first reading of *Naked* many years ago my surprise at Mailer's knowledge of officers' lives and of tactics and strategy. Mailer doesn't seem to miss much wherever he is (and in whatever condition of sobriety or inebriety). As Robert Lowell told Dwight Macdonald in *Esquire*, reflecting on the 1967 March on the Pentagon: "When you're with another novelist, you think he's so sensitive and alert and you find later he wasn't taking in anything, while Norman seems not to pay attention but now it seems he didn't miss a trick—and what a memory!" (Macdonald 42). But in Mailer's letters we see another reason for this low-level grunt's knowledge of the larger picture, a knowledge that proves crucial to his depiction of officers, operations, and tactics in the novel. His early assignment in Luzon, he writes to his parents in February of 1945, is in the Headquarters of the 112th Regimental Combat Team. He serves as a clerk in the Intelligence Section, "which is really a good break . . . It means being more in on things, and getting a completer picture of what is going on. . . . I'm seeing things. . . . and work directly under a Major and Lieutenant, which is closer than I've been to officers since I've been in the army" (*Selected Letters* 23–24).

Mailer describes for Bea his first view of a battle zone in a jeep ride out to the front with a captain and others from HQ. He first offers Bea a disquisition on battlefield strategy and tactics, including those leading to the localized defeat of the Japanese. But what he witnesses on that "first time out" to a devasted town where the Japanese had been holding out deeply entrenched is for him "a landmark" experience. At the time, it gives him a "strange elation," like that of "a youth after his first trip to a brothel." What he saw and smelled was "a hybrid of a junkyard and a charnel house," twisted machinery and corpses like "badly mutilated dolls." Only later did his unconscious, he reports, allow the shock to emerge into consciousness (ms. 24–26 February 1945).

From his experiences in combat and in Headquarters' Intelligence Section, Mailer's themes emerge first in the letters. One is the absurdity ("the familiar unreality of war") and dehumanizing destructiveness of mechanized warfare, an echo of Hemingway's own theme. The irrationality of war will climax, as I've said, at the novel's conclusion, but Mailer describes for Bea in a letter of 4 June 1945, just after he has become a *machine* gunner, the landscape after battle of "roiled bodies and the crickets in the bright green grass, the smoking charred tank with the stiff black corpses like articulated wire dolls and the scarlet peas lying sweet and clean near the turret," indicating not a God that is good but one that is "excited by the fascinating dualities he has created and very often sits back to see how the play will come out. . . . He is utterly without compassion" (*Selected Letters* 35–36).

He writes to Bea that he now agrees with Henry Adams on "the psychological relation between men and machinery" (ms. 11 July 1945). Then, in August of 1945 he is opining to Bea about "how I am becoming pathological about machines" and about when another war comes, if not in twenty then in another fifty years, it will be with the atom bomb as "the final victory of the machine." He sees our worship of the machine in the sailors and airmen who give their instruments personifying names, but the "machine is so deceptive a fellow, so benign for so long that they forget it has a fuse. . . . We have come to the age when we love machines and hate women. The next step is religious awe, and the atom bomb looks like the last deity." And in part through mechanization, we are arriving at the age of authoritarian rule, totalitarianism or fascism, where "the world will be controlled by a few men, politicians and technicians—Spengler's men of the late West-European-American civilization" (Selected *Letters* 38–40).

His next letter to Bea develops this theme. The allies are not winning the war against fascism so much as they are laying the groundwork for an organized state under a "triumphant Caesar . . . the leader symbol," embodied in the Army by the "mass-will in this nation . . . against the professed principles of the Democratic Christian state" (43). It will be General Cummings, starting with his conversations with Lieutenant Hearn in the first half of the novel, who will carry this theme of the looming, postwar authoritarian-organizational state. Not only the fascism the Americans are fighting but the new fascism and authoritarianism that is coming, that the armies of the world have prepared us for in our postwar world, "the Big Lie," as Cummings says, that kept Hitler in power over millions of his own people: "he was the interpreter of twentieth-century man." As Hearn learns, any hint of resistance or dissent is met with power disciplining downwards against resistance. To Cummings, Gandhi and passive resistance are laughable. "Historically the purpose of this war is to translate America's potential into kinetic energy," the organizational and coordinating energy of a country, Cummings points out. Man's "deepest urge is omnipotence. . . . To achieve God." And "the only morality of the future is a power morality. . . . You can consider the Army, Robert, as a preview of the future. . . . The only way you generate the proper attitude of awe and obedience is through the immense and disproportionate power" (*Naked* 313, 318, 320–24). At this point in Mailer's letters, we see two things: how an idea may also drive a character and how Mailer early on expressed his lifelong obsession (in both his writing and public statements) with authoritarian power, with fascism and totalitarianism, as transformed from the middle through the late twentieth century and beyond.

While in Japan formulating his novel, Mailer also becomes aware of a looming issue that is bound to stalk him throughout the composition and publishing of the novel—censorship. "The only question is how much profanity I'll be able to get into print. . . . it's impossible to get the G.I.'s speech across without larding in the fuck, piss, cock, shit, cunt which flows so naturally in the most basic sentences," he says in a letter to Bea (*Selected Letters* 56). Indeed, profanity was one of the problems that Little, Brown publishers raised when Mailer was back on the home front working on the novel. His October 1946 letter to junior editor Adeline Lubell Naiman (former Radcliffe roommate of Bea's sister and friend of Mailer's sister Barbara) addresses the issue: "On the profanity (here we go again) I am feeling weak and battered. . . . I've insisted all along that it's a pigment in the complete picture." He then cites Farrell's Studs Lonigan trilogy, "a successful novel," as part of a plea for better understanding on this point. He takes the opportunity to enter a complaint that he will charge against American publishers for the rest of his career: however "good or poor the novel may be it's a damn sight better than a lot of novels which are being advertised right now. . . . I do feel that if publishers have any driving ethic other than becoming big business they have as great a moral debt to an author as an author has to them. A serious author is a rare phenomenon today, and he ought to be nurtured" (59–60). He will repeat his complaints about censorship and publishers' duty toward serious writers a month later and with more efficiency to Little, Brown's Angus Cameron, editor-in-chief (63–64).

Later, when Rinehart takes the novel on, Mailer agrees to resolve the problem by way of making some cuts on his own, about one-fifth of the previous profanity, as he told Louise Levitas in 1948 (Levitas 3). In the published novel he will turn such phrasing as "blow it out your ass" to "blow it out" and use an occasional dash (—). He had previously decided to use "fug" for fuck. Still, a surprising number of profane words remain, given his initial problems with Little, Brown. The Rinehart editors were more tolerant, but in a long letter to William Raney, his Rinehart editor, Mailer insisted on delivering a long rationale about his fears of editorial cuts to profanity, asked for some deletions to be restored, and argued that legal history has made his work acceptable to pass through the mails. That letter of 7 February 1948 is worth reading as the most complete explication of his logic in the use of GI profanity (*Selected Letters* 67–72). But by March, after reading the galleys, Mailer sees that his novel has been left largely intact, despite his fears (72–73).

Censorship was an even more significant issue a generation earlier with *A Farewell to Arms*, as we will see. But Hemingway and Mailer shared another concern during the editorial process that Mailer expressed in that same long February letter to Raney—cover art. Mailer disliked the apparent fact that the phony "Ernie Pyle version" of the fatigued soldier to be used for advertising (which he was willing to accept for that purpose alone) was being carried over to the book jacket. He would prefer something plain to that, he would pay himself for an artist to do a cover he liked if necessary, and he would even prefer "some sort of mass ensemble of activity with a few soldiers in the foreground" to indicate America (70–72). (The first edition used a black cover with an abstracted line drawing of a soldier in a red rectangle, closer to one of Mailer's suggestions as being an acceptable design.)

F or Hemingway the censorship issue arose while he was doing final revisions and proofreading galleys. His letters to Max Perkins represent a substantial back-and-forth on the topic. Hemingway's concern heightened in February and March of 1929, well before the publication of the novel itself, while it was being published serially in *Scribner's Magazine*. Editor Robert Bridges had cut and replaced a number of words Hemingway had not approved, even though Perkins had assured him no changes would be made without approval (*Letters* v. 3, 527–28, 535–36, 549–50, 551). (The June *Scribner's Magazine* was banned in Boston anyway.) And if there are to be any substitutions of blanks (long dashes) for words, he tells Perkins, then "I want the blanks to indicate what the word is" (v. 4, 23). He later tells Thornton Wilder the novel "reads like tripe in the magazine. . . . They cut the guts out of it" (v. 4, 39). "I never use a word if I can avoid it," he had assured Perkins earlier, "but if I must have it I know it." In a later exchange in July, Hemingway reminds Perkins that he compared *Farewell* to Erich Maria Remarque's *All Quiet on the Western Front* as an example of a commercially successful novel despite the use of some of the same words, because "no words stood out and the sincerity of the book carried it." He had referred Perkins to a statement in Remarque's British edition: "The soldier is on friendlier terms than other men with his stomach and intestines. Three-quarters of his vocabulary is derived from these regions, and they give an intimate flavor to expressions of his greatest joy as well as his deepest indignation. . . . Here [on the front] it is the universal language" (v. 4, 19–21, 47).

Mailer, revisiting the profanity issue in *Armies of the Night* (1968), summed the issue up this way:

> [T]hat noble common man was obscene as an old goat, and his obscenity was what saved him. The sanity of said democratic common man

was in his humor, his humor was in his obscenity. And his philosophy as well . . . which looked to restore the hard edge of proportion to the over-blown values overhanging each small military existence. . . . a skinny Southern cracker with a beatific smile on his face saying in the dawn of a Filipino rice patty, "Man, I just managed to take a noble shit." Yeah, that was Mailer's America. . . . So after years of keeping obscene language off to one corner of his work . . . after *The Naked and the Dead* . . . he had come back to obscenity . . . he had kicked goodbye in his novel *Why Are We in Vietnam?* to the old literary corset of good taste, letting his sense of language play on obscenity as freely as it wished. . . .

The American corporation executive [however] . . . was perfectly capable of burning unseen women and children in the Vietnamese jungles, yet felt a large displeasure . . . at the generous use of obscenity in literature and in public. (61–63)

What had sparked Hemingway's reference to Remarque was a debate with Scribner's over the use of the bedpan and other words "of that aspect of hospital life," most of which Hemingway had already expunged. Hemingway then assures Perkins that it is not only the publisher who knows the risks but that an author knows and accepts the risks too in the use of words that might get the book banned (*Letters* v. 4, 49). There was some dickering, of course—the substitution of the word "scrotum" for the word "balls," the long dash for "shit" and "cocksucker," and so on—but the novel itself retained plenty of what Hemingway had originally put in. He does request of Perkins, however, to have one copy for himself of the galleys bound up before any "blanks" were employed (v. 4, 109).

Like Mailer, Hemingway before him also had issues with cover art: "It looks as though the Jacket designer had been so wrapped up in that beautiful artistic effort on the front that she tried to eliminate . . . the title and author's name so they wouldn't intrude on the conception of the nude figure with those horrible legs and those belly muscles like Wladek Zabyenko's . . . and the big shouldered lad with the prominent nipples who is holding a broken axle (signifying no doubt the defeat of the Horse Drawn Vehicle)." This strongly worded complaint to Perkins might have never been sent, however; a more professionally courteous letter registering the same dissatisfaction was sent two days later (v. 4, 107–14).

It's important to keep in mind that, unlike Mailer's letters, Hemingway's about the front in World War I were not *intentional* planning documents for a novel and are therefore not as strategic as Mailer's when referring to the men, women, incidents, and themes that will go into the composition of *A Farewell to Arms*, nearly a decade after his service. Nonetheless, readers find in his letters the whole backstory of Hemingway's wounding and recuperation, his ill-fated love affair, his experience of the landscapes of battle and of Italian towns, and several of the novel's characters. We also discover Hemingway, a year out of high school, as committed to the life and labors of authorship as Mailer was by his second year at Harvard, after reading Hemingway, Farrell, Fitzgerald, and Dos Passos.

Even Hemingway's later letters do not, as do Mailer's, reveal Hemingway's thinking about the composing process, under the principle that writing or talking about a book ruins it. What the letters contemporaneous to composition do show (volumes three and four) are the progress of the novel—page and word counts, frustrations and difficulties with the writing, and momentary elations as the months roll by. We follow Hemingway as he travels to and from Key West, to Arkansas, Wyoming, and so on, working on the book, even as he has finally given up on his manuscript for a "Tom Jones" novel. In a letter to Perkins on 17 March 1928, Hemingway first refers to having started on a good story, which then evolves into *Farewell* (v. 3, 374–75). And he will later announce on 22 January 1929, "Finished the book today" (v. 3, 509). After his epistolary chronicle of all his struggles to get the book written, by 16 February that year he now believes, as he tells Evan Shipman, the novel is "the best thing I've ever done" (v. 3, 530). But in order to fully appreciate Hemingway's depiction of the experience the novel is based on, we must turn to volume 1 of the *Letters*.

As general editor Sandra Spanier's introduction to volume 1 of *The Letters of Ernest Hemingway* puts it, these collected letters are "the last great unexplored frontier of Hemingway studies" (xii). The intent, she notes, of the ongoing collection of the Cambridge edition (which may run to seventeen volumes) is to allow scholars and readers alike "ready access to the entire corpus of Hemingway's extant letters," 85 percent of which were never before published. As Mailer's work will be in the second half of the twentieth century, Hemingway's work is "a chronicle of the twentieth century," at least to the mid-1960s, and (again as with Mailer's letters) the list of correspondents "reads like a twentieth-century *Who's Who*" (xiii, xxi). In her introduction to volume 3, Spanier quotes Patrick Hemingway saying that his father's "letters are a portrait of the first half of the twentieth century" (v. 3, xxxi). Linda Patterson Miller will add in her foreword to the first volume that "the interplay between his artistry and the life that shaped it remains only half understood. . . . A fuller understanding is needed and the complete letters of Ernest Hemingway . . . will help make that possible." She then adds, "Hemingway's exposure to the war and its relationship to his writing deserve to be reexamined in light of his wartime correspondence" (liii, liv). The relationship between the people in Hemingway's letters and the characters in his novel is, to a large extent, known, with a few fine distinctions in seemingly perpetual debate. But the range of letters here about his wartime service in the American Red Cross Ambulance Corps in Italy solidify our sense of the connections. None more significant, of course, than his fictional alter ego Lieutenant Frederic Henry, the narrator-protagonist of *A Farewell to Arms,* that so clearly distinguishes this war novel from Mailer's. In his introduction to the first volume, Robert Trogdon sums up the similarities the letters reveal between hero and author quickly: "a prolonged hospitalization in Milan, a trip to Stresa, a friendship with an elderly diplomat, and a desire to visit the Abruzzi to hunt. Hemingway also returned to the front after recuperating from his wounds . . . ; in a letter to his family of 1 November 1918 he reported that he was at the front for the final Italian offensive and assisted in the evacuation of the wounded before succumbing (like his character) to jaundice" (lxiv).

The prototype for Catherine Barkley, the other central character based in part on American Red Cross Nurse Agnes von Kurowsky, is less visible than Frederic in these letters alone. Seven years Hemingway's senior and his first great love, Agnes's later fiancé made sure Hemingway's letters to her were destroyed before the fiancé, Italian artillery officer and heir to a dukedom Domenico Caracciolo, in turn dropped Agnes. But Agnes is nonetheless a clear presence in Hemingway's surviving letters. The letters regarding Hemingway's convalescence in the Milan Hospital are remarkable for their parallels to Frederic Henry's convalescence: from his arrival as one of the first patients (v. 1, 116, 118) and his wounds and surgeries, to his associations with friends, to Miss Van Campen, the hospital superintendent and a Nurse Ratched figure based on Katherine De Long (known

---

17

to patients as Gumshoe Casey), to, all importantly, meeting Agnes von Kurowsky (v. 1, 165, 167). One significant difference between the letters and the novel is that in *Farewell*, Lieutenant Henry is a more mature figure, not a boyish high school graduate; before the war he had been studying architecture in Rome (242). There is no discernable seven-year gap between the lovers. This difference will color the nature and fruition of their fictional relationship, a sort of idealized version until Catherine meets her agonized end giving birth to their child.

Catherine is in fact an amalgam of Agnes and Hemingway's first two wives, Hadley and Pauline (to whom he was married while writing the novel). He also based Catherine on Elsie Jessup, a blonde British nurse whose fiancé died in battle like Catherine's, necessary because American nurses were not in Italy yet when the main action of the novel takes place in 1917. To take one example beyond Agnes for now, Catherine's death equates to Pauline's experience of the Caesarean birth of Patrick: an agonizing eighteen-hour labor producing a baby "too big in fact as he nearly killed his mother" (*Letters* v. 3, 402–3). These are the words, of course, Frederic Henry utters in the final chapter of the novel, before Catherine dies of hemorrhage (*Farewell* 325). Hemingway was present for the labor and birth, and as he writes to Guy Hickok on 27 July 1928 of the impact of the event: "It is a different feeling seeing the tripas [intestines] of a friend rather than those of a horse to whom you have not been introduced" (*Letters* v. 3, 416–17). Is it too much to speculate that his observation of Pauline's suffering, occurring while he struggled to write the novel, gave Hemingway an ending that both helped repress Agnes from the psychic territory of his wounded past and avoided a sentimental ending?

Hemingway will not mention his being in love with Agnes to his parents until the letter to his mother of 29 August 1918, well into his recovery (v. 1, 136). Later Agnes will be described to various correspondents, family very much among them, as the woman who has put him into "a state of dumbness," "my girl," "who I'm going to marry," "the wife," the one "who makes all Chicago femmes look like a shot of Karo Corn Syrup compared to '83 Burgundy," "The Girl," and "the Missus," among other descriptors. And it is "quite a miracle in it's self that she loves me" (v. 1, 153, 157, 165, 167, 170). When he returns home, it is to begin his writing career and make enough money to marry Agnes (v. 1, 162–63). Although his letters to Agnes were destroyed, her letters to him survived and are offered in full in Henry Villard and James Nagel's *Hemingway in Love and War: The Lost Diary of Agnes von Kurowsky* (1989). Her letters make clear that Agnes reciprocated his love while they were in Italy and for some time after Hemingway returned home to Oak Park. In short, the fictional relationship is not merely wish fulfillment. And his love affair, even while maintained at a distance, spurred his writing, as he reports to his old friend Bill Horne, "Really tho I'm writing stuff that I had no idea I could write" (v. 1, 174).

By the spring of 1919, however, the affair was over when Agnes sent a letter to America breaking it off, a second wound from his time in Italy. He reports to Bill Horne: "She's been my ideal and I forgot all about religion and everything else. . . . All I wanted was Ag and happiness. And now the bottom has dropped out of the whole world. . . ." (v. 1, 177). As Hemingway writes to his former commanding officer James Gamble, it is now clear to Hemingway that he needs love: "I'm not sorry it happened because, Jim, I figure it does you good to love someone" and, anyway, he is now free "to fall in love with anyone I wish which is a priceless privilege" (v. 1, 181–82). "The best writing," he will later tell George Plimpton in his *Paris Review* interview, "is certainly when you are in love" (223). The pattern being established will be the one Mailer will follow, that of a man who needs to fall in love, who finds creative energy in loving a woman while love lasts, but who will be both a serial monogamist and a serial philanderer. One of the many paradoxical dualities in both authors' lives.

More importantly, Catherine and Frederic in some of their infatuated moments and peregrinations during his recuperation cover the same ground Hemingway reported covering in his letters. Hemingway's reference in a letter to James Gamble on 3 March 1919 to "staying away from the ponies" to save money toward his marriage with Agnes refers to his and Agnes's visits to the San Siro racetrack near Milan, an event reiterated at length in the novel. Between the crooked racing and the crowds, Frederic and Catherine discover another disillusionment and the preference to be alone together (see *Farewell* 127–32; *Letters* v. 1, 170, 173). One of the more significant plot-related trips Hemingway took is to Stresa on Lake Maggiore while on convalescent leave for ten days before returning to Milan for his "mechanical" therapies. In letters to his sister Marcelline, his father, and then to his family in late September of 1918, Hemingway describes the resort as "of Great Beauty. Above the clouds in sight of Switzerland." A cog railway up Mount Mottarone would have given him a wide view of the Swiss frontier (v. 1, 141–43). Stresa and the Grand Hotel he describes in the letters are later used as the scene of several chapters in book 4 of the novel where Frederic and pregnant Catherine find their "home," "alone against the others," that made "all other things seem unreal," and then make their escape along the lake to Switzerland, to their separate peace and final commitment to one another. It is at Stresa as well that Hemingway meets Count Greppi, the model for the wise, aged, yet vital Count Greffi in *Farewell*. Greppi, Hemingway will later write to Charles Scribner, "brought [me] up politically" (v. 1, 143–46). "What do you value most?" the old Count asks Frederic during billiards and champagne.

> "Some one I love."
> "With me it is the same. That is not wisdom. Do you value life?"
> "Yes."
> "So do I. Because it is all I have. And to give birthday parties," he laughed. "You are probably wiser than I am. You do not give birthday parties."
> We both took a drink of the wine.
> "What do you think of the war really?" I asked.
> "I think it is stupid. . . ."
> "I had always expected to become devout. All my family died very devout. But somehow it does not come. . . ."
> "Mine comes only at night."
> "Then too you are in love. Do not forget that is a religious feeling."
> "You believe so?"
> "Of course. . . ." (*Farewell* 262–63)

This exchange echoes the priest earlier in the novel, a character based in part upon a priest Hemingway meets in the hospital and describes in his letter to his mother of 29 August 1918: "A peach of a Catholic missionary Priest from India, a regular good old scout . . . comes in to see me very often and we have great old gab fests" (*Letters* v. 1, 135). Early in the novel the priest, one who also suffers with quiet endurance and grace, tells Frederic that love is not "only passion and lust. When you love you wish to do things for. You wish to sacrifice for. You wish to serve." Frederic, understanding, says "I don't love," but then asks if loving a woman can be like that. But the priest, who has just defined the larger dimensions of love Catherine and, to a lesser extent, Frederic will come to understand (i.e., caritas and agape as well as eros) says he does not know about that: "I've never loved a woman" (*Farewell* 72). The priest, another mentor figure, also echoes the count's disillusionment with the war in the long conversation with Frederic in chapter 26 (177–80).

Milan, the setting for Frederic and Catherine's meeting, courting, and lovemaking while Frederic recuperates, Hemingway came to know well as he moved about the city on recuperative walks and rides. By September 1918, Hemingway reports to his father that he can now get around on the streets with "a cane or a crutch" (*Letters* v. 1, 139). A month later he reports to his mother that he is walking a half-mile to another hospital for physical therapy (v. 1, 155). To his family at Thanksgiving, he recounts his delight in attending the Italian opera at the Scala and getting to know the singers at the American Bar (v. 1, 160). And in November as well he is riding around Milan in a motorcycle sidecar driven by friend D. D. Lore, as a tipped-in photograph in this volume shows (v. 1, 205). There are also passing references to the Anglo-American club, restaurants, and Duomo di Milano. Much later in 1922 he will write to Gertrude Stein about his tour of his old city and battlefield sites with Hadley (v. 1, 345–46). Much of this familiarity with Milan is reflected in the novel as Frederic takes his first crutch and cane walks; as Frederic and Catherine take their carriage rides, walks, and dinners at the beginning of chapters 18 and 19; as they meet at the local wine shop, visit an armorer's shop, and rent a hotel room for few hours on the eve of Frederic's return to the front in chapter 23.

The similarities between Hemingway's wounding by a trench mortar during the battle along the Piave River in July of 1918 and Frederic Henry's "on the Isonze north of Plava" in the fall of 1917 are by now one of the better-known connections between the biography and the life, even though the time and the geography of both events are different. The letters to his parents especially include considerable detail, as one might expect. His friend Theodore Bromback's letter to the family (at Hemingway's prompting) lays it all out before Hemingway can write to them—the killed and wounded men nearby the wounded Hemingway, the heroic action of carrying a wounded man to the first-aid dugout, the medals in the offing, the nature of the flesh and knee wounds (v. 1, 114–16). Hemingway later clarifies the specific wounds to his family in several letters, none more so than the letter of 21 July 1918 (his nineteenth birthday), including a drawing of himself in bed with the 227 shrapnel and bullet wounds—his knee, his right foot, his legs—as the first American to be wounded and *survive* his wounds (v. 1, 117–19). In an August letter, he will even draw pieces of the shape and size of the shell fragments taken out of his legs (v. 1, 132). The wounding is obviously the central moment in his life and the novel, out of which the narrative emerges and the primal prism through which Hemingway will view the rest of his life. The well-known similarities of the trench mortar strike and wounding in *Farewell* occur at several points, in the sound of the arriving and exploding shell (54), the wounded men around him, without the heroic carrying of one to the first-aid post (55–58), the doctor's listing of the wounds, very like those described in the letters (59), and the description of the wounds after the X-rays in Milan (94–100).

The letters from Milan do not contain an original description of that famous passage in the novel where the wounded Frederic Henry feels himself rush out of his body, knowing he was dead, and float before sliding back into his body (55); that will be part of an in-person exchange and a letter from Johnny Miller, a wounded friend from the Milan hospital who accompanied Ernest on his leave to Lake Maggiore, where they discussed their wounding on the Piave. Miller, an aspiring artist with a dry wit, said when you died that was the end, but Hemingway spoke of his out-of-body experience as proof of something more about death. In *Along with Youth: Hemingway, the Early Years*, Peter Griffin references Miller's 16 November 1920 letter to Hemingway on the matter (89, 240). But in a letter to his family from the Milan hospital in August of 1918, Hemingway does recount details about his own battle wounding similar to his fictional hero's. Hemingway describes being struck by the blast from a trench mortar and machine-gun fire, not yet in pain but in shock, feeling as if his boots are full of water and his kneecap "acting queer." He describes his wounds, attending to a wounded comrade, and being sent on a stretcher to the dressing station to await an ambulance. He describes ordering the ambulance down the road to pick up wounded soldiers first, then being evacuated to a field hospital, and then on to the base hospital in Milan (*Letters* v. 1, 130–32).

Most of the details in the letter are repeated and fleshed out in the novel: the watery shoes, the waiting for treatment at the dressing station, the request to pick up others first, the doctor's cataloging of Frederic's wounds, and the ambulance ride to the field hospital (*Farewell* 54–61).

And Hemingway will slow his recovery by going back to the front on convalescent leave to be "in on the offensive" the Italian Army launched on 24 October 1918. Hemingway ends up back in the hospital with jaundice, as he informs his family on 1 November 1918 (*Letters* v. 1, 148–49). His experience at the front, however, will be greatly amplified in the novel by way of Hemingway's invention of Frederic's participation in the retreat from Caporetto (a retreat that took place before Hemingway was in Italy and on a different front from Hemingway's). But on the retreat is where Frederic is almost assassinated after mock trials, along with other Italian officers believed by fanatical "white-hatted carabinieri" to have deserted their men or assumed to be German infiltrators in Italian uniform (*Farewell* 214–25). Witnessing such events and narrowly escaping by diving into the river trigger Frederic's final disillusionment with war's absurdities and leads to his escape with Catherine to Switzerland—all of which consumes the final third of the novel.

The novel's tracking of Frederic Henry's series of disillusionments with the war to this point contrasts with Hemingway's own youthful illusions at the age of nineteen in his 18 October 1918 letter to his family where he uses language not unlike that of war propaganda: "We all offer our bodies and only a few are chosen. . . . I am proud and happy that mine was chosen. . . . And how much better to die in all the happy period of undisillusioned youth, to go out in a blaze of light" (*Letters* v. 1, 147). But by the time he composed the novel a decade later, Hemingway had traveled Europe and Asia Minor as a foreign correspondent, reported on the Genoa Economic Conference, witnessed certain horrors of the Greco-Turkish War and the corrupt politics of the Lausanne peace conference ending it, interviewed Mussolini, spent years in Paris learning from James Joyce, Ezra Pound, Scott Fitzgerald, and Gertrude Stein, and suffered through divorce and the uncongenial demands of fatherhood. No longer the callow high school graduate, he was by the time of composition a worldly man of experience.

In fact, the only time Mailer quotes at length from *A Farewell to Arms* is on this very point—the disillusionment of the young who experience war.

In a letter to the *Boston Globe* chastising "Republican toady" George Will, who compared George W. Bush's "terse" prose to Hemingway's, Mailer calls Will's praise for Bush's prose "the scurvy manipulation" of abstractions that endangers democracy. Against Will and Bush, Mailer places Frederic Henry's riff on the political manipulation of abstract and jingoistic language: "I was embarrassed by the words sacred, glorious, and sacrifice. . . . I had seen nothing sacred, and the things that were glorious had no glory and the sacrifices were like the stockyards at Chicago if nothing was done with the meat except to bury it. . . ." (Mailer, "For Whom the Will Tolls").

Hemingway's letters might not be a writer's intentional notes for a novel, as Mailer's are, but we see through both authors' side of the correspondence that experiences and people inform their war novels and, in turn, inform the reader's full experience of the narrative. Both men succeeded in what Hemingway said was the artist's task in *Death in the Afternoon* (1932): to "make all that come true again" (272). In Hemingway's case, the letters from Agnes reveal the degree to which her expressions of love for the younger man are legitimate and not Hemingway's nostalgic fantasies. Nor do they fit with Agnes's later-in-life dismissals of the affair. The best source of Agnes's language in her love letters is Villard and Nagel's *Hemingway in Love and War*, although Peter Griffin's *Along with Youth: Hemingway, the Early Years* (1985), makes effective use of the letters as well. Ernest is "my furnace," "oh Master Mine," "my darling," "the Light of my Existence," "more precious than Gold in Wartimes." She writes that "I am lost without you." Then, "I love you more and more and know what I'm going to bring you when I come home." And "I never pined for anyone in my life. I never imagined anyone could be so dear and necessary to me. . . . Last night I was wishing I was with you on the big couch on the terzo piano." She is "missing you quite as much as you will miss me tho' maybe not quite as wildly. . . . On the train yesterday I kept wishing I had you alongside of me, so I could put my head on that place—you know—the hollow place for my face—& go to sleep with your arms around me." Their war-sacrifice will be "to keep our secrets to ourselves—but, so long as you have no secrets from me, & I have none from you (. . . I can't think of anything you don't know already)." And "I love you so much. . . . I just began to hunger for you. . . . Sometimes I wish we could marry over here." She explains that she has written to her mother that she is "planning to marry a man younger than I." And if their hearts should ever change, they "would lose this beautiful world of us" (Villard and Nagel 99, 101–2, 104–8, 119, 127, 134–35, 140, 145).

There is more of the same, but the tone will alter later as Agnes is moving away from Ernest and toward her inconstant duke after Ernest has returned home, even before her Dear John letter to Ernest. Her diary is more restricted in passion despite the fact that she doesn't have to worry about the Red Cross censors as she does with letters, but she does mention in the diary that one of her hair pins was found under his pillow, that she has given him her "home ring," and that their "more real farewell" was in the privacy of an elevator (Villard and Nagel 77–78, 82).

I recall that before looking at Agnes's and Hadley's side of the courtship correspondence, I had always thought in reading the novel that the lovers' dialogue was over the top—a little too self-abnegating, too willing to be absorbed by the other. People in love, especially in the inebriations of early infatuation, say silly things, but isn't this a bit much? I thought. The language of passion and self-abnegation is even more Hadley's during their courtship, language imported into the novel after his marriage to Hadley has ended. "I'll eat you alive," Hadley tells him before he arrives in St. Louis for a visit. "Isn't it a good thing you and I know so well we love each other. . . . Don't let's ever die, Old Sweet. . . . I'm sure we're a pair preconceived by the Maker." And she says, "My thought is how tremendously when we're made into a unit or firm or whatever 'tis, gifted we'll then be. . . . We pool everything precious we've got. Everything I've got is yours. But I don't give it to you. There's no volition on my part. It just belongs to you, Ernest, 'count of love. . . . So I know nothing could shake me from my desire to be everything to you. . . . Being everything to you is the only thing that can satisfy me physically." Ernest doesn't reciprocate in the same emotional register (and he seems to be testing her constancy) in his few remaining letters to Hadley—no doubt because he's been burned before. As the French say, every relationship has one who kisses and one who is kissed. But he admits to Hadley that he is "stale, flat, tired, uncreative" and needs her to make things go again (Griffin 160, 168–70). There is, unfortunately, a dearth of letters to Hadley from Hemingway, accountable to the fact that she burned his letters after their marriage fell apart. Likewise, Pauline's family followed her wishes and destroyed her correspondence from Hemingway after her death, leaving only two letters from Hadley and nine from Pauline (see Sandra Spanier's introduction to the *Letters* v. 3, xvii–xviii). But there is more than a little Hadley in Catherine Barkley, who for both Ernest and Frederic share the same pet name, "Cat." Both women, we've seen, share a similar language of love: the expression of one who wishes "to sacrifice for, to do things for," as the priest puts it. There are also the similarities between the Swiss idyll (the good place) in book 5 of *Farewell* and Hadley and Ernest's time in Switzerland from Montreux to Lausanne in January of 1922. The descriptive details in Hemingway's January letters to his family and to Katharine Foster Smith describing Hadley and Ernest's vacation bear considerable resemblance to Frederic and Catherine Barkley's after their escape to Switzerland: the weather, the winter sports, the hikes, the cozy accommodations—complete with a proprietor who starts your wood stove in the morning before serving you breakfast in bed (see *Letters* v. 1, 318–26; *Farewell* 289–301).

It is, nonetheless, best to avoid innocent assumptions that a work of fiction is merely autobiographical without much invention or research. In Hemingway's case, the secondary research included histories and official military reports of battles, topographical maps, veterans' eyewitness accounts and memoirs, news reports, timetables, and photographs—not unlike Stephen Crane's research for *The Red Badge of Courage*, for which research Hemingway expressed admiration in his 1942 introduction to *Men at War* (xvii). Michael Reynolds in *Hemingway's First War* (1987) discovers such sources and the many temporal and geographical differences between Hemingway's war and Frederic Henry's. But what we can begin to see, especially through both authors' correspondence, is how some of their sources (autobiographical and historical) were transformed into works of art. In Mailer's case, the invented island of Anopopei gave him more factual leeway because he was not recreating on the page *actual* battles and the historical debacle of an Army's retreat he had *not* lived through, as Hemingway was.

AFTERMATH: THE DEMONS OF SUCCESS

After the enormous success of his first novel, Mailer was feeling his oats. He was also mired in his struggles to write and successfully publish his second novel, *Barbary Shore*. He was feeling a sense of competition with one of his literary fathers, Ernest Hemingway. As if clearing some space for himself, Mailer complains to Lillian Ross in a letter of 12 September 1952 that Hemingway is reduced to mere posturing in his latest book, *The Old Man and the Sea*, recently published in *Life* magazine. He is tired of Hemingway parading his manly life. Mailer "just can't stand his prose . . . of 1952" and "feel[s] nastily competitive, but it is his own Goddamn fault for writing such affected prose" (*Selected Letters* 124). But within two years as he works on *The Deer Park*, Mailer is more self-aware and humbled in a letter to William Styron. He could learn to accept other writers' gifts and success "if my own stuff would grow." He just "can't seem to enter people's heads," he laments of his own characters (137–38).

But that of course is the same criticism he makes of Hemingway to Ross, too much Hemingway's manly head and not enough of his characters'. Such competition with his literary father is deep and complex. As Michael Lennon points out in his introduction to the *Selected Letters*, Hemingway's suicide in 1961 "troubled him deeply, and he has more to say about Papa, his life, death, and work than about any other writer" (xvi). And that of course doesn't even mention Mailer's own cultivation of boxing, bullfighting, and displays of courage, like a son emulating his father for approval. "I know his flaws inside out," Mailer said of Hemingway. "I've loved and hated him as if he were my own father for years. There is so much he did for one, so much he didn't do. Truly the relationship you have with him is as a father. . . . His sense of the English language, I'd say, is virtually primitive in its power to evoke mood and stir the senses" (*Pieces and Pontifications* 161). It seems reasonable to say that there was more than a little of what Harold Bloom called the anxiety of influence, and its ambiguities, at work in Mailer's psyche. (For a fully developed assessment of Mailer's anxiety of Hemingway's influence, see Erik Nakjavani's "A Visionary Hermeneutic Appropriation: Meditations on Hemingway's Influence on Mailer" in the special Hemingway-Mailer issue of *The Mailer Review* in 2010, 163–93.)

Hemingway himself was, of course, highly competitive and had his own anxieties over literary fathers. "Writing whether you want it or not is competitive," he tells Max Perkins in September of 1928. "Most of the time you compete against time and dead men—sometimes you get something from a living competitor that is so good it jars you. . . . But as you read them dead or living you unconsciously compete" (*Letters* v. 3, 434).

———

Still, had a published cache of Hemingway's letters been available to the young Mailer at the time, he would have recognized the parallels between his own struggles to write his big war novel and Hemingway's, and he would have recognized Hemingway's experience as a young man publishing his first best-seller and the difficulties that flow from such success, not least postcelebrity writers' block and familial complications.

What to write next? A question that plagued both writers in their time after their breakthroughs. For Mailer's part, after *Naked*, he would never write a novel again (putting aside the "nonfiction novel" *The Executioner's Song*) where he was so able to avoid "projection." Projection is the word Mailer uses as he admires Somerset Maugham's avoidance of projecting himself onto his characters, the very thing he later accuses Hemingway of doing (*Selected Letters* 25). This lack of authorial projection Mailer greatly admires in Tolstoy, especially *Anna Karenina*, "a great and necessary sympathy that sees all people in their own eyes" (45). He later said, in the 50th anniversary edition of *The Naked and the Dead*, that he read from *Anna Karenina* "most mornings before he commenced work" for that very reason (xii). He knew even before working on *Naked* full time that he would also need Tolstoy to keep him "in a good humanistic mood" and to remind him of what he recognizes as the "lack of any tenderness in my writing. And I feel a little helpless before that lack." The best he could do, he told Bea while planning the novel from Japan is to generate some warmth by presenting each character in "the self-beloved circle of his own mind" (ms. late 1945 and 20 October 1945). But by May of 1948, Mailer is dithering over the next novel, as he tells agent Adelaide Scherer. He is hoping to get out to Hollywood to write about it because he has "several ideas" for novels but fears his ideas are "too small": after the success of *Naked*, "you get frightened if your next can is smaller" (*Selected Letters* 74). And a year later he tells Charles Rembar, his lawyer/agent, that he is trying to finish his final draft of "Mrs. Guinevere," the early title of *Barbary Shore* (80).

Indeed, the 1950s would become "Mailer's toughest decade as a writer," Michael Lennon tells us in the *Selected Letters:* "Wealthy and famous, he nevertheless felt disoriented and depleted; he didn't know what to write about next." Two false starts fizzled out; then, meeting intellectual mentor Jean Malaquais in Paris, Mailer tried to redirect their conversations on Marxism and history into a novel set in the Brooklyn rooming house where

---

he had written his best-seller. And when that second, claustrophobic novel was panned by reviewers, Mailer considered giving up writing altogether, as Lennon points out (93). "Now what in heaven will I write about for a third novel?" he asks Jean Cranford of Rinehart just before his twenty-eighth birthday in January of 1951 (102).

After his separation from Bea, in the spring of 1951, Mailer writes to her that he hopes that "psychologically the critical failure of *Barbary Shore* is a better climate for me" (105). He has just moved to New York and rented a loft, hoping that psychological climate will engender a new, better novel. But by the fall of 1951, the Hollywood novel is dying in his hands, the prose "only adequate." Still, he will try a couple of months more to see if it comes along. If not, he will quit writing for a while and spend the year on manual labor. "I'm getting awfully stale" (107), he notes. Merely a month later he tells Mickey Knox he has quit the novel and for now is writing short stories, five or ten, and then seeking an agent to sell them (110).

The work on the stories continues well into 1952. Beginning in January Mailer writes to his Japanese translator Eiichi Yamanishi that he is working on a book of short stories, mostly about the war (117). One cannot help wondering whether this collection shouldn't have been his second book and obviated the suffering and frustration he had to undergo for years. As he tells Charles Devlin, his friend and informal editor on the final *Naked* manuscripts, in February of 1952, writing stories has made him "think the thing I write best about is the war" (118). The reading public had been primed for more Mailer on the war from the striking success of *Naked*. A second book of war stories might well have been a follow-on success, instead of the critical creaming he had to endure on *Barbary Shore* and all the dead ends he kept running into with his "Hollywood novel." "What a torture writing is," he tells Bea. "I detest it." He says, "I'm terrified. I'll probably give it up" (119). He just doesn't have the material he had in *Naked;* he's lost "the simple humanity" of his characters. For months he was "convinced I was through as a writer" (123). Just after his thirtieth birthday, he tells her again that he is taking a new attack on the Hollywood novel that leads to an ambitious project of a projected eight (Balzacian?) volumes (131–32). Letters to John Aldridge and William Styron, among others, repeat much of the same lamentable story.

And when Mailer first contacts psychoanalyst and author Robert Lindner on 18 November 1952, we begin to understand that Mailer is by then making his way toward *Lipton's Journal,* the 1954–55 document of self-analysis that will pit Mailer against his society. "One must feel that a society which warps, corrupts, and 'adjusts' its members must either be destroyed, or to the contrary modified," an idea he tried to express "in my last book, *Barbary Shore*" (126–27). His later correspondence and meetings with Lindner as he worked on *The Deer Park* connect Mailer's personal literary struggles and his social rebellion as expressed throughout *Lipton's* with the direction of his future work.

Mailer will continue to wrangle *The Deer Park* for some time. But he might well have taken heart had he been able to read Hemingway's letters about his similar struggles after *A Farewell to Arms.*

H emingway was asking the same questions in his letters after the triumph of *A Farewell to Arms.* What's next? Should I just write short stories instead of starting on a new novel without fresh material? Should I quit? Hemingway's success seems all the more astonishing given that his novel landed in the public sphere on the eve of the Great Depression and most of the sales occurred after the October stock market crash.

But Hemingway had thought of quitting even as he was at work on the grinding revisions of *Farewell* in galleys. In a letter to Thornton Wilder on 26 May 1929, he complained of "all the little sniveling shit of literary politics" and asked, "What the hell does success get you?" He threatened to "quit the whole business and buy a boat . . . and shove off. Then have a book every five or ten years or whenever you have one and not have to write them because they bring so much bloody pressure on you" (*Letters* v. 4, 15). That July he writes to his editor Maxwell Perkins that he is feeling bad trying to write short stories now and *Farewell* "seems like my last book. . . . I'm sick of all of it . . . of writing . . . of the shit i-ness of critics" (v. 4, 49).

After publication in late September of 1929, Hemingway continues his exasperation and cynicism in another letter to Max Perkins, saying that Scott Fitzgerald tells him that the idea of living off royalties is "all bunk. . . . a book only sells a short time. . . . So I guess it's all just a damned racket. . . . I'm a professional writer now—Than which there isn't anything lower—I never thought I'd be it (and I'm damned if I'm going to do it any more)" (109). With sales of the novel soaring by mid-December, Hemingway still expresses exasperation to Perkins: "The idea that a writer can write a book and then become a businessman, then a writer again is all—as we say——. It's hard enough to write—and writing prose is a full time job and all the best of it done in your subconscious and when it is full of business, reviews, opinions, etc., you don't get a damned thing" (v. 4, 203).

As Mailer will think a generation later, Hemingway believes maybe all he can do for now is short story writing. Letter after letter reveals the difficulty of choosing what might come next after the big war novel. Even in his July letter to Perkins, Hemingway complains of not getting the juice when he tries to write short stories every day, "not being able to write a damned bit and so . . . this seems like my last book" (v. 4, 48). He repeats the same phrasing to Owen Wister the same day (v. 4, 52), to Guy Hickok a few days later (v. 4, 57), to Sylvia Beach in mid-August (v. 4, 66), to Fitzgerald on the eve of the novel's publication, saying that depression over not being able to write is "The Artist's Reward" (v. 4, 93), and to his sister Madelaine, "my next book but how to write it—and about what?" (v. 4, 99). Even into the next year nearly four months after publication of *Farewell*, he tells his mother, "Have been unable to write since Nov." (v. 4, 215). This block even though, or perhaps because, *Farewell* has sold over 70,000 copies by early January 1930, to extraordinary reviews (v. 4, n. 1, 218).

Nonetheless, during this dry spell Hemingway does manage to draft "Wine of Wyoming," "A Natural History of the Dead," and "After the Storm," all published after 1930, the same year he tries to begin *Death in the Afternoon* (first conceived in 1925 but published in 1932). He also in 1928 finally abandoned a novel he had been trying to write earlier recounting in part precombat experiences, *A New-Slain Knight*, the unpublished manuscript of which resides in the JFK Presidential Library Hemingway collection in Boston (Griffin 54, 236). It is also revealing that his next novel and intended comeback, *To Have and Have Not*, did not come out till 1937 and to, mostly, critical scorn, even if the sales were fine for a time. It will be, moreover, three more years beyond that before the triumph of his next big war novel, *For Whom the Bell Tolls*. Jeffrey Meyers reports that the novel would have won the Pulitzer for 1940 had not the archconservative president of Columbia University nixed it, but it sold 500,000 copies in the first five months, compensated for the books of the 1930s, and established the Hemingway legend and the public self-advertising persona that helped sell books (Meyers 239, 339). In fact, Meyers also points out a celebrity author phenomenon that one might argue Mailer did not entirely escape either— the convergence of fictional protagonists and the author's legendary public figure. It was not Hemingway's wish to have his personal biography exposed and probed, particularly if he had to be psychoanalyzed on paper by unqualified critics, but he did wish to have his legendary persona publicized to boost sales (453, 462). Publicity is one thing, probing biography quite another.

Given what the letters reveal, it seems reasonable to suggest that if *A Farewell to Arms* and *The Naked and the Dead* had not been such financial and critical successes, both young authors would have experienced less writer's block. Mailer's wildly successful novel being his first published made it more difficult for him. In a letter to Bea's parents, he jokes that he woke up a celebrity and brags that Lillian Hellman is working on a theatrical version of the novel even while the first negotiations with Hollywood have begun (*Selected Letters* 76). Michael Lennon calculated that on a scale of 1–5 the sixteen major reviews have graded Mailer a 4.031 score (752, note to letter #58). But he will also learn, as Hemingway did before him, that such rewards exacerbate familial problems as well. In Hemingway's case it was his mother, in Mailer's his father, who expected financial help from the recently celebrated son. Both celebrated sons will help, but both will draw hard boundaries to restrain the parental supplicant.

Barney Mailer, a compulsive gambler, turned to Norman to help him out of debt in, as Mailer puts it, a "bullshit" and "masterful document of the English colonel writing to his son." Mailer delivers a harsh lecture to his "Jewish accountant in Brooklyn" father and tells him, "it is time for you to grow up." He then proceeds to lay out five "principles" he is going to hold to "until hell freezes over": 1) He will give the three thousand dollars owed only to those his father owes, not directly to him; 2) Norman's mother must be included in his father's bank account; 3) the money sent must not be considered a debt to the son; 4) Norman will let Barney go to jail—or never speak to him again—if he starts fooling around with accounts of people he works for; and 5) his father needs to sit down and understand a few fundamentals about himself, such as he'll never be a rich man, he is neurotic, and his son will never pay another debt (85–87).

When Hemingway experienced similar high praise from reviewers, substantial sales, and rumblings of interest from Hollywood, he too had felt it necessary to compose and an equally excoriating letter in response to his mother's assumptions regarding financial help. It should be said that Hemingway voluntarily wanted to help his family clear debts (*Letters* v. 4, 121), he had granted his former wife Hadley all royalties from *The Sun Also Rises* (v. 4, 133), and he had set up a trust fund to help support his still-young sister Carol and his mother, Grace. But in a yet unlocated letter, his mother apparently made some comment about what "Justice demands" apropos her and Carol's support. That set Hemingway off. He did not retract the trust fund but complained bitterly of his mother's expectation of financial "justice" toward his family, in the wake of his father's suicide in December of 1928. He took the opportunity to throw back at her (in quotations) his mother's previous complaints about his fiction ("you'd 'rather see me dead in my grave rather than writing as I am,' etc."). He lays out precisely the terms of the trust fund, stresses that Grace as Carol's mother is not released from the obligation to provide for her daughter while she is underage, and emphasizes that he now has two books whose profits he has given away. "So much for 'Justice demands,'" he crows.

In the same letter he then assures his mother that he has made no money yet from any movie deals and that he and his wife, Pauline, have no home, no property, and have two children of his own to raise and educate. He is particularly resentful of his mother's expectation of financial help—which he is giving her—after her complaints about his "disgraceful" writings. He tells her he is retreating to Key West "to have some tranquility to write." What he will have to live on, he tells her, is only what he can earn from his writing from now on (v. 4, 219–20).

For the serious artist, celebrity authorship—like writing itself—has its rewards as well as its afflictions. It was only during the composition and publication of their breakthrough war novels that Hemingway in his generation and Mailer in his experienced such a blessing and curse. But it was the experience of war itself that gave them the material they needed to write their big novels. Just as it did for Mailer's contemporary Kurt Vonnegut, whose breakthrough war novel *Slaughterhouse-Five* (1969) was based on his own experience as a soldier, POW, and witness to the firebombing of Dresden (just one city of several in Germany and Japan where Allied aircraft firebombed civilian populations and centers of culture in a final frenzy of total war). As for Hemingway and Mailer, for Vonnegut war was embedded in the psyche. It took Vonnegut twenty-five years finally to get the war out of his depths and onto paper and then published in manageable form. The style he would use in that novel turned out to be the same he used in his now famous 1945 letter to his family about what had happened to him, one of the few survivors from his unit, as a soldier and POW. His characters also are based on other soldiers he knew. It is, moreover, their immersion in war as young men that motivated Mailer and Vonnegut to come out publicly (and early) in the 1960s against the catastrophic blunder (including more firebombing) of the Vietnam War.

Mailer knew war was a gift to him, as he tells Bea while still in the Philippines. He saw, first, "the universality of military life" in its dull collective labors, marches, and routines organized by leaders around a mission, an "emotional climate" as familiar to Roman legionaries as to twentieth-century grunts. And he also saw, as Hemingway did, the value to a writer of combat experience: "Much as I hate the army, I've learned certain kinds of knowledge that would have taken me years any other way" (mss. 20 June 1945 and 24 July 1945). Here Mailer was echoing, perhaps unwittingly, Hemingway when he wrote to Fitzgerald on 15 December 1925 that "War groups the maximum of material and speeds up the action and brings out all sorts of stuff that normally you have to wait a lifetime to get" (*Letters* v. 2, 446).

But we should not forget that if Hemingway, Mailer, and Vonnegut knew that war could be a gift of material for a writer, they also knew war's criminality. Hemingway expresses it best, I think, in his introduction to the 1946 postwar essay collection *Treasury for the Free World*. So, with thanks to Erik Nakjavani for pointing me to the quotation, let's give the literary father, Papa Hemingway, the last word on what they who have suffered in battle know about war.

"*Never think that war, no matter how necessary, nor how justified, is not a crime*" (xv; my emphasis).

2

LIPTON'S JOURNAL

Mailer's Quest for Wholeness and Renewal

The modern mind has forgotten those old truths that speak of the death of the old man and the making of a new one, of spiritual rebirth and similar old-fashioned "mystical absurdities." My patient, being a scientist of today, was more than once seized by panic when he realized how much he was gripped by such thoughts. He was afraid of becoming insane, whereas the man of two thousand years ago would have welcomed such dreams and rejoiced in the hope of a magical rebirth and renewal of life. But our modern attitude looks back proudly upon the mists of superstition and of medieval or primitive credulity and entirely forgets that it carries the whole living past in its lower stories of the skyscraper of rational consciousness. Without the lower stories our mind is suspended in mid air. No wonder it gets nervous. The true history of the mind is not preserved in learned volumes but in the living mental organism of everyone.

CARL JUNG, *Psychology and Religion*

AUTHOR'S NOTE: *During the thirteen weeks spent composing his private journal of self-analysis and personal growth between December of 1954 and March of 1955, Mailer, at age 32, recorded his discovery of various pathways to tap into his libidinous, instinctive, rebellious, and liberated self as an artist. I'll examine here Mailer's* Lipton's Journal *from two complementary perspectives: 1) how Mailer used a Jungian self-analysis to change his life and work, and 2) how Mailer recorded his discovery of jazz as one of the most significant pathways to artistic renewal.*

MAILER AND JUNG

In the mid-1950s Mailer employed creative methods and goals that are significantly like those Carl Jung employed through his own journal of self-analysis earlier in the century. Both Mailer and Jung seek to discover neglected and undeveloped elements of their personalities; both are in search of wholeness and renewal; both are in search of their deepest selves. Both, by their own testimony, are in search of their souls. In short, Mailer initiated a Jungian analysis on himself, though it is unlikely he was fully aware he was doing so in 1955.

Mailer's self-analysis through *Lipton's Journal* was transformational and foundational; it would become the key to all his future work, beginning in the 1960s. Reading it, we witness both the *how* and the *why* of Mailer's personal transformation. Mailer began *Lipton's Journal* during a turbulent and disappointing time in his life—after the collapse of his first marriage and the bleak reception of *Barbary Shore,* and in the midst of his anguished attempt to find a publisher for his third novel, *The Deer Park.* "For the first time in my life," Mailer writes in journal entry #157, "I have come to realize that I, too, could go mad or commit suicide." He recognizes that *Barbary Shore* and *The Deer Park* had expressed his few ideas, "only through great pain, and the most stubborn depression. . . ." That *The Deer Park* "is an enormous lie," and that he must break free of such dishonesty and such worrying over "bad receptions of my books" because such worries tend to make him "go on and try to be more dishonest at an even higher level" rather than becoming a rebel artist connected to an independent, whole self (#250, #460). He writes, "I am analyzing myself in order to become a real rebel, not just an adjusted rebel" (#276).

Mailer found his journal to be "a refuge . . . giving him a clean feeling" (#218). He began to see that "Only through understanding myself can I come to create. . . . As I understand myself . . . so I can waste less time" (#582). He was on a quest through self-analysis for potential sources of rebellion against the claustrophobia he was feeling about his life as a rejected, perhaps even failed, artist. "*The Deer Park* is a failure, but I have discovered myself," he writes, and adds that he will no longer need "to protect myself against quitting the values of the world" (#145). His self-analytical journey in *Lipton's* would be his turning point, the source of his personal transformation (#155). He sees himself as "shoving off into a total re-evaluation of everything. . . . I must trust what my instincts tell me is good rather than what the world says is good" (#159). In the same entry, Mailer notes that he considers *The Naked and the Dead* to be an "imposture" he tried to hide behind, but he now is committed to going forward. He wants his work now to become less derivative, more rebellious and outrageous, more instinctual and deeper, foretelling not only *Advertisements for Myself,* but *An American Dream, Why Are We in Vietnam?* and *Armies of the Night* in the coming decade. Mailer also believes such "self-analysis will make me a happier more effective rebel . . . because I will be less afraid" (#623). He predicts, "I believe I'm going to come out of this bigger than I went in" (#262).

Mailer was opening himself to—was indeed ardently seeking—a means of integrating, of better balancing, the powers of his conscious and unconscious life. He was seeking rapprochement between the two. He was seeking, therefore, an integration or "individuation" of psyche. In "The Relations between Ego and the Unconscious," in *Two Essays on Analytical Psychology,* Jung defines individuation as "embracing our innermost. . . . becoming one's own self. . . . coming into selfhood or self-realization" (173). "The unconscious is a process," Jung writes in his autobiography (*Memories, Dreams, Reflections*), "and . . . the psyche is transformed or developed by the relation of the ego to the contents of the unconscious," which contents in humanity's "collective life . . . has left its deposit principally in the various religious systems and their changing symbols" (209). Jungian therapist and scholar June Singer, in *The Boundaries of the Soul,* emphasizes the psychological dynamic of growth and change nicely: "The starting point of understanding the analytic process is the concept of the psyche as a self-regulating system in which consciousness and the unconscious are related *in a compensatory way.*" Singer, as we'll soon see, could have been describing Mailer and his journal when she adds that as the "resources of the unconscious" integrate with consciousness, *the conscious psyche can release the "attitudes, modes of behavior, that are no longer necessary or desirable,"* realizing the individual potential "which has somehow gotten lost" (10–11; my emphasis).

In his own journal of self-analysis, entitled *The Red Book,* Jung demonstrates his motivations and processes in search of a more integrated self, a quest not unlike Mailer's own forty years later. The "self" in Jung's psychology "is produced through the synthesis of conscious and unconscious elements of the personality," as Jung explained in "On the Psychology of the Child Archetype" and *The Red Book* (136). The self is therefore a potential for and a result of the individuation process. Self is the wholeness of psyche or "the subject of my totality"; whereas the "I" is "the subject of my consciousness." The "persona" is the "conscious attitude," essentially the mask we wear as social beings (59).

Jung's more extensive journal, first composed in a series of six small "Black Books," began at the end of 1913, on the eve of the first world war and after he had parted ways with his mentor, Freud, a stressful time when Jung, much like Mailer, feared he was susceptible to a nervous breakdown. In his autobiography Jung describes his feelings as he embarked on his journal as "uncertainty" and "disorientation," as if he were living "under constant pressure" and in a "state of tension" and "psychic disturbance." He experienced "a feeling of panic" and became "afraid of losing command of myself." He then started his journal as "a voluntary confrontation with the unconscious as a scientific experiment" on himself. "I was in effect writing letters to the anima" or "the soul, in a primitive sense," to "she who communicates the images of the unconscious to conscious mind" (170–87). Jung's journal itself demonstrates his nonlinear process, continued off and on with greatest intensity until June of 1917, when he began to understand the material arising out of his experiment. In his earliest journal entries Jung describes his "unbearable inner longing" for something more than his professional accomplishments, some potential enrichment of his soul, an enrichment he has "long discarded." He felt as if he were "half a man" stuck in his own time (127–28). The inexplicable brooding darkness he felt eventually manifests in the reality of world war, and by 1914 he comes to believe that wars, as with any human conflict, are an external projection of the unbalanced duality within human beings. That inner struggle, that imbalance, is "the wellspring of the great war" (199–200).

For many years thereafter, Jung revised, added commentary and graphic images, extended the journal, and eventually produced a single text of his entire, decades-long journal in a folio calligraphic version, bound in red leather, but unpublished until the twenty-first century, when it was *The Red Book: Liber Novus, A Reader's Edition.* Jung's experiment in self-analysis was for him a frightening confrontation with his unconscious, that potent and creative layer of the psyche. In one of his dialogues with his soul, Jung was clear about his fear of such a journey into the depths: "You dread the depths; I [the Soul] should horrify you, since the way of what is to come leads through it." Opening to the deepest layers of your psyche allows "the dark flood of chaos to flow into your order and meaning" (138–39). But through several dialogues, Jung decides to trust his soul "even if you lead me through madness." If you enter the world of the soul, you are "like a madman" (148–51). Later, he describes the process of opening himself to his psychic depths as "a civil war in me" (159). Part of the fear is also a lack of easy understanding as the inner material first reveals itself: "the meaning is dark to me" (184–85). Later, when he has the opportunity to reflect on the journal, he comes to see the need for integrating conscious and unconscious psyche—the process of individuation. Similarly, Mailer writes in his journal that "I will journey into myself with the hope that I, the adventurer, can come out without being destroyed. But I am terrified. I don't think I have ever been so frightened in my life" (#103).

To aid his journey into deepest self, Mailer used cannabis (hence the title "Lipton's" or "tea," as well as the moniker—General Marijuana—he soon gave himself in his *The Village Voice* column, later collected in *Advertisements for Myself*). "Lipton's seems to open up one to one's unconscious," he writes. Cannabis "destroys the sense . . . of society and opens the soul." He continues, "Lipton's is a great aid given my intellectual and verbal mind" to "my great adventure." Mailer compares smoking tea to hypnosis because it "opens man to his soul, immediately, powerfully, and perhaps irrevocably." "Administered properly," he goes on, "Lipton's has excellent therapeutic qualities," allowing him to "ideate so profusely" because it releases his "normal state of muscular tension" (#2, #63, #103, #275).

One can't help being struck by the way Mailer discovers what Jung called "the collective unconscious," that layer of psyche deeper and broader than Freud's version of the personal unconscious. Freud's unconscious is, essentially, a layer beneath consciousness developed through the experiences and environments of one's life, whereas Jung's unconscious includes a layer below the personal that taps into the larger, archaic history of humanity as evinced in world mythologies through archetypes—those similar mythic forms (characters, quests, images, and tropes) appearing in the record across many cultures, traditions, and epochs. Jung's sense of the collective unconscious, then, taps into myth-forming structural elements of the unconscious. In 1909 Jung began to shift his research to what he believed to be that larger phylogenetic layer of psyche consisting of mythological images that he analyzed, over decades and voluminous works, though comparative anthropology. He used his studies—stimulated by his journal—to transform not only his own life but psychotherapy, especially his treatment of his own patients, through the creative use of those primordial images that arise not only in art, literature, and religion, but in our fantasies and dreams, as well. June Singer gives a proper emphasis to the images and figures from the unconscious as actors in "the archetypal drama" that move us from psychic "separation and loss of integrity and despair" and lead ultimately to "the drama of transformation . . . and regeneration" (250).

Near the start of his own journal Mailer also writes of his belief in a "stratum of the collective unconscious" that connects us all "independent of [one's] will" (#24). His earliest theories suggest many layers of the unconscious, each one buried deeper in the psyche and closer to what he was at the time calling "homeostasis" (the deeper layer of illogical, intuitive, and irrational power in the psyche), which opposes "sociostasis" (the layer of psyche where reason becomes rationalization and serves as "a bulwark of society") (#245, #282). Mailer suggests that sociostasis and homeostasis are engaged in "trench warfare" as the "condition of the soul," and it is "the deep collective truths of the soul" that will provide the "clue" to the time to come (#342).

Indeed, the conflict between the soul and society, which echoes Emerson as much as it does Jung, is the central theme and insight of *Lipton's Journal*. Mailer writes of "the cry of the soul against society" and "the anger of the soul" forced to "travel the roads of the social world." Soul and society comprise but one dualism Mailer examines throughout his journal, the extreme opposition to the soul is totalitarianism, the greatest state of imbalance. He places "the soul's insights against the world's insights." The individual's soul is "part of the collective soul" that society opposes. Mailer goes so far as to declare that a writer's "style gives the clue . . . to what happened to the soul" (#45, #59, #250, #255). Mailer also concluded, as Jung did, that although the underlying symbolic structures of the archetypes endure, the symbolic forms are colored by, shaped by, the society in which one lives: "No matter how deeply we dip into . . . our collective wisdom," Mailer writes, "the particular insights we return with to the world are colored by our S," our dominant society (#606). Most people probably know of the symbols and archetypes that unfold across millennia through the work of Joseph Campbell, but Campbell based much of his own work on his predecessor Jung, even if he carried Jung's work further.

Like Mailer's journal, Jung's is full of raw material that can be difficult to judge or comprehend, but the editor for the published version of *The Red Book*, Sonu Shamdasani (professor of Jung History at the Center for the History of Psychological Disciplines at University College of London) is an excellent guide to Jung's. In his nearly 100-page introduction, Shamdasani points out that *The Red Book* depicts the rebirth of God in the soul, a "hermeneutic experiment" not unlike Yeats's automatic writing experiments that published as *A Vision* reveal the creation of an individual cosmology (30–31). Although Yeats's cosmology was fully formed once published, as was William Blake's in his illuminated works, Mailer reveals in *Lipton's* merely the seeds of his own cosmology, seeds that will begin to bear fruit in "The White Negro" (1957), "Hip, Hell, and the Navigator" (1958, 1959), and his work of the 1960s. In "Navigator," published in *Advertisements*, we encounter Mailer's emerging cosmology, which posits a God in danger of dying and in existential battle with a Devil—as two "warring element[s] of the universe" that place mankind in a "staggering moral" position, to be navigated by unconscious messages to consciousness (380–83, 386). Like Blake, but unlike Mailer's mere doodling, Jung adds extensive drawings and paintings in the process of developing his integration of soul and consciousness, individuality and society. "The overall theme of the book," Shamdasani writes of Jung's *Red Book*, "is how Jung regains his soul and overcomes the contemporary malaise of spiritual alienation. . . . a new worldview in the form of psychological and theological cosmology. . . . a prototype of Jung's conception of the individuation process. . . ." (48).

Jung would have his patients follow a journaling process similar to his own, complete with drawings, to illuminate dreams and images arising out of their confrontations with the collective unconscious. As therapist, Jung helped his patients toward self-transformation by enabling them to interpret and integrate into the self the unconscious materials (fantasies and dreams, often in dialogue form) called forth by the creative journaling process he called "active imagination." The creative goal, as Shamdasani puts it, is to use the mythopoeic imagination (a "higher wisdom") that has been lost to the modern age in order to "reconcile the spirit of the time with the spirit of depth" (39, 49). Let me offer a few words of explanation regarding Shamdasani's distinction. The spirit of the time (more commonly the Zeitgeist) is the general spirit in which we act and think as we live in our era; the spirit of depth, Jung writes, "evokes everything that man cannot" and speaks "in riddles," often in dreams, "the guiding words of the soul" (132, 154–55). The spirit of depth is thereby the gateway to the soul, the nourishing unconscious. But out of balance, the unconscious is less nourishing than dangerous: "The spirit of this time is ungodly, the spirit of the depths is ungodly, balance is godly." Understanding this, Jung adds, "is how I overcame madness" (150). The fusion effected by individuation, then, inspires a break with social conformity, bound by time (204–7). Individuation is, therefore, a transcendent function for the individual, a function Mailer was obviously seeking throughout *Lipton's*.

Mailer's desire, as he later said in *Advertisements for Myself,* to find "the courage to pay the high price of full consciousness. . . . and to make a revolution in the consciousness of our time" (17) was necessarily based first on making a revolution in his own consciousness through *Lipton's* in the mid-1950s. Speaking of the collapse of former civilizations and the old order in World War I, Jung too understood that no social revolution is possible without internal revolution first in individuals' consciousness. He put it this way: "Too many still look outwards. . . . But still too few look inwards, to their own selves, and still fewer ask themselves whether the ends of human society might not best be served if each man tried to abolish the old order in himself, and to practice in his own person and in his own state those precepts . . . which he preaches at every street corner, instead of always expecting these things of his fellow men" (*Two Essays on Analytical Psychology*, 5).

Mailer's work in the sixties represents not only a significant change in style, but the breaking through of a new self, a self that includes qualities his former self lacked and that now give "rise to images assumed worthless from the rational perspective," as Shamdasini describes the phenomenon. Shamdasini then adds, "The first possibility of making use of them is artistic" (Jung, *Red Book* 60). The archetypal imagery in Mailer's fiction, as in any archetypal art, is imagery that can educate the spirit of an age, offsetting its one-sidedness. It is art that can synthesize dualities by resetting the balance against imbalance and disproportion. "If society is allowed to-tal reason, it will destroy itself," Mailer writes. "I am a revolutionary be-cause only by revolution, and probably not political revolution, can the S [Society/Sociostasis] be set back . . . and put into serious retreat, thus opening larger H [Homeostasis or later in the journal "Homeodynamism"] gambits for future generations" (*Lipton's* #353). Mailer argues that without the counterpoise of homeodynamic psychic force, Reason becomes Soci-ety's Rationalization, "so H turns to the illogical, the intuitive, the *irratio-nal*" (Mailer's emphasis) (#250). The dialectic he was drawn to he found in himself: "I am the rationalist who is drawn to mystery" (#289). For Mailer it is "the extraordinary contradiction of my personality . . . that gave me strength as a writer," (#316).

In early 1955 while waiting for the galley proofs of *The Deer Park,* Mailer comes to understand that *Lipton's Journal* is showing him the way forward as a rebel artist: "Doing my analysis in the way proper for me . . . is through creativity—taking into self, synthesizing." He comes to see that in our psychic duality ("the polarity, the double") the conscious and the unconscious reflect one another in the manner of "a dialectic." Mailer puts it this way: "What I believe is true of psyche and of dialectic" is that "as we plumb . . . the unconscious, states of consciousness appear" (#379, #440). As a psychotherapist, June Singer describes the therapeutic process, like-wise, as the "dialectic between ego and the unconscious" that has the poten-tial to "result in a transformation of the personality" (29). Jung called this nourishing and rebalancing of consciousness "*mysterium coniunctionis*"—wholeness of self through the synthesis of opposites. "My mind is deeply dialectical," Mailer later writes. "The whole journal has been a dialectical illumination" (#404). Right to the end, this duality/dialectical theme re-appears in Mailer's journal. "We dip into our er, our collective wisdom," Mailer says, and return to the world "with insights . . . colored by our S" (#606). ("Er" becomes one of Mailer's words for vital force in the uncon-scious, just as S becomes his shorthand for Society/Sociostasis.) This vital duality within us, this "lore of the mind-body . . . is the source of all cre-ativity to us" (#645). The exploratory processes, his adventures, in *Lipton's* will become ever more the processes of his later books, just as archetypal imagery will reflect that creative narrative process. "The novel goes from writer's-thought to reader's-thought by the use of oblique (obliging) symbol, expression, or montage," Mailer writes. The creative process must be authentic (i.e., autonomously archetypal), fed by the unconscious, not constructed by the rational mind alone. And that is why Mailer says he can't write a fully outlined novel knowing "what I want to say," because "it comes out too thin, too ideated. My best scenes are the ones where I didn't know what I was doing" (# 698). Those interested in pursuing a detailed analysis of how archetypes function and cohere throughout Mailer's writings (up to 1980) may refer to my book, *Acts of Regeneration: Allegory and Archetype in the Work of Norman Mailer.*

Jung, like Mailer, began to profoundly adjust his life and work as a result of his experiment in self-analysis. Within a year of beginning his journal he resigned in 1914 from the medical faculty of the University of Zurich and as president of the International Psychoanalytic Association so that he could focus on what he believed was his more creative work on the collective unconscious and its historical manifestations in world art and religion. And he would thereafter focus his therapeutic work with his patients on their confrontation with the deepest unconscious material in their own search for psychic integration and balance. "It will be no joy," Jung says of "my transformation. . . . But a long suffering since you want to become your own creator. If you want to create yourself, then you do not begin with the best and the highest, but with the worst and the deepest." He later writes, "Incidentally, mustn't it be a peculiarly beautiful feeling to hit bottom . . . at least once, where there is no going down any further, but only upward beckons at best?" (188–89, 235). In *Cannibals and Christians,* Mailer put it this way: "Postulate a modern soul marooned in constipation, emptiness, boredom and a flat dull terror of death. . . . It is a deadened existence, afraid precisely of violence, cannibalism, loneliness, insanity, libidinousness, hell, perversion, and mess, because these are the states which must in some way be passed through, digested, transcended, if one is to make one's way back to life" (269–70). *An American Dream* is Mailer's first fully realized fictional narrative of such descent and transcendence, a modern retelling of the ancient heroic journey.

For both Freud and Jung, making one's way back from the depths to life requires the integration of one's dualities. But one must first recognize the dual nature of one's personality and allow each element of the duality its time, place, and energies. Jung saw his own dual personality, on the one hand, as the accomplished schoolboy, his failings and ineptitudes, but also his love of and success with science. The second personality was the man full of theological reflections, in communication with nature and cosmos, the lover of art and humanities. Jung found psychiatry a means of integrating his interests in both science and art, his rational self and his intuitive self. For Mailer the personal duality is most readily expressed, as he wrote in *Lipton's*, as "the neurotic little boy" and "the sweet clumsy anxious to please Middle-class Jewish boy" (#187, #228) who will go to Harvard to pursue his scientific interests, but who began studying American literature in 1939 and, as he put it in *Advertisements for Myself*, realized he wanted to become "a major writer" (27). But through *Lipton's*, he will go on, more importantly, to become a rebel writer challenging his society and, in Jung's words, "his time."

Mailer's Jungian discoveries and sympathies stem in part from Mailer's problem with Freudian psychoanalysis as it was generally practiced. Mailer read Jung in his search for a deeper, more congenial understanding of the psyche. The Farley Library at Wilkes University now has a Mailer Reading Room on the second floor that is a replica of Mailer's study and library in Provincetown, Massachusetts, including all Mailer's books from that study. Although I had been in Mailer's study in Provincetown once, I didn't have the time to peruse the shelves properly. But in that Wilkes replica I had the time to discover that Mailer had a significant collection of Jung's collected works, published in twenty volumes in its Bollingen Series by Princeton University Press. These include the handsome, durable paperback editions of *Freud and Psychoanalysis, Symbols of Transformation, Alchemical Studies, Mysterium Coniunctionis, The Archetypes of the Collective Unconscious, Two Essays on Analytical Psychology, The Development of Personality, Aion*, and *The Practice of Psychotherapy*.

On Mailer's shelves I also found books about Jung: Barbara Hanna's, Aryan Christ's, and Frank McLyan's biographies, as well as Jung's own autobiography, *Memories, Dreams, Reflections*, which received an asterisk signifying its importance in the bibliography at the end of Mailer's last novel, *Castle in the Forest*. Other related works, such as Claude Levi-Strauss's *From Honey to Ashes: An Introduction to a Science of Mythology*, sat nearby on these same shelves, as if to emphasize Mailer's interest in the mythological and archetypal levels of his own work. We know Mailer was contemplating a sequel to *Harlot's Ghost* (*Harlot's Grave*) with a Jungian protagonist. Moreover, Susan Mailer reported at a Mailer Society conference that her father questioned her (his psychotherapist daughter) rather pointedly about Jung in the 1970s. And in January of 2007, during one of his last interviews, Mailer told Michael Lee in *Cape Cod's Literary Voice* that he decided "on my own" that it's as if "an unconscious was lent to us, almost like a Jungian notion," but "I didn't have to read Carl Jung to decide this." Mailer's 2007 "notion" that "the unconscious taps into a deeper realm of knowledge that we possess," if the unconscious "trusts you," is also close to a classical sense of the Muse. Nonetheless, we do not know conclusively whether Mailer had read much or any Jung by 1955, although it's obvious from the journal he knew *about* Jung, as so many knew generally of Freud and Jung (among other psychoanalysts) at the time. My speculation is that Mailer came to his self-analytic journaling technique by his own path, not by Jung's, whose own journal wasn't published till 2009.

For Mailer, the problem with Freudianism was that it seemed to be a kind of "ideational lobotomy," severing man from his deeper world, his soul, and leaving him adjusted to, marooned in, the "dead world of society" (#35). He accuses one New York psychoanalyst of being afraid of "taking a wild plunge off the Freudian board into the oceanic unconscious," a plunge Mailer is himself now taking through his journal (#529). Mailer, who mentions in *Advertisements for Myself* that he once considered abandoning writing for a career as a psychoanalyst (108), sees himself through *Lipton's* as "embarking on the second Freudian expedition into the unknown" (#159), just as Jung did in his journal, as well as in his decades of studying comparative anthropology.

Jung's own "second Freudian expedition" also credits Freud for his bold accomplishment, as stated in *The Spirit in Man, Art, and Literature:* "Like Nietzsche, like the Great War, and like James Joyce, his literary counterpart, Freud is an answer to the sickness of the nineteenth century" (37). I would add Marx to this list. Jung writes, "The Victorian era was an age of repression, of a convulsive attempt to keep anaemic ideals artificially alive in a framework of bourgeois respectability by constant moralizings" (34).

Jung's self-analysis, however, instigated his own break with Freud. Jung not only became disenchanted with the limitations of experimental and statistical psychiatry. Even though Jung began his research into deeper layers of unconsciousness before he met Freud, he turned from Freud in 1910 because he believed that Freud reduced all psychic distress to sexual repression or trauma and because of Freud's emphasis on the personal unconscious to the exclusion of transpersonal elements of the psyche. For Jung, psychotherapy could no longer be solely preoccupied with the treatment of psychopathology; rather, psychotherapy becomes for Jung, in Shamdasani's words, "a practice to enable the higher development of the individual through fostering the individuation process" (*Red Book* 75). It is not enough for therapy to adjust one to society. Creativity, psychic integration, and balance constitute larger goals for mental health. Mailer's friendship with psychiatrist Robert Lindner—who read and discussed installments of *Lipton's* as they were being written and figures prominently in it—began when Mailer saw that Lindner understood the shortcomings of any therapy that merely adjusts the individual to the world, to the time and society in which one lives. Lindner agreed with Mailer's feelings (expressed in *Lipton's*) that *The Deer Park* was "a phase, a necessary step in your development. . . . Now that this [book] is well on its way, you're free to grow a new self."

I am quoting from Mike Lennon and Susan Mailer's recently available online edition of the Mailer-Lindner correspondence (25 January 1955), appended to the published edition of Mailer's *Lipton's Journal*. Eventually Mailer and Lindner had a falling out over the journal's contents. In Lindner's view, the problem was Mailer's "insistence on projecting some of your doubts about the 'new' self you are discovering on me" (14 March 1955). But Lindner's private responses to the journal were by and large helpful to Mailer's development, though they in no way constituted a professional psychoanalysis of Mailer's psychological state at the time.

The insights Jung gained from his journal, as I indicated, changed his professional life and priorities; those insights also informed all his writings thereafter. Jung described in his autobiography those years between 1913 and 1920 spent "pursuing my inner images" through his journal as "the most important in my life . . . with the goal of psychic development of the self" (*Memories* 196, 199). I would argue the same might be said of Mailer's life and self-induced therapy merely beginning in 1955. Although *Lipton's Journal* is more compact, much less filled with dramatic confrontations and dialogues with archetypal figures, and covers a shorter time devoted to the self-analytical journaling experiment, a case can be made that *Lipton's* (which, in a letter to Lindner, Mailer called his "internal dialogue between the doctor and the patient in me") is merely a "catalyst" (to use Mailer's description to Lindner), a first draft of a larger, multivolume project (*Selected Letters*, 183, 193,. for Mailer extended his self-analysis beyond *Lipton's* per se and into the next decade of his fiction and nonfiction. For practical purposes here, I can only suggest what I mean by Mailer's extended and public self-analysis through the 1960s.

That public self-analysis was collected and launched in 1959 with the publication of *Advertisements for Myself,* a first fleshing out of the ideas and the new consciousness Mailer was first approaching in *Lipton's* in 1955. His introductions ("advertisements") to each section of the book are his "muted autobiography," a continuation of self-analytical moments as he looks back on his earlier life and work, a sort of confessional analysis more fit, however, for public self-revelation than for the private meditations of his journal. He tells us in one advertisement that his journal of "self-analysis" with "marijuana, my private discovery," led him to evolve into "a psychic outlaw," a "changed writer" even as he worked on the page proofs of *The Deer Park:* "Finally, I was learning how to write." His new outlaw voice and style began to emerge in his *Village Voice* column in 1956 as the opening salvo of his battle for a revolution in consciousness, "a seed ground for the opinions of America." The new style was "a purgative to bad habit" and an expression of "rage against the national conformity which smothered creativity, for it delayed the self-creation of the race." That new style became "the first lick of fire in a new American consciousness . . . I was gambling all I had" (219, 234–35, 277, 283–84, 335). We also see in *Advertisements* the emergence of the dialogue form that Jung had used so often in his self-analysis, but the real "seeds" of his future work, Mailer points out, are collected in the last half of the book—"The White Negro," "The Time of Her Time," and "Advertisements for Myself on the Way Out" (335). It becomes more obvious that *Advertisements,* the first progeny of *Lipton's,* is *the* transitional book for Mailer and that his 1959 book looks particularly toward *An American Dream,* the first fictional development of the themes begun in *Lipton's Journal* and given initial public airing in *Advertisements for Myself.*

Cannibals and Christians (1966), a collection of diverse pieces, can be read as a sort of exegesis for *An American Dream* (1964, 1965). The two books function like artistic pendants, parallel texts. The extension of speculations and meditations begun in *Lipton's* are developed much further in *Cannibals* for publication. And just as Mailer began to make use of the dialogue form in his published existential and psychological musings in *The Presidential Papers* (1963), in *Cannibals* the technique—echoing the many dialogues in Jung's *Red Book*—comes to full fruition. Two dialogues are of particular significance. "The Metaphysics of the Belly" posits intuition as messages from the unconscious that can transform perception, perception that is both physical and psychic, i.e., integrated (*Cannibals* 263–65). It is such messages from the unconscious that continually urge themselves on the hero Rojack in *An American Dream*, the potential source of his transformation: "I felt as if I had crossed a chasm of time and was some new breed of man" (81). In the other major dialogue, "The Political Economy of Time," Mailer explicitly connects body and soul into a "being" and connects the soul with the unconscious (287–373). This dialogue particularly is in turn strikingly (if annoyingly, as some of Mailer's critics claimed) similar to the dialogue in chapter 6 of *American Dream* between Rojack and his heroine, Cherry, a dialogue that repeats much of what Mailer wrote in *Lipton's* about the struggle between Soul and Society.

During the writing of *An American Dream*, Mailer was in a state of personal crisis once again, perhaps even worse than that during his writing of *Lipton's*. Looking back on that period in *Existential Errands* (1972), Mailer described it as one of the lowest, despairing points of his life. The tone of *The Presidential Papers* reflects that crisis, as *Lipton's* reflects the earlier one, but his collections of poems *Deaths for the Ladies (and other disasters)* (1962) strikes the tone even more emphatically. His failing marriage to Adele ended with him stabbing her in 1960 during a drunken fight, his 1962 marriage to Lady Jeanne Campbell had collapsed, and in late 1964 he had married Beverly Bentley. Though he had found his voice, he was still a man who had not yet come through.

American Dream can be read as a fictionalized extension of *Lipton's*, another public development. But this time, in *American Dream*, the book foregrounds all the archetypal figures and dialogues of mythopoetic art. The unconscious material is fully fleshed out in narrative. It does the

———

novel no disservice to argue that it is a deeply if partially autobiographical plunge into powerful unconscious material and filled with figures who test, threaten, and help the hero in his extreme state of (as Mailer put it in a letter of 3 June 1965 to his translator Eiichi Yamanishi) "emotional exhaustion and existential disorientation" during his quest for renewal. Mailer described the novel's originality as his attempt to write "the dramatic history of a man's soul over thirty-two hours . . . a time of intense despair" (*Selected Letters* 350). *An American Dream*, then, rewards archetypal analysis as a story of the classic hero's journey (crisis-descent-return), a quest and battle for wholeness arising out of traumatic psychic disruption. At the same time, it represents the commonplace, almost banal, reading experience of the much-worked-over conventions of crime fiction and the familiar elements of the mythic heroic quest. But it is this very narrative mundanity that also makes the novel one of Mailer's most mythopoetic. As Mailer put it in his 23 April 1965 letter to John Aldridge, "The narrative clichés were chosen precisely because I felt they had been despised so long that a novelistic magic had returned to them" (*Selected Letters* 346).

Similarly, in one of Jung's dreams entitled in his *Red Book* "The Castle in the Forest," (as Mailer's final novel is titled), during Jung's dialogue with an old hierophant/scholar/scientist/Logos figure and his daughter, a Salome/anima/Eros figure, Jung at first feels outrage at the "common" folklorish, "hackneyed nonsense"; by the "sentimental romance," the "hellish banality," and the "pulp fiction" of the visionary experience. It was "enough to make me laugh." But such familiar narratives "on everyone's lips for millennia," Jung comes to understand, offer the ancient lore and wisdom of "a collective vision" of opposing forces that are "universally human," primordial, and which teach us that "Balance is the way" (220–24).

Two years later Mailer writes a novel of a very different kind that nonetheless also carries forth the themes first arising out of *Lipton's Journal*. *Why Are We in Vietnam?* (1967) is Mailer's Swiftian-satirical, libidinous, Dionysian, darkly humorous rant, complete with mythic rituals, dialogues, and confrontations among archetypal figures. It is Mailer's rant against the status quo of the military-industrial society that peaked in the 1960s. A spontaneous rant in the form of an inspired tour de force of youthful alienation from a murderous, hypertechnological society that desacralizes all elements of the ancient hunt ritual in a rapacious desire for complete domination over man and nature. It is the cry of Mailer's soul-rage (embodied in the trickster-fool narrator D.J., "disk jockey to the world"). Mailer's rage expresses his homeodynamic "er" (the vital force of his unconscious, as he describes the "er" in *Lipton's*) pitted against a corporate America that chose devastating technological warfare in a far-off Asian jungle. Warfare America would eventually lose. The satirical obscenity in the novel is nothing compared to the obscene lies and acts that enabled the war in Vietnam and took more than three million lives (half a Holocaust) and wasted millions of other lives of survivors and their families. Back in 1955 in *Lipton's* Mailer also had been already trying out part of his narrative strategy in *Vietnam?*—that is, his theory of human beings as "receivers and senders of electric waves" and of the radio as providing "an ear" into one's unconscious, "a vital experience longed for," giving us "electric communication." Mailer went so far as to propose in *Lipton's* that his wife Adele could be "a hipster-lady" if she could "m.c." her own radio program (#344, #681). Adele, thereby, might be seen as an early prototype in Mailer's mind for the narrator of *Vietnam?* as a D.J. who beams her/his "grassed out" hipster rant across the collective "magnetic-electro fief" to the American ear.

Although after *Vietnam?* Mailer would give up fiction per se for a decade, *Armies of the Night* (1968)—again with brio, élan, and outrageous humor—is more than a little filled with Mailer's continuing self-analysis, with personal tests of courage and displays of incapacity, with analytical insights into various Mailerian personae, and with new rebellious energy in Mailer's more intuitive, more Melvillian, post-1950s style. In short, the self-analysis begun in *Lipton's* and carried forward into the autobiographical introductions in *Advertisements* continues here. He even takes up the question of obscenity so prevalent (and apparently so troublesome) in the literary satire of *Why Are We in Vietnam?* The real obscenity in American life is done to humanity and nature by those politicians and corporation executives who are "perfectly capable of burning unseen women and children in the Vietnamese jungles, yet feel a large displeasure . . . at the generous use of obscenity in literature and in public" (*Armies* 47).

But *Armies*, more than *An American Dream* or *Why Are We in Vietnam?*, reads like the work of a man who has come through. Mailer discovers, in an event filled with absurdity, compromise, and mass movements, hope for a renaissance of integrated consciousness. The book is a record of a war, a war between a dead world and a living one, during the "long dark night of the soul" in America. Mailer from the start realizes he had been dragging his own bad image around like a sarcophagus, that he has often been his own worst enemy, that he has been a man of self-defeating unintegrated polarities. In book 1, "History as Novel," he plays both observer and actor, and it is as actor that his flawed personae emerge. But in Mailer's flaws lie his strengths; he becomes a fool-hero, a persona not unlike D.J.'s outraged fool, full of comic flaws and disproportions but nonetheless encouraging and participating in the symbolic rites and revels that, in *Armies*, confront the center of military-industrial-technological power, the Pentagon. As a fool-figure, both absurd and prophetic, Mailer assumes the potentialities of that mythic character of universal dimensions, as Enid Welsford points out in *The Fool*, based on a long history and mythology of fools as agents of human emancipation from stifling order, from leviathan states and their representatives. The fool's wisdom is not of the intellect but of the spirit; he draws from mankind the self's inner antagonism against the oppressive social order. In one incarnation, the holy fool, he represents a receding of the "logical soul" or consciousness and advances the inspired, irrational soul. Satire is one of his natural modes of expression (Welsford 315–19). He is, then, a representative of what Mailer called back in 1955 homeostasis, the ranting, romping enemy of sociostasis. Especially as he observes the antagonistic battles, rites, and rituals of the demonstrators in book 2, Mailer realizes he is witnessing an historical moment when "the radiance of some greater heroic hours may have come nonetheless to shine along *the inner space* [Mailer's emphasis] and caverns of the freaks. . . . some refrain from all the great American rites of passage. . . ." Despite their flaws, the protesters, reinvigorating Dionysian symbolic warfare in a "crazy time" of history, have found the endurance and courage "in a painful spiritual test" where "some part of the man has been born again, and is better" (*Armies* 280–81). Mailer too has been changed: "he felt one suspicion of a whole man closer to that freedom from dread which occupied the inner drama of his years . . . than when he had come to Washington four days ago" (212–213).

Mailer seems to have discovered in his march on the Pentagon and in his writing about it new energy and a new faith in nonfiction, the genre that would consume his next decade. By his immersion in historical experience, he discovered the primordial order of energizing archetypal ritual, he discovered wholeness and purpose in a world apparently without wholeness and purpose, and he discovered that through the unifying force of his art he could give meaning to the events of his time. Mailer discovered in writing *Armies,* therefore, that imagination and reality can unite to produce a new foundation for narrative structure and theme and a new complication in his relationship to his characters and material. Enlightened by Mailer's previously private journal, I'd like to propose that Mailer's books of the seventies through the nineties might be read profitably anew with a full recognition of the extended experiments in individuation, private and published, in which Mailer engaged from 1955 through 1968.

MAILER AND JAZZ

AUTHOR'S NOTE: *This portion of the essay was delivered in an earlier draft at the 2017 Mailer Society Conference in Sarasota, Florida. As people filed into the room, I played Sonny Stitt's "Autumn in New York," a Stitt tune Mailer loved and which played at the Mailer Memorial Tribute at Carnegie Hall in April of 2008. This rendition is available on Stitt's CD* Personal Appearance, *track 3. At the end of my presentation, I played Dizzy Gillespie's "We Love to Boogie," available on his CD entitled* School Days, *track 10. Both are also available on YouTube.*

During the thirteen weeks spent composing his private journal of self-analysis between December of 1954 and March of 1955, Mailer recorded his discovery of jazz as one of the most significant vehicles to tap into his libidinous, instinctive, and liberated self as an artist. Mailer considered and analyzed many topics that might open pathways into his deepest self: language and style, sexuality, Wilhelm Reich, gender and bisexuality (close to Jung on our inner gender duality), the Holocaust, humor, hip, courage, Marx, and the visual arts among them. Any of these topics will reward further analysis of Mailer's journal, but jazz music will be my focus here as one of the most important topics as Mailer prepared himself to emerge from the 1950s a rebel writer whose language can now be as much or more concerned with rhythm and sound as it used to be concerned with literal sense.

How did jazz become one of the most important vehicles for Mailer's literary, psychological, and even spiritual transformation? Mailer was tone deaf and never played an instrument. Nonetheless, in the fifties he and his new wife Adele went on weekends with friends into such Village and Harlem jazz clubs as The Village Vanguard, Five Spot, and Jazz Gallery. Mailer met some of the musicians and ultimately became friends with saxophonists Sonny Stitt and Sonny Rollins. Mailer's 1957 essay "The White Negro" (collected in *Advertisements for Myself*) is but one product of Mailer's jazz experiences. In "White Negro" Mailer writes that the "presence of Hip as a working philosophy in the sub-worlds of American life is probably due to jazz . . . its subtle but so penetrating influence on an avant-garde generation." Jazz, he continues, is the black man's connection to survival through "the art of the primitive," the voice of all the highs and lows of his existence, the music of orgasm, good or bad, the communication of "instantaneous existential states" (340–41). The jazz musician "is the cultural mentor of a people" (348). *Lipton's Journal* is the very seedbed of such ideas expressed in that notorious essay, as indeed Mailer's journal reveals the processes of germination for one writer's acts of self-creation and regeneration. Over the length of *Lipton's*, we see the direct influence jazz musicians had on Mailer himself, teaching him some things he was ready to learn, or relearn, about existential art, about taking risks whether you succeed or fail, about art as antitotalitarian force, and about the sound and rhythms of improvisational language.

He writes of his coming to understand that "jazz consists almost entirely of surprising one's expectations" and that "the artistry lies in the degree to which each successive expectation is startled." It is an art form that "has risen to the crisis of modern painting" by "changing the audience's expectations nightly. . . . a self-accelerating process," that is not without risk and is now blending all the arts (#8).

The surprising risks jazz musicians take display the existential nature of their art, through the immediacy of improvisational creation. "Instead of trying to understand the beauty of jazz," Mailer writes, "one should understand it as something which is constantly triumphing *and* failing." Victory is simply the "effort to keep musically alive." To flesh out these insights, he offers the example of Dave Brubeck and Paul Desmond improvising together "entirely off on their own with nothing but their nervous systems to

sustain them wandering through jungles of invention with society continually ambushing them." Brubeck, Mailer adds, might "wander into a cliché,
then investigate it, pull it apart . . . put it together into something new."
Sometimes Brubeck succeeds, sometimes he fails, but whether he fails or
succeeds he accepts the risk and creates "a communication between the
soul and the world." Caution is the "high priest of society," Mailer continues,
and "swing is a distillation of competitiveness in social life," but "jazz is the
soul" (#47, #50). Here Mailer echoes a quip often attributed to Duke El-
lington when asked about the difference between swing music of the thir-
ties and forties (the pop music of Mailer's generation) and jazz: Swing is
business, jazz is art.

Mailer more than once compares playing jazz to bullfighting, another
existential art, and posits that jazz, bullfighting, and cosmopolitanism are
the three "culture bearers of the hipster," culture bearers that "Stalinism
[i.e., totalitarianism] will continue to war against" (#57). Mailer will follow
up this thought later, writing that Be-bop "is a hybrid art (like opera)," expressing a distrust of society, a sort of decadence that allows the soul of the
musician to be expressed (#422). These thoughts lead Mailer into meditations on the language of jazz and the hipster, the language of antitotalitari-
anism. Hipster speech contains "fucking rhythms . . . almost as powerful as
music." About the be-bop jazz chorus, he writes, "You get me bee-bopping
too." It was the energized be-bop form of jazz in the early fifties that helped
him feel his way beyond "the sweet clumsy anxious to please Middle-class
Jewish boy" (#186, #187).

As he would later say in "The White Negro" about hip language, Mailer
first says in his journal that there is a poetic diction in improvisational be-
bop, especially, where the words, whether sung as jazz scat or played on a
horn, "can mean two or three things at the same time," and may bring us
all to a point where we "speak in the style of *Finnegan's Wake*" (#242). Be-
bop, he later writes, "is the first popular and tentative expression of Joycean
language . . . Which is why I prefer it to cool, which while technically advanced is nonetheless a retreat from a more advanced state of perception"
(#667). If Rojack in *An American Dream* might well represent Mailer's first
fictional hero as hipster and psychopath seeking regeneration, it is D.J. in
Why Are We in Vietnam? who to my mind best represents the jazzman
or hipster's improvisational, instinctual, free-flowing font of language and

sound. *Vietnam?* is his hipster novel, his rebel novel, his be-bop novel, his most improvisational novel, that novel he said on several occasions was the only book that came to him on a wave of inspiration without the hard and dreadful labors so many of his other books required.

Dizzy Gillespie, the trumpeting prophet of the be-bop style with a dizzying range, Mailer much admired, calling him a genius, and noting that jazz is "more creative, the more responsive to genius than classical" even if "it [jazz] is a degraded expression," the only kind of expression left to genius in our time (#134). One thing Dizzy seems to have taught him appears shortly after his notes on the Diz: "I suspect," Mailer writes, "that the frequency of sound has some relation to the depth of one's *unconscious*. As frequency is stepped up so the notes rise [as in the upper registers and limits of the trumpet or saxophone].... Low notes are progressively more *conscious*" (#668; my emphasis). So be-bop, especially in the highest ranges of an instrument, becomes yet another source, a hip source, into the unconscious of the artist, and perhaps of the listener. Jazz, then, became for Mailer one avenue into the unconscious and instinctual life, into rebellion, into existential and risky artistry. Into what—finally by 1959 in *Advertisements for Myself*—would become Mailer's own, true voice. And Dizzy, I'm going to speculate, is the one whose brash be-bop trumpet playing gave Mailer the clue to his famous line near the end of *The Deer Park*. For Mailer found his voice and his rebellion in *Lipton's Journal*, in large part through jazz, and like Sergius O'Shaugnessy at the end of *The Deer Park*, emerged better prepared "to blow against the walls of every power that exists, the small trumpet of his defiance" (374).

3

MAILER AND MILLETT

Sex Prison

Women and Men who were born during or after the political and social unrest of the 1960s and '70s may find it hard to relate to the debates over second wave feminism during that time. The flagrant level of the economic oppression and political exclusion of women that ignited the women's liberation movement in the middle of the twentieth century would be barely recognizable by the 2020s. And unrecognizable to the older generations of the sixties and seventies would be our current sense of gender fluidity in our more inclusive culture today. However, as people born after the mid-century look back, they might be able to gain some purchase on the issues of that earlier women's movement if they can connect those old issues to our own lingering aftermath of gender inequity, to the predatory misogyny that the Me Too movement has exposed and confronted, and to such events as The Women's March against sexism and misogyny the day after Donald Trump's inauguration in 2017.

In the early 1970s Mailer found himself in the middle of the often-rancorous debates over second wave feminism after he discovered female social and literary critics took him as their literary bête noire. After reading Kate Millett's *Sexual Politics* as a part of his research into feminist authors to find out how he had become feminist anathema, he decided to have his say, as we might expect, by writing a book about what he had learned. He found some easy targets, such as Valerie Solanis's *SCUM Manifesto* arguing for the elimination of men as a biological accident, an incomplete female, and a "walking abortion." But Mailer preferred to devote most of his attention to Millett's book as a more well-researched historical attack on institutionalized misogyny and as a sustained criticism of male writers, including himself.

There is no question that Kate Millett's *Sexual Politics* is an important document for its time and for ours, primarily due to its exhaustive account between the covers of a single book of the historical subjugation of women. After the somewhat more tentative assertions in the fifty-eight pages of part 1, "Sexual Politics" ("instances" and "theory"), the book takes off in part 2, "Historical Background," for the next 175 pages, covering 1830–1930 as "The Sexual Revolution, First Phase" and covering 1930–60 as "The Counter Revolution." Throughout this most developed part of the book the prose is lucid and convincing, the assertions well-documented; here Millett's highly specified litany of the violations of women's rights flesh out our more general sense of the horrors of Victorian and late Industrial employment (and unemployment) for women.

Unfortunately, Mailer did not with any substance address this second, largest section of Millett's book. It was the final third of the book, part 3, "The Literary Reflection," that Mailer took issue with. He did so by not addressing what Millett had to say about his own work through the late 1960s; he avoided that defensiveness by offering a strikingly different view of two other authors Millett had attacked, D. H. Lawrence and Henry Miller. This he did after his account of reading certain current feminists and his reaction to them, and after expressing his support for economic and political equity for women. It was, then, against Millett's reading of Lawrence and Miller, not the substance of her detailed historical analysis, that Mailer launched his counterpolemic. I will let Mailer speak for himself in a moment, but I must admit I too found this final third of Millett's book oddly, after its earlier substance and merit, less than convincing. Briefly, to take Millett's approach to Mailer, since he avoided doing so, I had the reaction teachers of introductory literature classes would recognize when students confuse an author with his or her characters, mistake satire for literal polemic, or in other ways misunderstand the deeper ambiguities of imaginative literature.

That an author has the temerity to explore the dysfunctions and gross imbalances in human nature would seem to set him, or her, up as an easy target. Mailer, as Millett acknowledges, had long studied the schizophrenia in the American psyche, its divided conscience, its dualistic qualities (315). The saint and psychopath, the seer and the beast, in all of us. But to read *The Naked and the Dead* as "a militarist" brief in favor of the "cancerous personalities" and "cheap patriotism" of Croft or Cummings, for their ultimately positive representations of incipient fascism and humanity's totalitarian impulses, is to misread the book rather remarkably (314, 316). True, after Mailer's modest Brooklyn boyhood, his years at Harvard, and then his sudden immersion in the violence of the Pacific Theater in World War II, Mailer's work became obsessed with the theme of violence, especially the pathological backlash to combat and to the stifling of social, economic, and sexual fulfillment. His admitted fascination with characters (heroic villains) like Sergeant Croft and General Cummings is not to condone them but to penetrate to the heart of the malevolent, and powerful, forces buried in humankind. And to discover psychosocial oppressions that prompt such forces to emerge, even as their purgative, to the extent there is one, can be shocking, violent, and oppressive. Mailer's lifelong political anxiety was that America would indeed become either a full-blown fascist or totalitarian polity. I would suggest another chapter-length reading of the novel as counterpoise to Millett's approach—Robert Merrill's second chapter in *Norman Mailer Revisited* entitled "*The Naked and the Dead:* The Beast and the Seer in Man" (11–29).

Millett's study of "WASP male psychosis" in Mailer's *Why Are We in Vietnam?* seems to me equally tendentious. Is that novel condoning wars instigated by patriarchal psychopathology? The novel is a raucous, ranting, scatological Swiftian tour de force satirizing the violent, competitive psychopathology of the American corporation and its top executives, the pathology Mailer saw as the root of our blunder into the wholly unnecessary, extraordinarily cruel, and mendacious war that killed three million people (half a Holocaust) in far off Asia. Mailer also was publicly against that war way before most Americans finally turned. Yes, the ancient rituals of the hunt under the psychotic leadership of the executive-fathers do turn narrator D.J. (and sidekick Tex) into, as Millett puts it, "the murderous order of his peers" and mentors (Millett 319). But that is precisely the point, not a condoning of the murderous order founded on toxic masculinity and patriarchy. A ranting half-mad narrator might be extolling the virtues of

---

59

eating Irish babies (or even abolishing Christianity in another rant), but the *author* of Swift's satires is not condoning the eating of children or the abolition of *true* principles of Christ's teachings (the rarest of practiced principles among "Christians"). If Mailer argues that one has to earn one's manhood, as Millett keeps reminding us, it does not mean that one must earn it only by unleashing the beast in oneself at the expense of other lives. But it does mean that, in twisted social and economic circumstances, manhood might emerge in toxic, violent ways. And even then, the victim of a patriarchal toxicity sometimes strikes the final blow, as "a Jewish college girl," who goes nameless in Millett's account of Mailer's story "The Time of Her Time," does when she, Denise Gondelman, on the way out the door tells her orgasmic violator Sergius O'Shaugnessy, "Your whole life is a lie, and you do nothing but run away from the homosexual that is you" (Millett 324–25). The Vietnam novel, as I argued at length in my first book on Mailer, is a narrative of a *failed ritual* of regeneration precisely because of the toxic masculinity heaped on D.J. by his father and other men on the Alaskan big game hunt.

To be fair, Mailer could subvert his own breakthroughs, too. After breaking through the Dark Night of His Soul in the 1950s, Mailer gained newfound success in the 1960s—only to founder on the rock of women's liberation, circa 1970. He lurched into the feminist bull's-eye without sufficient self-awareness, preparation, or public sobriety. One could not help wondering whether Mailer would ever be forgiven for his shortcomings, his wild blurting, in how he sometimes approached women's liberation—even though he was out front, often at personal and professional risk, on such fraught issues as civil rights, the Vietnam War, our nationalistic blunders abroad, economic injustice, environmental degradation, and the proxy and corporate-protection wars of our own often paranoid government.

Following a description of his discovery that feminists considered him their "major ideological opposition" in part 1 of this four-part *Prisoner of Sex*, parts 2 and 3 take us to the heart of the matter. Looking first at part 2, "The Acolyte," we see Mailer running headlong into voluminous reading to find out what indeed 1970s feminism/liberation is, as best he can discern it. Here Mailer lays out his first admission that should hint to his "opposition" that he is no cartoonish misogynist smugly accepting the economic exploitation of women, who, Mailer tells us (by available 1964 figures), are making only 60 percent of the wages of men, and only 2 percent of whom are earning in America's workforce over $10,000 a year. Any "everyday common conscience," Mailer writes, would recoil from such a "condition in need of amendment" (40). It seems reasonable to make allowances for the justifiable strain of feminist misandry in the 1970s, given the state of female exploitation and inequality on many fronts. But given also that things have not changed more than 17 percentage points on the issue of gender pay equity in half a century, it seems also reasonable to suggest to my academic colleagues that in any practical sense we should by now be more concerned (or even outraged) about the real-world exploiters of women (and children and men) and less ruffled about the fictional narratives of canonical and noncanonical male writers. According to the US Census Bureau, for example, the gender pay equity gap went from 60 percent to 77 percent (*Income, Poverty, and Health Insurance Coverage in the United States: 2009*, 11). And The World Economic Forum's most recent data available on their website (*The Global Gender Gap Report* 2014) puts the USA at number 20 out of 142 countries in gender equity, behind such countries as South Africa, the Philippines, Ireland, Rwanda, Latvia, Burundi, Ecuador, Bulgaria, and Slovenia.

Mailer also agrees in part 2 of *Prisoner* with feminist Linda Phelps that women should not merely emulate men, not live in positions of power in men's world, but that the society men have created must be changed before a just and humane world can be built for both women and men (43). Mailer is nothing if not, by his own lights, a revolutionary; he seems, however, to have been too easily baited and missed his chance to engage publicly with feminism in a wider, more nuanced, revolutionary cause.

Mailer, furthermore, in part 2 refutes, as the feminists did, Freud's theories of human (especially female) sexuality. He calls Freud's theories "cruel and unreasonable" (64–65). He also implies in the second part of the book what he will state explicitly later: his agreement with his "ideological opposition" in his attitude toward the 1950s domestic servitude of "the ranch house and plastic horizon." All "his enthusiasm for the mystery of the womb is not to squeeze women back into that old insane shoe," an insane shoe Betty Friedan called the Feminine Mystique. That Mystique, as Mailer puts it, is a creation of men, a "tool of still unsophisticated technologists and totalitarians." It led to a 1950s "hygienic and anti-sexual society" that "he [Mailer] hated . . . as few men alive" (128).

Is it not possible to say, at the least, after rereading part 2, that Mailer's attitude toward women's rights is a little more complicated than often portrayed? In fact, there is a basic distinction we need to make for clarity's sake. On one hand, Mailer's position on *women's rights* by 1970 is, as he admits, close to NOW's legislative agenda for the Equal Rights Amendment that in 1973 started down its decades-long, futile struggle for passage (40). He does suggest, however, that NOW's legislative initiative will probably fail in the political process and that nothing short of changing the whole economic system will serve the intent of the ERA (43). On the other hand, his attitude toward the coeval *women's liberation* movement is far less agreeable; he finds this postwar wave of feminists too often technophilic, tending toward a "unitary" or "totalitarian" vision of men and women. If we are going to critique Mailer's position on women, we should at least be attuned to such basic distinctions.

Much of the rest of part 2 consists of Mailer's examination at length of the women's liberation movement's specific cures for the social and political inequity he agrees they have correctly identified. But it is what he finds in his examination of the cures, as I've suggested, that gives him pause concerning the proposed solutions to men's historical exploitation of women. Using textual evidence from feminist writings, he makes the case for what he sees as a "Utopian" effort to alter the "design of human beings" in the "struggle with men" on the economic, corporate playing field in order to relieve "the damnable disadvantage" and "burden" (the feminists' word) of the womb. In short, he discovers an underlying theory ever tending (in varying degrees depending on the feminist author) toward human uniformity and technological solutions to exploitation and injustice. Ti-Grace Atkinson becomes Exhibit A in the effort to discredit sexual intercourse "as a means of population renewal" and as a rationale for "extra-uterine solutions" to the uterine "burdens" of our political economy (50–51).

And it is in chapter 5 of part 2 that Mailer presents through extensive quotation an ancillary tendency in liberationist writings to technologize sex, particularly the female orgasm by denying any experience of orgasm within the vagina through intercourse, a unitary theory of female orgasm

that even Germaine Greer disputes and whom Mailer quotes at considerable length (61–62). In Mailer's view, the case for limiting orgasm to the cli-
toris only is based on data from laboratory experimentation (or "laboratory
libido") and is an effort, by the testimony of some of his quoted sources, to
eliminate men from the sexual equation—one more example in Mailer's
view of the drive toward a unitary vision of women and humanity, which
is to say a fundamentally totalitarian impulse. Mailer sees any impulse to
homogenize sexual polarity as "a world where men and women were as
interchangeable as coin and cash." Is it possible on the other hand, Mailer
wonders, to believe that "God might have established man and woman in
some asymmetry of forces"? He also argues that the technological solutions
to sexual "asymmetry" are part of the effort to remove the mystery from
sexual experience (63, 65).

It might be helpful to pause a moment to remind ourselves that by 1971
Mailer had argued for years, and would continue to argue most cogently
in his nonfiction, against the dangers, even the evils, of the technological,
totalitarian, and mystery-denying impulses in *men*.

Part 3 of *Prisoner*, "The Advocate," is Mailer's head-on confrontation
with literary criticism, in this case feminist criticism, that relies on po-
lemical distortions of texts; that confrontation consumes 40 percent (or
seventy-one pages) of his book. His confrontation in part 3 is with Kate
Millett and her 1969 book, *Sexual Politics*. His strategy is to turn to the
other two male authors Millett excoriates. He struggles mightily to make
lengthy restorations of Henry Miller's and D. H. Lawrence's texts from Kate
Millett's quotations out of context and out of order, her truncated passages,
and her insinuated paraphrases or summaries in *Sexual Politics*. He writes:
"Her lack of fidelity to the material . . . was going to be equaled only by her
authority in characterizing it . . . jeering at difficulties which were often the
heart of the matter . . . the bloody ground strewn with the limbs of every
amputated quote. Everywhere were signs that men were guilty and women
must win" (72). Every reader will have to decide for herself whether the
fifty-three pages Mailer packed with restored texts beside Millett's truncated texts represent a fair, accurate, or even convincing case.

Laura Adams, to take one example of a female critic, said in *Existential
Battles: The Growth of Norman Mailer* that Mailer's case against Millett
is a fair and credible restoration of the male authors' works, even though

Adams disagrees at several points with Mailer's more speculative sexual theories (165). In her book *We Must March My Darlings: A Critical Decade,* Diana Trilling writes that it is "difficult to exaggerate the disorder . . . the raucousness" of the infamous April 30, 1971, town hall meeting in New York where Mailer stood his wobbly ground against a panel of four women (including Trilling) and a room full of women taking on his ideas in *A Prisoner of Sex.* It was more like a bearbaiting than a debate. (For anyone interested, D. A. Pennebaker's documentary record of the event, *Town Bloody Hall,* is readily available by typing in the title on YouTube.) Although Trilling too dissociates herself from Mailer's ideas at the time about contraception and conception, she also dissociates herself from the crowd's efforts to "wipe out all sexual differences . . . not merely on behalf of equality for women . . . but for all purposes of life itself" and in a context where half the human race was "expendable." Instead, and as Mailer had in his book, she was going "to put myself on the side of sexual duality" as well as the "individual complexity" of the female orgasm. All this does not mean, Trilling emphasizes in closing, that she does not oppose the "repressive, life-diminishing culture" that restricts the full range of opportunity and freedom for women (*Prisoner* 199–210). Neither did Mailer, as anyone who actually reads his book might see.

Given the tenor of the debates at the time, it seems important to understand also that Mailer does not present Miller and Lawrence as paragons of humanity or authorship. He specifically charges Miller, for example, with redundancy and with a lack of female characters "equal to Ibsen's Nora to stand against his men" (91). And he is quite critical of Lawrence's weaknesses as a writer: he could be pedestrian, didactic, "a pill and humorless nag," even at times "pathetic" but with an intellectual ambition sufficient to overthrow European civilization. He was "perhaps a great writer," but like Miller on a different, also flawed exploration in his life and work, Lawrence struggled to define himself and the deepest potential relations between men and women (100). Lawrence's quest, his experimentations, took wrong turns, revealed weaknesses, but he was courageous in his repressive historical moment, as Miller was in his. But *"Millett concealed the pilgrimage, hid the life, covered over that emotional odyssey,"* to make her reductive ideological point (102–3; my emphasis).

One feels curious to think of a later meeting between Mailer and Millett, which Millett generously initiated. As reported in Michael Lennon's biography of Mailer, Kate Millett (who was his daughter Susan's professor at Columbia University) first invited Mailer for a friendly drink in 1974. It was a remarkable peace offering after they had engaged in literary combat in their books, and Mailer appreciated it. But he had to decline, by way of a friendly letter, because he was on his way to Africa to cover the Frazier-Ali fight, which would result in his 1975 book *The Fight* (Lennon, *Norman Mailer* 478). Nonetheless, another invitation for a drink from Millett did result in a later meeting in Provincetown, Massachusetts. According to Millett, however, Mailer was condescending and kept the meeting brief (see http://localeastvillage.com/2012/06/06/35371/). The actual nature of their dialogue remains unclear since Millett's account is merely a passing remark and there is no record of their exchange.

These are the basic lineaments and strengths of Mailer's book through the second and third parts. Dare one hope that a new generation of female readers and critics might look at Mailer—at his arguments in *Prisoner* and at his larger body of work—with a more sympathetic response than their sisters of the 1970s? Part 4 entitled "The Prisoner," however, does less to help encourage hope and seems to my mind to be a flawed authorial strategy that might sink the ship Mailer had been so far carefully constructing. It's not that the final part is entirely without moments of merit. Mailer does try to advance reasonably his earlier argument that the womb attaches a woman to forces larger than the individual herself—to forces of biological creativity, gestation, and the birth of another living being. But wouldn't this be a better book if he had never written part 4 or had written it closer to his own advice to Miller? Like Miller and Lawrence, Mailer's own explorations as a human being and writer are of course flawed. Here, in the final section, he moves over from criticism and textual evidence to his outermost speculations regarding the mystical/cosmological implications of sex and conception. The speculations might be well-meaning as part of his effort to argue that "either sex had meaning which went to the root of existence, or it did not . . . and if human beings are not absurd . . . then sex cannot comfortably be absurd . . . and therefore best shunted over to semen banks and extra-uterine receptacles" (136–37). But in speculating over such a perhaps reasonable point, Mailer sounds at times like one of those clueless, old-school bishops or a zany right-wing politician on a roll using conception versus contraception as a ploy to fire his zealous base. Women, some of his less mystical speculations run, once had a natural internal ability to avoid or abort pregnancy; women at the top of the economic ladder would become a "gestation free elite," hiring others to have their children; children would be raised by the "collective professionalization of the care of the young." And Mailer would not marry a woman whose prenuptial demands, or contract, for division of labor would cause his "work to suffer" (142–44, 154, 161, 164). His final statement that he "would agree with everything they asked but to quit the womb" (168), to consider it nothing but "a burden," is perhaps unlikely to mitigate for most contemporary female readers the mystical and biological speculations that preceded such an ultimate "agreement."

The second misstep, as I see it, is that Mailer nowhere—and part 4 would be the natural place—offers women alternatives to being trapped in either domestic *or* corporate servitude. How might they best be liberated? What are the responsibilities of institutional and corporate chieftains and legislators to offer correctives for financial inequity, to offer solutions to problems of familial childcare? What is a feasible alternative, in Mailer's view, to a woman's technological separation from her womb, as he argued certain feminists were propounding? And wouldn't it be better to rally male authors—including himself—to be more attuned to some of their female characters and offer at times "women equal to Ibsen's Nora to stand against [their] men"? Given what comes before, why not propose answers to those questions, if there must be a fourth part of the book?

The Prisoner of Sex leaves me, at least, with several questions about critical approaches to Mailer. If by his own testimony Mailer would have women freed of economic exploitation, if he would rather they seek their liberation not through cultural and technological uniformities, if he would have feminist theoreticians at least play fairly with male authors when revealing their shortcomings, how might critics today confront Mailer on his "women's issue" fairly, honestly, and productively? How might they best illuminate for readers the true strengths and true weaknesses of this writer in his own experimental journey, in his own repressive historical moment, along the thorny path of one of literature's oldest themes: how to make sense of—and perhaps restore health to—relations between men and women?

4

MAILER
AND DIDION
Against Prevailing Winds

L
ike Diana Trilling, Joan Didion saw merit in Mailer's critique of what he saw as the strategies and unitary philosophy behind the 1970s women's liberation movement. Neither of these women nor Mailer had any intention of condoning the economic or social oppression of women. Of course, the corporate cultures of a WASP-patriarchal system in the postwar decades kept many women and minorities from achieving equal opportunity and pay. And Mailer, who could have become a revolutionary ally, was intemperate when he took on those who had attacked him and other male authors as among their misogynistic oppressors. Beyond that, Mailer, like most men of his generation born within a few years of women earning the right to vote—a long painful battle for suffrage that today seems outrageous to have been necessary, as much as the goals of the suffrage movement now seem eminently reasonable and obvious—still had some evolution in his thinking to undergo. Women did need another political and economic revolution by the 1960s. If they had emerged during the war into previously unknown employment opportunities on the home front's industrial boom, they were too often in the fifties being subordinated in the workplace again and "squeezed back into that old insane shoe," as Mailer put it, of suburban domesticity.

But when the feminists of the 1960s and 1970s appeared to Mailer, as he began to read them, to be insisting on unitarian theories of gender, biology, and sexuality, as opposed to polarity and diversity, he saw an opening and entered the fray. He had developed an ethic of risk-taking both as a man and a writer, even though taking risks at times led to embarrassment or failure. Didion too developed her own ethic of writing as the taking of risks, a point worth developing shortly. But in 1971, it was Didion who defended Mailer in an interview with Trudy Owett in *New York*. Mailer's position in *Prisoner of Sex*, Didion said, "strikes me as exactly right. I know he was picked by Kate Millett as one of the prime examples of male chauvinism and yet he is one of the few people who can write about sex without embarrassing me. I think sex is a lot darker than Kate Millett does. I think there is a lot more going on than meets her eye" (Owett 41).

I n fact, Didion went on to cover this territory herself in "The Women's Movement," a 1972 essay collected in *The White Album*. Here Didion sees the root of the movement as essentially a Marxist theory of creating a revolutionary class. However, "one oppressed class after another seemed finally to miss the point. The have-nots, it turned out, aspired mainly to having." And "just as disappointingly they failed to perceive their common cause with other minorities." She then turned to a critique reminiscent of Mailer's in *Prisoner of Sex*.

> If the family was the last fortress of capitalism, then abolish the family. If the necessity for conventional reproduction of the species seemed unfair to women, then let us transcend, via technology, "the very organization of nature," the oppression, as Shulamith Firestone saw it, "that goes back through recorded history to the animal kingdom itself". . . . Burn the literature, Ti-Grace Atkinson said in effect when it was suggested that, even come the revolution, there would still remain the whole body of "sexist" Western literature. But of course no books would be burned. The women of this movement were perfectly capable of crafting didactic revisions of whatever apparently intractable material came to hand. . . .
>
> The idea that fiction has certain irreducible ambiguities seemed never to occur to these women, nor should it have, for fiction is in most ways hostile to ideology. . . . Nonetheless it was serious. . . . Attention was finally being paid, and yet that attention was mired in the trivial.

Even the brightest movement women found themselves engaged in sullen public colloquies about the inequities of dishwashing and the intolerable humiliations of being observed by construction workers on Sixth Avenue. . . . They totted up the pans scoured, the towels picked off the bathroom floor, the loads of laundry done in a lifetime. Cooking a meal could only be "dogwork". . . . Small children could only be odious mechanisms for the spilling and digesting of food, for robbing women of their "freedom." It was a long way from Simone de Beauvoir's grave and awesome recognition of woman's role as "the Other" to the notion that the first step in changing that role was Alix Shulman's marriage contract . . . a document reproduced in *Ms.*, but it was just toward such trivialization that the woman's movement seemed to be heading. (109–13)

Diana and Lionel Trilling became Mailer's personal friends and correspondents, as Didion did not, but Mailer had enormous respect for Didion as a writer; they did become friendly, with only one bump in the road, as we say. Mailer interacted with Didion and her husband John Gregory Dunne when they were writing the screenplay for *The Deer Park*. Who better to take on Mailer's Hollywood novel for a screenplay? In an interview for *Variety* in May of 1987, Mailer spoke of Sidney Lumet possibly directing the film (McCarthy 2, 13, 14). The movie would never be produced, however, because Mailer did not like the screenplay. He told Michael Lennon in an unpublished interview during 13–14 August 1990, in Provincetown, that Didion and Dunne misunderstood two characters. Mailer said they made Lulu Meyers "into only a cocksucker, and she's more than that," and they never grasped "the centrality of Elena," a major character. This misunderstanding did not come between Mailer and Didion, but Mailer said he was now "feeling tender" about *The Deer Park* during the interview (Lennon, E-mail, 21 Mar. 2021).

Didion first came on Mailer's radar as a young editor for *Vogue* when she published a review of *An American Dream* (1965) in William Buckley's *National Review*. The novel had plenty of detractors and some defenders, but Didion's take caught Mailer's eye, as he wrote to Buckley on 20 April 1965: "What a marvelous girl Joan Didion must be" (*Selected Letters* 343).

Didion in her review, "A Social Eye," compared *An American Dream* to *The Deer Park* as each representing "in many ways a perfect novel." Moreover, *An American Dream* captured the incipient fragmentation and roiling revolt of the mid-sixties, just before, we might add, all hell broke loose. Didion called the novel "the only serious New York novel since *The Great Gatsby*," a work sharing Mailer's knowledge that "the essence of New York is celebrity, and that its true genius is tabloid melodrama." Both authors also shared a "fascination with the heart of the structure, some deep feeling for the mysteries of power . . . [and] there remains something sexual about money." Fitzgerald and Mailer display "the immense technical skill, the passion for realizing the gift. The deep romanticism. And perhaps above all the unfashionableness, the final refusal to sail with the prevailing winds" (329).

Barbara Lounsberry recognized a similar connection to Fitzgerald in Didion's own work. Didion, Lounsberry wrote in *The Art of Fact*, is "devoted to exposing misapprehension and mirages of every American hue." Like Fitzgerald, Didion exposes our illusions and their fallout. If Didion presents us with no final truth or answer, if she admits her own errors and illusions to help gain readers' trust, she also endeavors "to discipline her own personal illusions," as we might well do ourselves. But she never accepts ideologies of "human improvability" and "melioration for America" (109–11, 123, 136–37). In that sense we might see, I would add, Didion's conservative strain and recognize another correlation with Mailer in his self-proclaimed "left-conservativism." All this does not mean that elusive truth is not sought. But using Didion's own phrasing from her 1976 essay "Why I Write," Lounsberry points out that, like Emily Dickinson, Didion seeks elusive truth slantwise, "on the periphery" by its mere "glimmers" being obliquely glimpsed, often "shimmering" forth by what is not said. By the "white spaces," the gaps, the inferences in "works of high compression" (107–8).

More than a decade after her review of *An American Dream*, Didion reviewed *The Executioner's Song* in *The New York Times Book Review* of 7 October 1979. As "a novel of the West," she was interested from the start to see Mailer enter her own territory, how he would, in the first half of the novel, capture "the authentic Western voice . . . rarely heard in literature." She was the first to recognize that "the strongest voices in it . . . [are] those of the women. . . . Women pass down stories." Only Mailer, she said, would have dared it, taken the risk. She thought it was a fourth example of his promised "big book," which big book he had written already, against the critical consensus, "three times now": *The Deer Park, An American Dream,* and *Why Are We in Vietnam?* And in *The Executioner's Song,* it was all accomplished in a limited vocabulary and flat rhetoric, unlike the more torrential Melvillian style Mailer had become known for, "a writer for whom the shape of a sentence is the story," as she put it. "When I read this," she went on to conclude, "I remembered that the tracks made by the wagon wheels are still visible from the air over Utah, like the footprints on the moon. This is an absolutely astonishing book" (1, 26–27).

Together Mailer and Didion contributed to the creation of that sixties and seventies literary movement Tom Wolfe dubbed the New Journalism. It is another point of sympatico between them as laborers in the same vineyard. Beyond Wolfe's own anthology of the genre, there have been over the decades so many analyses of what has also been called immersive journalism, participatory journalism, saturation reporting, etc., that one risks sounding obtuse in repeating definitions of the "new" genre. Complete with dramatic techniques, intensive reporting, and acknowledged subjectivity, Mailer's coverages of presidential election politics, the march on the Pentagon, and the moon shot and Didion's coverage of the war in El Salvador and the upheavals of the sixties and seventies in *The White Album* and *Slouching Towards Bethlehem* would be prime examples. Jason Mosser's *The Participatory Journalism of Michael Herr, Norman Mailer, Hunter S. Thompson, and Joan Didion* (2012) is a good twenty-first-century examination of the genre, with attention in depth to rhetorical devices and the theoretical underpinning of Kenneth Burke's "poetic" ideal as carrying emotional experience versus the journalistic ideal of "semantic detachment." The protean genre served both Mailer and Didion's interest in entering and exposing the moods, as well as the deeper realities, of significant historical moments. And their mutual engagement in the new nonfiction was just one more correlation between the two, an aid to Mailer's respect for Didion, and vice versa. A respect that ran deep both ways.

Didion's *Salvador* (1983), to offer an example, is a slim masterwork of montage with judicious, thought-provoking juxtapositions—an understated yet terrifying account of her and her husband Dunne's time reporting in El Salvador, a hallucinatory locus of grotesque violations of human rights. The place above all at the time where a reporter had to control her fears in the face of grotesque risks. A country whose corrupt government is heavily supported by the Reagan administration in America's lingering Cold War paranoia over "communist" incursions south of the border. Unlike Mailer's engaged and often exaggerated personae in his reporting, Didion's persona is typically self-effacing. But the book exemplifies what Mailer admired about her work. She is completely immersed in spine-chillingly dangerous circumstances, yet she is also an artist with great capacity for letting the material speak for itself. Among other subjects of her montage technique are the juxtaposition of body dumps and Reagan advisors working with Salvadorian Intelligence Officers (20–28); the execution of Roque Dalton Garcia by leftists and Central America's largest shopping mall complete with American muzak (32–36); the rapacious massacre of Mozote and the Reagan administration's certification of human rights progress (37–38); the showpiece Human Rights Commission and its membership including the Director of National Police (64); bumper stickers demanding "Journalists Tell the Truth" and an utter lack of information, even while disinformation is plentiful (66–67); the execution of Bishop Romero and thirty others set beside troops moving into the National University to kill fifty and to smash laboratories and offices in one more campaign to destroy the country's literary and academic intelligentsia (78–84).

There are a few moments of commentary, as particularly the summing up near the end following the Kurtz-like report by the Permanent Select Committee on Intelligence of the House of Representatives—"a dreamwork devised to obscure any intelligence that might distract the dreamer" (see esp. 92–96). The unreality and ultimately the unknowability of the dystopian country is the emergent theme, perfectly adumbrated by her book's epigraph from Conrad's *Heart of Darkness.* "All Europe contributed to Kurtz," who had been entrusted by "the International Society for the Suppression of Savage Customs . . . with the making of a report, for its guidance." A report that with its "unbounded power of eloquence—of words—of burning noble words. There were no practical hints to interrupt the magic current of phrases. . . ." Its message was simply "Exterminate all the brutes." Those burning noble words justifying horrors, words the young Hemingway and his hero Frederic Henry would finally learn to reject, but words millions of adult Americans would accept and support in a state of utter ignorance about what was taking place in El Salvador, why, and supported by whom.

As Mailer told Barry Leeds in 1987 (an interview reprinted in Leeds's *The Enduring Vision of Norman Mailer*, 2002), it was this power of montage at every level of Didion's writing that he most admired.

> I have a lot of respect for her work. I once said that if there were a particular woman writer today in America whom you could compare to Hemingway, it'd probably be Joan Didion.
>
> . . . . She has that same sense of the power of the sentence sitting by itself and the power of the next sentence. There's no accident that she writes movies and lives with film because her work, like Hemingway's, is montage. That is, there's an assumption that the reader's going to pay enough attention to each sentence so they'll feel the next sentence come into place. It's very much like cuts in a film. Sentences don't have to exist entirely by themselves; they exist by their relation to the next sentence and the echo of the sentence that just passed. She writes marvelous prose. Another thing about Hemingway that I liked so much after I finished *The Executioner's Song* is that I was doing that a little bit in *The Executioner's Song* but it just didn't compare. Pick up Hemingway and read him, and boy, you feel the montage. . . . You can't write in a simple style and get away with it unless you can do that. Those choices have to be exquisite—what goes next to what. (133–34)

Chris Anderson in *Style as Argument: Contemporary American Non-fiction* further analyzes to good effect what Mailer was talking about in describing Didion's montage: her use of the "rhetoric of gaps," the empty space between clustered details ("the rhetoric of radical particularity"), the refusal to use traditional transitions and reader signposts. Less reader guidance and explanation, more reader participation and interpretation (133–73). Didion agreed with Hilton Als in her 2006 interview: "Yes. I learned a lot of fictional technique" from movie work (Als, "Joan Didion" 114).

Didion's "The White Album," the title piece of *The White Album* book collection, is a key example of what she at the time called "flash cuts," the essence of her cinematic montage (14). The need for such technique, she tells us, is that so many encounters have only "the logic of dreamwork," causing her to "stop looking for logic" at a time when "all narrative was sentimental . . . all connections equally meaningful, and equally senseless"

(19, 21, 44). Earlier in the essay she had prepared us for her technique: "I was meant to know the plot, but all I knew was what I saw: flash pictures in variable sequence, images with no 'meaning' beyond their temporary arrangement, not a movie but a cutting room experience" (13). Although she does not take on personae as Mailer does in *Armies of the Night* or *Of a Fire on the Moon,* she interweaves deeply personal information and brief responses to events she is immersed in and to people she meets. From her psychiatric report (verbatim), to the Ferguson brothers' Laurel Canyon murder, to Linda Kasabian of the Manson murders, to her mother-in-law's house with its maudlin "framed house blessing," to The Doors in a practice session ("the Norman Mailers of the Top Forty"), to Janis Joplin at a party, to Huey Newton's gunfight with officer John Frey and the subsequently engaged Black Panthers and Eldridge Cleaver, to her highly personal list of what to pack quickly for journalistic travels, to the demonstrations at San Francisco State College where human folly is revealed in seekers of political ideals through descriptions of "industrious self-delusion," to her medical difficulties and tests revealing she has multiple sclerosis, Didion jumps the reader from one element of her montage to another. Such flash cuts between what is being covered reveal the illogic and fragmentation of the times perfectly, as well as what many of us would recognize as our own fuguelike understanding (or memories) of what was happening as America seemed to be coming apart at the end of the sixties.

Mailer not only respected Didion's montage technique; he also admired her equally filmic ability to create superb dialogue, as he said in *The Spooky Art:* "If one wants an example of superb dialogue where the bar is set about as high as it can go, then read William Kennedy or Joan Didion. But make no attempt to imitate either. Superb dialogue is inimitable. It is the indispensable aid, however, to most short stories" (79).

Mailer and Didion share a further connection in their analysis and coverage of politics. Didion began in 1977 in her novels with *A Book of Common Prayer* and continued through *Democracy* (1984) and *The Last Thing He Wanted* (1996), often probing the theme of the role of domestic politics on foreign policy, a theme carried through in such nonfiction books as *Miami* (1987), *Political Fictions* (2001), and *Fixed Ideas: America Since 9.11* (2003). Like Mailer she also covered presidential campaigns and conventions, beginning, long after he did, in 1988.

One sees, then, many sources for Mailer's respect for Didion. That respect was further indicated when, as President of PEN America, Mailer invited her—along with Susan Sontag, Alice Walker, and Eudora Welty—to be one of sixteen headliner speakers at the 1985 fundraising event in New York City for the 1986 PEN Congress. And he included Didion again—this time along with Diana Trilling and Frances Fitzgerald—when in 1989 he organized the PEN America rally to support Salman Rushdie, after Ayatollah Khomeini, supreme leader of Iran, issued a fatwa against Rushdie for his *The Satanic Verses*. (Perhaps an echo of the earlier literary fatwa Millett had issued against Mailer?). For more details on the organizing and execution of these events see J. Michael Lennon's *Norman Mailer: A Double Life* (600–603, 637–38).

Mailer was right, moreover, about Hemingway's powerful influence on Didion, a student of Hemingway from the age of twelve or thirteen, as she reports in her 1998 essay "Last Words," collected into her 2021 book *Let Me Tell You What I Mean*. The essay begins with her brief analysis of the opening paragraph of *A Farewell to Arms*—"four deceptively simple sentences, 126 words. The arrangement of which remains as mysterious and thrilling to me now as it did when I first read them." She goes on to do an analysis of the words themselves (syllables, rhythms, deliberate omissions, punctuation) and of the premonitory inferences looking ahead to the whole novel itself (99–101). After stipulating Hemingway's enormous influence on the prose of two generations, Didion points out that "the very grammar [one might say the rhetoric] dictated . . . a certain way of looking at the world, a way of looking but not joining, a way of moving through but not attaching, a kind of romantic individualism distinctly adapted to its time and source" (103). Cannot the same be said of Didion's grammar or rhetoric? The rhetoric of making one's separate peace with a deeply flawed, fallen world. Her prime example of such rhetoric carried well into the twentieth century is George Orwell, but she might just as pertinently have used herself.

Later in her essay on Hemingway, Didion brings in Mailer, not as a writer whose style was influenced by the master but as one who took on the risks of a similar stance of romantic individualism. She quotes Mailer: "All writing is generated by a certain minimum of ego: you must assume a position of authority in saying that the way I'm writing it is the only way it happened. Writer's block, for example, is simply a failure of ego" (115–

16). This follows Didion's own discussion of "the risk of publication" for even those "writers less inclined than Hemingway to construe works as the manifest expression of personal honor." One opens oneself to "the mortal humiliation of seeing one's own words in print," made all the riskier now that "the increasing inability of many readers to construe fiction as anything other than roman a clef, or the raw material of biography, is both indulged and encouraged." An inability, Didion sets out to demonstrate, even abetted by the *New York Times* as it brands the publication of Hemingway's unfinished manuscripts as autobiographical (106, 120–21). On the eve of the publication of *Ancient Evenings,* Mailer described to me his own sense of compositional risk this way:

> There is always fear in writing a book. If I had tried to write the book in a year, the fear would have been so great it couldn't have been written. But over ten years you can carry the fear. *Writing* a book is the fear. . . . [W]riting is not a comfortable or attractive profession day to day. Then you add to it the fear. . . . Most people take pride in the fears they can endure. It's obvious that you can't be a professional writer for as many years as I have been without taking a certain pride that I can endure those fears. I would say that writing is like all occupations that have some real element of risk. You really don't want to write a book in which you're not taking on some risk, especially a long book. You can write a book quickly in two months, six months, or a year in which the risks are minimal. But to do a long book, you would want to take risks. . . . How dignify it if large risks aren't being taken? ("Twelfth Round" 48)

That necessary strength of ego to endure the risks of writing is in part what Didion meant in her now famous essay "Why I Write" (also collected in *Let Me Tell You What I Mean*) when she opened with the point that the writer asserts her "I" as well as her eye. Writing is "the act of saying I, of imposing oneself on other people. . . . It's an aggressive, even hostile act. . . . an imposition of the writer's sensibility on the reader's most private space" (44–46). But in her case, as in Hemingway's, she will not deal in abstractions and thoughts but in "physical fact." And it is here, perhaps, she most deviates from Mailer's more philosophical, discursive, ever-amplifying work. Yet like Mailer, she can only write to discover what she sees and thinks; she describes herself in the essay well into her novels *Play It As It Lays* and *A Book of Common Prayer* not knowing yet where she is going, who the characters really are, what the relationships among characters are. And here, in the compositional processes of discovery, she is closer to Mailer once again, as he explained his compositional process in *The Spooky Art:* "I look to find where my book is going. Plot comes last. I want a conception of my characters that's deep enough so that they will get to places where I, as the author, have to live by my wits. That means my characters must keep developing. So long as they stay alive, the plot will take care of itself. . . . For that matter, the moment I think of a good plot, I find that the book becomes almost impossible to write, because I know I won't believe it" (92–93).

I would like to amplify a point by circling back to where we started. Given Mailer's ill-advised public imbroglio with the women's liberationists, we should note that Mailer acknowledged his respect (beyond Didion and Trilling and the other women he invited to the PEN events) for the work of Jean Stafford, Carson McCullers, Mary McCarthy, Iris Murdoch, and Erica Jong (Lennon, *Norman Mailer* 249). But when he was attacked by Millett and others as the feminists' bête noire, he reacted not only in self-defense but in defense of other writers he believed had been unfairly attacked and truncated as well—Lawrence and Miller especially. It is completely reasonable to see Mailer's reaction in public as a miscalculation, as one of those intemperate errors in one's life most of us admit only to ourselves. As a public figure—even a television personality—Mailer's improvident miscalculation was something he has never completely lived down. It is such a miscalculation that has motivated too many to adopt a distorted, unfortunate view of his large body of work as *nothing but* the labors of an unreconstructed misogynist. During the memorial for Mailer at Carnegie Hall in 2008, Didion, offering a single corrective to that view, read from her review of *The Executioner's Song*. Perhaps turning to Didion's analyses of Mailer now would help readers understand the shortcomings of such a limited view of him.

5

MAILER AND EMERSON

Lipton's Journal and the Dissident Soul

The great day in the man is the birth of perception, which instantly
throws him on the party of the Eternal.

— RALPH WALDO EMERSON, *Journals*, May, 1859

*M*ailer opens *Of a Fire on the Moon* (1969) recalling his reaction of "horror" and "dread" at the news of Hemingway's
suicide: "Hemingway constituted the walls of the fort:
Hemingway had given the power to believe you could still
shout down the corridor of the hospital, live next to the breath of the beast,
accept your portion of dread each day. Now the greatest living romantic
was dead" (3–4). The Romantic mantle Hemingway dropped at the moment of his suicide is something Mailer coveted at least as early as 1954–
55 when he began his self-analysis through *Lipton's Journal*, his effort to
regenerate and transform himself after the failure of his work subsequent
to *The Naked and the Dead* and the dissolution of his first marriage. Might
not he, Mailer, after Hemingway's death in 1961 become the greatest living
Romantic?

"I have always been the romantic masquerading as the realist," Mailer
writes in *Lipton's*, as if in preparation for his future role, seven years before
Hemingway's suicide. "That is what has given the peculiar tension . . . to my
work. Now as I become aware that I am really an enormous romantic my
work may suffer tremendously for some time" (#229). Later, Mailer adds:
"I was the romantic sent out to discover realism—which is *Naked*. But once

a realist, I had to become the realist going out to understand the romantic, which is my present state" (#345). Mailer might well have donned Hemingway's mantle of Romantic rebellion to face the modern world and to face, near the end of the century, the postmodern pall descending like some dark night of the soul. Mailer's prose, however, takes an alternative tack from his literary hero's, reflecting instead (with a nod to Thomas Wolfe) the elaboration and orotundity of Melville, Coleridge, De Quincey, Ruskin, and Carlyle. These authors also believed in "God's Broadsword" of "Almighty prose," as Mailer put it in his introduction to the second edition of *Death for the Ladies (and Other Disasters)*. Mailer's Romanticism, moreover, echoes the British Romantic tradition not only in prose style but in theme as well. Like Emerson, Mailer sips from that font of British Romanticism William Blake. We only have to think, for example, of Mailer's Blakean view of orthodoxy and fundamentalism as repression of creative libidinal energy; of Mailer's development, like Blake's, of an antinomian, personal cosmology in his investigations into good and evil (energy and entropy); of Mailer's "rage" and "anger of the soul at being forced to travel the tortured contradictory roads of the social world," as Mailer put it in *Lipton's;* of Mailer's view that the nineteenth century ushered in the revolution against overweening Reason that led to his "hope that the future lies with monsters and mystics" whose "seemingly irrational" rebellion "only can fuck up the progress of the state"; of Mailer's metaphysics that, like Blake's, does not dismiss the world as illusion but as shot through with eternity, with infinity in the present; and of Mailer's vocation for creating art as an alternative for religious duty (#45, #332). In fact, the German and British Romantic movements deeply informed the American. Nonetheless, it is "in the American grain" that I want to focus my discussion of Mailer's Emersonian Romanticism, as developed, largely, through the formative process of writing his self-analytical journal.

THE DISSIDENT SOUL

Both Mailer and Emerson used their journals to think through the concepts that would inform their future work; the journals of both authors, in short, demonstrate the mind in action, the creative energy of thinking, as Stephen Whicher described Emerson's. I'd like to recommend the old Riverside edition of *Selections from Ralph Waldo Emerson* (1960) whose editor, Stephan Whicher, placed Emerson's relevant journal entries (and some excerpts from relevant correspondence) before and after the famous essays and lectures Emerson eventually delivered to the public. Though I will use Emerson's journals, my focus here will be on the published product of Emerson's journals rather than the journals themselves, as those well-known published artifacts are what entered the American literary consciousness, including Mailer's.

Emerson's journals do, of course, reveal a dialogue with oneself, as does Mailer's *Lipton's*. It's as if both authors have a neo-Socratic faith that the seeds of truth are within us and are best elicited by interrogation (in this case *self*-interrogation) and free association. Socratic self-knowledge then becomes the inner truth that is the source of a philosophy—an approach to life and literary work—in opposition to the society within which one lives. The rebellious path to such a journal is through solitude, as Emerson argued in "Experience": "[I]n the solitude to which every man is always returning, he has a sanity and revelation which in his passage into new worlds he will carry with him. Never mind the ridicule, never mind the defeat; up again, old heart!" (273). In "Self-Reliance," Emerson announces this theme of inner, rebellious self-reliance and revelation with greatest clarity.

> Society everywhere is in conspiracy against the manhood of every one of its members. Society is a joint-stock company, in which the members agree, for the better securing of his bread to each shareholder, to surrender the liberty and culture of the eater. The virtue most in request is conformity. Self-reliance is its aversion. It loves not realities and creators, but names and customs . . . Nothing is at last sacred but the integrity of your own mind. (149)

That quotation might well serve as the epigraph to a published version of *Lipton's Journal*. Here is the beating heart (and the heart's renunciations) of Emersonian Romanticism, as it would be for Thoreau, Whitman, and Dickinson. And for Mailer.

The central theme running through *Lipton's* is the conflict between the energies of the creative psyche or soul and repressive "caution . . . the high priest of society" (#48). For people "to live with their soul . . . means to war against society" (#137). Mailer returns again and again to his developing theories in *Lipton's* about the conflict between what he terms "Homeostasis" —or later in entry #214, "Homeodynamism" ("the personal healthy rebellious and soul-ful expression of man," or individual creative energy) and "Sociostasis" (the repressions of society, the "element in man placed there by society"). Mailer adds, "The tendency of society is to make all of mankind neurotic-conformist—the tendency of man, as viz. his modern heroes and celebrities, is to liberate the saint-psychopath present to some degree in everyone" (#194, #369). Other Emersonian themes surface in *Lipton's* (such as the hermaphroditic potential of the human psyche, the necessity of exaggerated expression to break through to one's audience, and the law of life that one must grow and change, to suggest three examples). But what gives this rambling—often frustrating—document a degree of coherence is Mailer's quest for the means to liberate the socially repressed psyche, above all, his own.

Among his earliest journal entries Mailer sets the stage for his liberation theme: "So far as we act to fulfill the needs of society, we are actually no more than a part of the net with which society keeps men from developing. We have the illusion of action, of motion; in truth we are merely lines of cord in the net." When "society wins," he continues, "the saint is ignored, the psychopath is shunned, and the purity of the human soul is concealed. We are returned to a world where we must be practical, mature, pluralistic, and confirmed in abysmal and false humilities—in return for agreeing to admit that we know nothing, we are offered the comforts, the securities, and the prestige of society." Society is "opposed to the soul . . . attempts to destroy the soul in order to maintain its stability"; society is "the concretion of the collective surrender of man's will." But "the soul fights back." Unfortunately, the revolution of the soul "never took place. . . . those who had souls retreated, or gave themselves up to being the machines of society," and "the polarity" of this soul-revolution is "totalitarianism" (#23, #43, #57). That totalitarian polarity of the soul is the force, the dark angel, Mailer would wrestle with for the rest of his life.

Mailer entitled his journal "Lipton's" (tea, marijuana) because cannabis, "which destroys the sense of time [and] also destroys the sense of society and opens the soul," was his aid to deeper self-explorations and growth. He is speaking here not of intimate personal relations, which cannabis can of course enhance, but of the oppressive Collective Society and its "war upon each individual." He then gives the example of modern advertising as one means by which society "reaches deep into each man's soul and converts a piece of it to society." Advertising coopts the soul's longing for "love and power, the two things the soul seeks for in life, legitimately, finely," by attaching that longing to commodities, which tempt the soul to "enter its contract with society" (#64). Modern advertising becomes for Mailer but one soul-trapping tool of Emerson's nineteenth-century joint-stock company.

For a novelist who by 1954 is wondering whether he might be a failed artist, who is fighting depression and felt suicidal (#157), Mailer's evolving theories of homeostasis/dynamism in conflict with sociostasis become of central importance to his whole project of psychic and artistic renewal. He now finds himself disappointed with the derivative *Naked and the Dead* ("an imposture"), the abortive *Barbary Shore*, and the "enormous lie" and "failure" of *The Deer Park* (#159, #460). By "imposture" Mailer is referring to his recognition that he was imitating his literary heroes in his most successful novel so far, a literary procedure Emerson often warned against. Emerson's broader argument throughout *Nature* is for the individual to create an original relation to the universe; in "Self-Reliance" he proclaimed that "imitation is suicide" and "insist on yourself; never imitate"; in "The American Scholar" Emerson warns, "in a degenerate state, when the victim of society, he [the scholar] tends to become a mere thinker, or still worse, the parrot of other men's thinking" (65, 148, 165). Imitation, for Emerson as for Mailer by the 1950s, becomes a type of literary failure.

By questioning his previous work, Mailer is also questioning the success or failure of his rebellious soul: "A novel is the record of a sociostatic retreat if it is a great or good novel. A bad novel is the record of a sociostatic advance" (#243). This is an attitude toward the novel since 1954 that Mailer would carry for the rest of his life, variously rephrasing the journal entry he made a half-century earlier. In *The Big Empty* (2006), for example, he would say: "The good novel, the serious novel, is antipathetic to corporate capitalism. The best seller is one of the props of corporate capitalism precisely because it's an entertainment. . . . Well, every time there's a page turner to read for too little, someone's mind is being dulled. Even page-turners can get into interesting questions, but dependably, they will always veer away from moral exploration" (129). The essence of genius, for a novelist, is "to make a voyage which is opposed to society. . . . He is

always attacking society because he is always carrying further our knowledge of the Self." And courage is the virtue most in demand for such self-
knowledge and self-reliance: "What makes a genius" Mailer continues, "is
his incredible courage, for he is a man who lives always in fear, and yet he
continues" (#337). Such Emersonian courage, based on self-trust, is what
inspires Mailer's hope for rebellious transformation—his twentieth-century
heroic adventure.

Emerson specified the soul as our inner resource of rebellion, a theme
best expressed in his "Divinity School Address": "In the soul then let the
redemption be sought. Whenever a man comes, there comes revolution."
Those who "love to be blind in public. . . . think society wiser than their
soul, and know not that one soul, and their soul, is wiser than the whole
world" (112). Emerson then exhorts his Harvard audience of graduating
seniors and their faculty mentors: "Oh my friends, there are resources in
us on which we have not drawn. . . . All attempts to contrive a system are
as cold as the new worship introduced by the French to the goddess of
Reason. . . . Rather let the breath of new life be breathed by you through
the forms already existing. For once you are alive, you shall find they all become plastic and new. The remedy to their deformity is first, soul, and second, soul, and evermore, soul" (114–15). For his efforts, Emerson then had
to deal with reviews and reactions to his words as negative as those Mailer
had faced in the wake of *Barbary Shore* and *The Deer Park*, including the
well-known troubles Mailer had in getting *The Deer Park* published. Emerson withstood the onslaught better than Mailer, by the testimony of his
journals, as in Emerson's 31 August 1838 journal entry: "Steady, steady. . . .
Who are these murmurers, these haters, these revilers? Men of no knowledge and therefore no stability" (116). Still, the critical onslaught against
Mailer sparked his "soul rage" and became the very catalyst for his self-
reliant transformation through the analytical processes of *Lipton's*.

"THE DOORS OF DISCOVERY":
THE POWER OF INSTINCT AND INTUITION

Reflecting in his journal on a visit to his parents, Mailer notes with empathy that his sister Barbara feels betrayed because his advice and example
had "made her a rationalist over the years—I took her sensitive delicate

nature and hammered my harsh mind into hers. No wonder she's furious at me now that I say Reason is bad, Instinct is good" (#400). Mailer then associates thinking with fucking as a species of intuitive leap, where "thought like fucking is dialectic but directed. The ultimate end of the fuck like the ultimate end of thought is to comprehend the universe as a whole" (#526). Mind and body collaborate in the processes of comprehension: "Indeed, no human can enrich himself without returning and dipping into the lore of mind-body. It is the source of all creativity available to us, outside of what we intuit from nature when we personify it. For indeed man is a part of nature and so can comprehend nature by understanding himself" (#645). Emerson phrased the point this way in his late essay "Fate": "Let us build altars to the Blessed Unity which holds nature and souls in perfect solution" (351). Mailer had prefaced the above journal entry seeking wholeness and unity by a speculation that "the closer man approaches to the infinity of God the more he will live in passivity." That is, the war of soul against society begins to resolve itself as we more fully approach infinity, comprehend intuitively the divine in the particulars of the natural world and in ourselves.

We begin now to understand better Mailer's earlier (Blakean/Thoreauvian) comment that "in the tiny is the profound. Those things which are too insignificant to notice are always *the doors of discovery*" (#352; my emphasis). Or, as Emerson put it in *Nature:* "1. Words are signs of natural facts. 2. Particular natural facts are symbols of particular spiritual facts. 3. Nature is the symbol of the spirit" (40). The reason so many academicians are dull, Mailer argues, is that there is no pursuit of such intuitive unity (or psychic integration) in their professional lives: "they have given themselves over to a subject they are not close to spiritually—usually to hide some other deeper drive of their nature. They conceal the rampant murderer, lover, adventurer, etc. within themselves from themselves. . . . There is a war mounting between the academicians and the ones with true vocation" (#213). Mailer then provides a litany of specialists who understand nothing deeper (spiritual, loving, intuitive, hence truly "vocational") about the subject of their life-work—from psychoanalysts, to editors, to sociologists, to anthropologists, to historians. Here we might be tempted to launch a Swiftian riff on certain ideological literary theorists as "Projectors" obsessed with their clever reductive grids, or a George Eliot riff on the Edward Casaubons of academic criticism, striving to hold "the Key to all Mythologies"

---

or literatures, without any loving or spiritual attachment to literature. But to honor the reader's patience so far, we will resist the temptation.

The preeminence of intuition and instinct over rationalist materialism that Mailer approaches in his journal is also fundamental to American transcendentalism. As early as "The American Scholar," Emerson says: "I believe man has been wronged; he has wronged himself. He has almost lost the light that can lead him back to his prerogatives. . . . If a single man plant himself indomitably on his instincts and there abide, the huge world will come around to him" (75, 79). In "Self-Reliance," Emerson asks, "What is the aboriginal Self, on which a universal reliance may be grounded?" Then he answers, "The inquiry leads us to that source, at once the essence of genius, of virtue, and of life, which we call Spontaneity or Instinct. We denote this primary wisdom as Intuition, whilst all later teachings are tuitions. In that deep force, the last fact behind which analysis can go, all things find their common origin" (156). In "The Transcendentalist," Emerson clarifies the point further: "Transcendental from the use of that term by Immanuel Kant . . . who replied to the skeptical philosophy of Locke, which insisted that there was nothing in the intellect which was not previously in the experience of the senses, by showing that there was a very important class of ideas or imperative forms, which did not come by experience, but through which experience was acquired; that these were intuitions of the mind itself" (197). For Emerson, an ordained American divine who had despaired of organized religion, doctrine, and orthodoxy, who resigned his ministry in 1832, and who outraged many in his "Divinity School Address," Jesus was an example of the highest "moral sentiment," the "indwelling Supreme Spirit" that should "not be attributed to one or two persons, and denied to all the rest" because "the doctrine of inspiration is lost." Rather:

It [inspiration] is an intuition. It cannot be received second hand. . . . Jesus Christ belonged to the true race of prophets. He saw with open eye the mystery of the soul. Alone in history he estimated the greatness of man. One man was true to what is in you and me. He saw that God incarnates himself in man, and evermore goes forth anew to take possession of his World. . . . He felt respect for Moses and the prophets, but no unfit tenderness at postponing their initial revelations to the hour and the man that now is; to the eternal revelation in the heart. (104–5)

———

For Mailer, Jesus (both man and symbol of the liberating power within) is similarly "the rebel, the anarchist, the saint, the compassionate, the life-giver . . . [who] was put on the cross and all his teachings were reversed. Christ became Christianity just as Reason became Rationalization" (#376). This early insight would inform Mailer's later work on Jesus a half century later in *The Gospel According to the Son* (1997) and *On God* (2007).

Though *Gospel* flummoxed some critics by the audacity of Mailer writing the novel in the first person, the first-person Jesus story goes back in the English tradition at least as far as "The Sacrifice" by George Herbert (one of Emerson's favored poets), likely composed about the time the Pilgrims were settling in America. Other reviewers were more concerned with the execution of Mailer's novel, a more legitimate concern. Be that as it may, Mailer's Jesus is an Emersonian prophet, "Even mightier than the prophet Ezekiel" (*Gospel* 36). Not unlike what Mailer recognized in himself during the 1950s, Jesus is filled with both Apollonian and Dionysian impulses: "If his [Satan's] odor could leave me uneasy it also offered sympathy to desires I had not yet allowed myself to feel." Jesus embodies the kind of "double life" Emerson thought open to us all: a man living the human, sensuous life but with divine energies (a dissident, transcendent soul) within. Jesus, Mailer asserts, is of the Gnostic Jewish Essene sect. Like Emerson's Jesus in the "Divinity School Address," Mailer's Jesus is the foe of orthodoxy, law, and nominal piety as exemplified by the Pharisees and the Synagogues, and as opposed to the interior experience and love of God (see *Gospel*, 48, 72, 80, all of chapter 35, and 239), and as opposed to the wealthy and powerful coopting for their own purposes desires in the human soul (152–53).

In *On God*, Mailer puts it this way: The "two elements now on the horizon that can destroy the world as we know it . . . [are] technology and . . . organized religion. The second drives people to stupidity" (119), not to mention violence. It is not far off the mark to speak of Emerson's and Mailer's Jesus as a Gnostic—one who seeks enlightenment *within* the deepest self, but *outside* institutions and doctrines. For both Emerson and Mailer, the process of journaling is one road in. "I have proceeded to ponder these questions without being qualified," Mailer says in dialogue with Michael Lennon in the chapter on Gnosticism in *On God*. "Yet my basic argument is that of course I am qualified all the same. We all are. That is why I can say yes, if you want to get down to it, I probably am a Gnostic in the sense that the inner feeling I have about these matters is so clear and so acute to me" (195). Indeed, while working on *The Gospel,* Mailer read Elaine Pagels's *The Gnostic Gospels* and *The Origin of Satan* (see Lennon, *Norman Mailer,* 696). In *Why Religion?* Pagels, Professor of Religion at Princeton, underscores that the Gnostic Gospels, those uncanonized gadflies of Christianity, and particularly the Gospel of Thomas, emphasize the Kingdom of God within you, not above or beyond you. It is also the Essenes who turned Satan, as Mailer did, into God's cosmic Antagonist. It is Gnosis, or "knowledge of the heart" and *Epinoia* (creative intelligence), that turns the deeper psyche or soul into the source of wisdom within us, a source we must find a way to awaken (see Pagels 44, 56–57, 146–49, 156–57, 176–78).

It is worth emphasizing here that for Emerson and Mailer, writing their journals does more than generate ideas. Writing a journal is an approach, an awakening, to the deeper psychic territory of the soul, to whatever revelation may be found within; it is a private act of self-examination, an act of devotion to one's vocation, the completion of one's being or identity. It is not so much a "religious" act because it is outside any practice, doctrine, or sect; it is not an interlocutory psychoanalytical act so much as a private spiritual act, a return to that inner vitality that participates in the transcendent soul, an alternative to traditional prayer. Like Emily Dickinson's poems, a journal can be a solitary practice of self-reliance against the vagaries and expectations of the social world. As British psychotherapist Anthony Storr describes it in *Solitude: A Return to the Self:*

> The creative person is constantly seeking to discover himself, *to remodel his own identity,* and to find meaning in the universe through what he creates. He finds this a valuable integrating process which, like meditation or prayer, has little to do with other people, but which has its own separate validity. His most significant moments are those in which he attains some new insight, or makes some new discovery; and those moments are chiefly, if not invariably, those in which he is alone. (xiv; my emphasis)

The inner truths revealed in solitude, however, may result in social action—a distinction George Kateb makes in *Emerson and Self-Reliance* between Emerson's "mental self-reliance" and his "active self-reliance" (or "democratic individuality"). Active self-reliance is *based* on the prior intellectual independence of mental self-reliance (Kateb 134–36). Emerson was wary of being drawn into politics and social movements, but he did protest (in public to President Martin Van Buren) the displacement of the Cherokees in 1838, was a vociferous abolitionist in the 1850s, and supported women's rights as they were defined in his time, defined not least by his friend and editorial colleague Margaret Fuller.

Neither Emerson's nor Mailer's journals were intended for publication, yet once published we come to see how they aid our understanding of the origins of both authors' published work and the processes through which inner revelation and disciplined self-examination eventually become literary artifact.

A PHILOSOPHICAL NOVELIST

For all his "soul searching" for psychic integration in *Lipton's,* Mailer is not a nineteenth-century transcendentalist. He is a twentieth-century philosophical novelist whose nonfiction often acts as exegesis to his fiction. The philosophical concepts he developed in *Lipton's* inform much of his later work. In fact, Mailer's work by the end of the twentieth century was also becoming more and more informed by his reading of Jung. In a 1999 interview with his biographer J. Michael Lennon in the *New England Review,* Mailer admits to spending a lot of time reading Jung in the last year of the decade (Lennon, "Conversation" 138–48).

We have seen that he was coming to understand more fully his motivations as a writer in 1954 and 1955 in the process of composing his journal. *Lipton's* became his philosopher's stone, with for him that stone's reputed transformative, invincible power.

What Mailer saw in Hemingway—and sought for himself—is an exemplary self-reliance and self-definition ("the sacred integrity" of his own mind) against the soul-crushing realities of the twentieth century: mechanized global warfare, economic depression, totalitarianism, genocide, gulags, and the ever-expanding commercialization or commodification of everything. The costs of developing from within a strength of ego to resist such forces and define oneself can, of course, be crippling. Only integration of ego and the deeper psyche can provide a basis for survival, but whether human beings can live up to such a challenge is an open question. Here and there, perhaps, an individual manages to live up to the challenge, but he or she is not likely to emerge unscathed.

A further distinction seems necessary here. Seeking freedom from society's domination of the individual, including the oppressions of society's political and economic engines, is not merely an expression of egotism or selfishness. The "Emersonian" individualist—the intellectually and spiritually free person with a strong identity—seeks to redress an imbalance or, to use one of Mailer's favored words, a disproportion. Mailer, like Emerson, is on a quest for the psychic balance and strength sufficient to resist the burdens of social and psychological conformity. Just as reason may become rationalization for the status quo, for the inflexibilities of society and for those who exercise power over, and benefit from, the status quo, so too might instinct and intuition (the counterpoise to rationalization) become so disproportionate that the benefits of reason are lost. But for Emerson, as for Mailer (trained at Harvard as an engineer), we are not in danger of disproportionate intuition or instinct; on the contrary, we suffer from disproportionate reason or rationalization at the expense of our intuitive powers and at the cost of our souls.

We have no evidence that Mailer ever read Emerson's journals, and that seems unlikely. On 16 November 1954, a month before he launched into his self-analysis, Mailer in a letter to one "Mr. Cole," refers to F. O. Matthiessen's *American Renaissance: Art and Expression in the Age of Emerson and Whitman* and the influence of that book's themes regarding Melville on *Naked and the Dead,* but Mailer also gives one mention of Emerson as among Matthiessen's important Romantics (see *Selected Letters*181). We don't know how much Emerson Mailer read before *Lipton's,* but Michael Lennon tells me that Mailer read a few of Emerson's essays at Harvard. Much later when Mailer read a collection of Emerson's works, Lennon reports that Mailer was "startled by how much Emerson's ideas seemed to mirror his own. I remember this vividly" (Lennon, E-mail, 2 Dec. 2019). We also know, as Lennon points out in *Norman Mailer: A Double Life,* that Mailer was influenced by F. O. Matthiessen. Mailer was impressed by Matthiessen's public lectures at Harvard; Mailer's writing mentor, Robert Gorham Davis, was a member of Matthiessen's Harvard faculty group; Mailer read Matthiessen's seminal book; Mailer campaigned with Matthiessen for Henry Wallace in 1948; and Mailer in Paris in 1948 reconnected with Stanley Geist, a Harvard acquaintance and author of *Herman Melville: The Tragic Vision and the Heroic Ideal* (first written as a thesis at Harvard in 1939), who worked as research assistant to F. O. Matthiessen on *American Renaissance* and commented on *The Naked and the Dead* in manuscript. Like Geist, Lieutenant Hearn in *Naked* is also a Harvard grad with a thesis on Melville. Obviously, the two friends would have discussed the making of *The American Renaissance* and its interpretations of American Romanticism (see Lennon, *Norman Mailer* 35, 90, 99, 116). What we do know, then, is that some degree of intellectual stimulation from American Romanticism was psychically embedded, so to speak, well before Mailer began *Lipton's*. Nonetheless, that journal is a true journey into self, not—for all its echoes of Emerson's own truths arrived from his own inward-turning journals—a mere parroting of Emersonian pensées. I would go so far as to say that Mailer's lack of substantial reading of Emerson prior to *Lipton's* freed him from concern that he would be merely imitating Emerson. Still, it is reasonable to argue that when the American Academy of Arts and Sciences gave Mailer the Emerson-Thoreau Medal in 1989, the Academy was acknowledging Mailer's "Emersonian" role in American literature a century after Emerson's.

Although Mailer's journal and books are darker than Emerson's works, we might do well to remember that Emerson's own darker vision in the late essays and lectures ameliorates our temptation to view Emerson as a naive idealist. Think, for example, of Emerson's "Life," "Fate," "Skepticism," and "Experience." Think of Emerson's own later journal entries:

- Conservatism has in the present society every advantage. All are on its side. . . . the voice of the intelligent and the honest, of the unconnected and independent, the voice of truth and equity, is suppressed (April, 1845).
- The name of Washington City in the newspapers is every day of blacker shade. All news from that quarter being of a sadder type, more malignant (May, 1847).
- The badness of the times is making death attractive (April, 1850).
- The world is babyish, and the use of wealth is: it is made a toy (June, 1851).

- A man [fugitive slave] who has taken the risk of being shot, or burned alive, or cast into the sea, or starved to death, or suffocated in a wooden box, to get away from his driver: and this man who has run the gauntlet of a thousand miles for his freedom, the statute says you men of Massachusetts shall hunt, and catch, and send back again to the dog-hutch he fled from . . . I will not obey it, by God (1851).
- It will always be so. Every principle is a war-note. Whoever attempts to carry out the rule of right and love and freedom must take his life in his hand (October, 1859).

Moreover, Emerson was as fully aware as Mailer of the dualities (the double life, the psychic dialectic) within each of us: "Man is not order of nature . . . but a stupendous antagonism, a dragging together of the poles of the Universe. . . . here they are, side by side, god and devil, mind and matter, king and conspirator, belt and spasm, riding peacefully together in the eye and brain of every man" (*Selections* 340). Still, Emerson's oeuvre accentuates the salutary, self-creative powers of transcendentalism. "The American Scholar" is our rousing Declaration of Intellectual Independence.

Mailer more often accentuates the violence of revolutionary consciousness and regenerative, libidinal force in his characters and protagonists. The powers discovered deep within can both destroy and create. Nonetheless, what Mailer discovers in *Lipton's* and the work that follows is fundamentally part of an American literary tradition. Mailer's opposition to the values of a dominant American culture during his lifetime places him in the company of a long lineage of writers who have sought to awaken (or revolutionize) the consciousness of their people, who have sought to attach words, through image and symbol, as Emerson said, to visible things, who have depicted the journey of the individual soul as connected to the journey of America. In the works of the Puritans, Emerson, Thoreau, Hawthorne, Melville, Twain, Fitzgerald, Faulkner, and Vonnegut, the pilgrim soul confronts extremes of good and evil, at times divided as God and Devil. The pilgrim, like some Old Testament hero ("a stranger and pilgrim on the earth," as Hebrews 11:13 has it), often undergoes an apocalyptic voyage in which the expansion of self and soul, and the integration of nature and God and self, are all part of the same process of growth and the same possibilities of defeat. It bespeaks a quest to define America's most liberated, most creative self. Such heroes partake, as well, of mythic odysseys—violent, libidinal, liberating, archetypal, shocking, beneficial for the hero's compatriots and culture—of the ancient heroes of Western literature. "The adventurer," Mailer wrote early in *Lipton's*, is "he or she [who] always has a very strong urge from the soul" (#87). The "Emersonian" and mythic soul-lore Mailer worked out for himself in *Lipton's* was an important stop along Mailer's own way, his personal quest to fashion a self and a body of work that would reflect that self truly. *Lipton's* is the seed ground for Mailer's protagonists in his fiction and nonfiction after the 1950s and for their often rebarbative, unseemly, disturbing-yet-creative journeys.

6

MAILER AND WHITMAN

The Interview on Democracy in America

True liberty will only begin when Americans discover IT . . . IT being the
deepest *whole* self of man, the self in wholeness, not idealistic halfness.
. . . The wholeness of a man being his soul.

    —D.H. LAWRENCE, *Studies in Classic American Literature*

AUTHOR'S NOTE: *My goal is to present Whitman in his own words, allowing for
occasional elisions, transitional phrases and sentences, and similar unobtrusive devices of coherence and clarity, so that modern readers might measure for themselves
the currency and significance of our most Emersonian poet's ideas on American democracy. The means to this goal of allowing Whitman to speak his own words is
rooted in his prose, none more so than* Democratic Vistas, *his "Preface" to the 1855
edition of* Leaves of Grass, *and the rendition of his late-life conversations with his
Boswellian acolyte Horace Traubel, published, beginning in the early twentieth century, in nine volumes as* With Walt Whitman in Camden.

    *Might Walt Whitman's body of work, even as glimpsed through the limited por-
tal I offer here, represent one of those potentially salutary "wisdom texts" you will
notice referred to during the interview with Mailer? Readers decide for themselves,
of course, just as they will decide as to the relevancy of Whitman to twenty-first-
century America. As one contemplates that relevancy or lack of it, one might want to
keep in mind that the hope for the progressive evolution of a culture is not necessarily limited to a sealed time capsule labeled "Nineteenth-Century Idealism." Everyone
who ever dissented, protested, or placed his or her body as "a counter friction to stop*

---

the machine," in Thoreau's formulation, in the quest for humane change from the injustices of the status quo has accepted, and today still does, the proposition that things can get better (not that they will but that they can).

Whitman's interviewer here, Norman Mailer, I treat with shameless freedom. Mailer's readers will note points of convergence between Mailer's own ideas and body of work and Whitman's side of the interview. Mailer's role here, however, is to engage and provoke Whitman to speak on the many facets of our living American experience that either enlarge or diminish, or even despoil, the republic (still far from flawless) first given to us by the American Revolution and those subsequent documents that established the foundation of our ever-evolving democratic freedoms and responsibilities.

MAILER

[Entering from stage right, Mailer sees a wicker armchair stage left, sits, settles a reporter's notebook on his lap, and glances at his notes. As Walt Whitman walks in from stage right, carrying an old-fashioned, collapsible, cloth-seated, wooden beach chair, Mailer looks up and stands.]

Mr. Whitman!

WHITMAN

Norman!

MAILER

Walt!

[They shake hands. Seat themselves.]

WHITMAN

[Breaks into sonorous recitation of lines from "So Long."]

94

"My songs cease, I abandon them,
From behind the screen where I hid, I advance personally solely to you
Camerado, this is no book,
Who touches this touches a man."

We are finally face to face. I've felt there's a certain simpatico. *Song of Myself. Advertisements for Myself!* [*Laughs*]

MAILER

[*Joining in the joke*]

Brooklyn!

WHITMAN

Brooklyn Heights. New Jersey.

MAILER

Manhattan.

WHITMAN

The soul-wounds of war.

MAILER

Witnesses to suffering. So, Walt. You knew of *Advertisements?*

WHITMAN

Certain rumblings, let us say, reached the netherworlds.

MAILER

I always hoped *Advertisements* might have sent certain reverberations—

out to various layers of existence, or, if you prefer, consciousness. That book was *my* Barbaric Yawp—far too long in coming. My own Cri de Coeur shouted over the rooftops of my repressed compatriots.

WHITMAN

One's Barbaric Yawp may be good and necessary, but too much anger, sheer effrontery, small-minded criticism of your peers is more rebarbative Rant than Yawp. Rant does not satisfy the Soul.

MAILER

Still, I stand by that book. The times called it forth from me. After the Great Depression, World War II, something broke in the American spirit. And the writers, intellectuals, and critics left their artists' opposition to society to embrace "the American Century," as it was called. The writers who inspired my generation had grown too accepting of things as they were shaping up, like a collective paterfamilias. And we younger writers were being pushed toward social acceptance and integration. So I struck out.

WHITMAN

And fear of failure? Fear too makes us lash out. We are all, as Emerson pointed out, creatures of a dual nature.

MAILER

I won't deny it. But making a reconnaissance into my deepest self changed me. I'd created a new, combative, determined self. No longer Mr. Nice Jewish Kid. Like me, Walt, you had dived into your deepest self in your mid-thirties and that process changed your work forever too. Two swaggering Romantic rebels, we might say.

[Whitman holds up his arms in a caricature of a carnival strongman and grins. Mailer rises out of his chair and shadowboxes, continuing his response as he dances and strikes out with his fists.]

Two authors of epic ambitions. Portraying ourselves as representatives of our time, our people. In their liberated state.

WHITMAN

We both had our hopes for some larger sort of consciousness, some new American breadth of scope. Some new, unfettered candor. To justify what we say by our deeper consciousness, a sort of heroic animality. But didn't you request, Norman, that we speak of democracy, Democracy in America? [*Breaks into sonorous recitation, again*]

"For you, from me, O Democracy, to serve you ma femme!
For you, for you I am trilling these songs."

MAILER

[Resuming his seat]

Such is my assignment. *[He flips his notepad back open.]*
The idea is to posit your analyses, in song and in prose. Readers in the twenty-first century will have to calculate for themselves the remaining distances we have to travel. I've noticed that like me you change your views over time, even contradict yourself. Ever testing hypotheses, ever the over-arching dialectic.
But indeed, let's talk democracy. You placed your hope in the future, some evolution of the American Revolution, even if you saw every fault line and flaw in the state of American democracy in your time. Your time pre-dated mine by a century. So, a reader might ask, was your hope misplaced? Though I take it you had in mind centuries upon centuries. Maybe even some sort of Vedic cycle of 25,000 years! For the moment, however, let's ignore the twenty-first century, trusting our readers, as I say, to make what-ever leaps are to be made. Begin with the Dream of Prosperity. The ma-chinery of democracy intersecting with those dreams of shared prosperity.

WHITMAN

Well, there are different kinds of prosperity, not only material but moral

---

and spiritual, as well. Have we Americans ever understood that, Norman? The prevailing delusion is always that free political institutions, plentiful intellectual smartness, with general good order, physical plenty, industry, etc. do, of themselves, determine and yield to our experiment in democracy the fruitage of success. Yet the moral conscience, the most important, the vertebrae, to State or man, seems to me either entirely lacking or seriously enfeebled.

Genuine belief seems to have left us—in our underlying principles (for all the hectic glow and melodramatic screaming). Nor is humanity believed in. The spectacle is appalling. We live in an atmosphere of hypocrisy throughout. The men believe not in the women, nor the women in the men. A scornful superciliousness rules in literature. A lot of churches, sects, etc., the most dismal phantasms, usurp the name of Religion.

MAILER

Had you felt the reverberations of D. H. Lawrence? I once made my own study of Lawrence. This novelist and poet followed in your wake and wrote that "as a great poet" you "meant so much to me . . . as the one man breaking a way ahead . . . the pioneer" among classic American authors. Like you, he saw the function of art as moral, not aesthetic only. And above all *not* didactic. Rather, an "implicit morality" which "changes the blood" before the mind. And you he found in this sense "the great moralist."

He saw that the other classic American authors of the nineteenth century had attacked the old morality (of church, of society's proprieties) through their passions, but they still gave "mental allegiance" to the old morality those passions would destroy. But you, Lawrence believed, were the first to break that mental allegiance, to smash the old moral conception of the soul as superior to and above the flesh. You kept the soul *in* the flesh!

WHITMAN

Then perhaps he understood me, Mr. Lawrence. *Leaves* was for me a necessary religious root ground, but we have to get rid of all our dogmas and hypocrisies and superstitions. My time demanded readjustment, not least of the democratic ensemble of science and religion, of reason and mystery.

MAILER

The biggest problem for Christianity is Christians, someone once said. One imagines the rage of Jesus. But you don't let the political and business leaders off the hook, either. I make so bold as to quote you President Herbert Hoover—no less! "The problem with capitalism is capitalists. They're too damn greedy." The American Dream became the people's nightmare.

WHITMAN

It's unfortunate, appalling. The official services of the state are steeped in corruption and bribery. In business (that all-devouring modern word, business) the one sole object is, by any means, pecuniary gain. The magician's serpent in the fable ate up all the other serpents; and money-making is our magician's serpent, remaining by my day the sole master of the field. The best class we show is but a mob of fashionably dressed speculators and vulgarians. It is as if we were somehow endowed with a vast and more and more thoroughly appointed body, and then left with little or no Soul.

I wanted the arrogant money powers disciplined. That's why I rejoice in anything the people do to demonstrate their contempt for the conditions under which they are despoiled. Our politics are degraded by wealth unbounded, greed unbounded. If anything will destroy us it will be fraud in the service of wealth.

MAILER

I've said as much myself: "the shits are killing us." Yet somehow you never gave up hope during your lifetime, despite all the flaws and wrong turns of our national experiment. All the ways a corrupt polity can destroy our humanity, much, say, as a war can. Whether that war is fought in our streets or on foreign shores.

WHITMAN

But America cannot afford to despair. Without hope, dreams, what do we have? I have dreamed of a little or larger band of brave and true, unprece-

———

dented yet—the members separated by different dates and states—north, south, east, west—a year here, a century there, but always one compact Soul, conscience-conserving, God-inculcating, inspired achievers, not only in Literature, the greatest art, but achievers in all art. A Soul Culture, if you will.

MAILER

That's how you kept your faith in American democracy—in this "band," as you say, within this larger sweep of time. In artists.

WHITMAN

Yes. The seeds of any evolution would have to be within those of larger consciousness. Otherwise we remain where we are. Permanent stasis. Culture as a class of supercilious infidels who believe in nothing. I should demand a program of Culture drawn out not from a single class, or of the parlors and lecture-rooms, but with an eye to practical life, the West, the workingmen, the facts of farms and jackplanes and engineers, and the broad range of women also of the middle and working strata. Culture as a deeper principle. Based on Individuality, a towering Self-hood (yes, that swagger as you say), the female equally with the male, possessing the idea of the Infinite. The Individual Personality of mortal life with reference to the Immortal, the Unknown, the Spiritual. Fear not, my brethren, my sisters!

MAILER

I'd make a distinction: small business can be a part of a new polity, a new equity, but the corporation is psychopathic. So, we would in your time and in mine have had to address more pungently the problems of capital and labor—more accurately, the corporations and labor—if a people were to be rescued, allowed to develop the culture you dream of.

WHITMAN

Certainly. Have I not said as much just now? The immense problem of the relation and conflict between Labor and its status and pay, on one side, and the Capital of employers on the other looms over these states like an ominous cloud. The many thousands of decent working people trying to keep up a good appearance but living in daily toil, from hand to mouth, with nothing ahead, and no owned homes—the increasing aggregation of capital in the hands of a few—the chaotic confusion of labor in the southern states, consequent on the abrogation of slavery, the growing alarming spectacle of countless squads of vagabond children, the hideous squalor of certain quarters of the cities and the increasing frequency of these pompous, nauseous outside shows of vulgar wealth (What a chance of a new Juvenal!), wealth acquired perhaps by some quack, some measureless financial rogue, triply brazen in impudence, only shielding himself by his money from a shaved head, a striped dress, and a felon's cell, those enormous fortunes for the few and of poverty of the million—all these stand as impedimenta of America's progress.

And there is no remedy in too much flag waving. In the easy hurrah. That is not patriotism in any sense I accept.

MAILER

I call them flag-patriots, Walt. But as I understand you, you see as corollary to the development of conscience the role of literature and of suffrage in dismantling these impedimenta. Consider suffrage first.

WHITMAN

Without fair suffrage there is no hope for controlling our own destiny as a nation beyond its stagnations. But first we cannot gloss over the appalling dangers of universal suffrage, the dangerous state of the gap between democracy's convictions, aspirations, and the people's crudeness, vice, caprices, evil wills, venoms—below which reside the good nature, integrity, and sanity of man. We are destined either to surmount the history of Feudalism or prove the most tremendous failure of time.

I would add, America means, or should mean, above all toleration, welcome, freedom, a concern for Europe, for Asia, for Africa. We are not all in all. We are to make our contribution to the big scheme. I say let that contribution be something worthwhile—something exceptional, ennobling. We cannot love America, desire American prosperity, at the expense of some other nation. We are all sailing together on the same ship.

"Joy, shipmate, joy!"

MAILER

Even if you make allowances for our essential duality, for the folly (or gullibility) of the masses (as you suggest), or at least of a substantial segment of the voting populace, you still have the errors of the officials—I refuse to say "leaders"!—they elect. Voters may be too easily conned, bamboozled. But it's their officials who did the con and then acted otherwise than the expectations they raised through bromides, pandering promises, and plain old jingoism. I'd argue that the officials' con game is one key to democracy's failures, as well.

WHITMAN

That is the state of the matter so far. We have a long evolutionary path to trod. I speak of an evolution of Conscience and discernment the likes of which we might well look to history for examples and come up short. The din of disputation ever raged around me. And rages still? Acrid the temper of the parties, vital the pending questions. Fortunately, time will dispose of Presidents, Congressmen, party platforms. But the people remain. And there is an immortal courage and prophecy in every sane soul that cannot, must not, under any circumstances, capitulate.

But yes, I have everywhere found, primarily, thieves and scallywags arranging the nominations to offices, and sometimes filling the offices themselves. The North as full of bad stuff as the South. Not one in a hundred has been chosen by the outsiders, the people, but most have been put through by little or large caucuses of the politicians and have got in by corrupt rings and electioneering, not by capacity or desert. And I noticed more and more the alarming spectacle of parties usurping the Government, and openly and shamelessly wielding it for party purposes. But a well-contested American election? I know of nothing grander, better exercise, better digestion, more positive proof of the past, the triumphant result of faith in humankind. I have written that the Poet "sees eternity in men and women; he does not see men and women as dreams or dots. Faith is the antiseptic of the soul."

We have yet to achieve what I call a third stage of our development, however. The first being the political foundation rights of immense masses of people, the organization of a republic, embodied in our Declaration of Independence, for example. The second being material prosperity, including intercommunication and trade, general employment, organization of great cities, the health of books, newspapers, currencies. Technical schools. But the third stage I would promulgate is a native Expression of Spirit, different from others, more expansive, evidenced by original authors and poets to come, by American Personalities, plenty of them, male and female. Entirely reconstructing Society, rising above all errors and wickedness. We have not yet exhausted the progressive conception of America, but rather arise, teeming with it. Daughter of a physical revolution—Mother of the true revolutions, which are of the interior life, and of the arts. For so long as the Spirit has not changed, any change of appearance is of no avail.

MAILER

A revolution of consciousness! My own battle cry. Of deepest consciousness, of soul. The first necessity for political and economic change. Because mere politics as politics is too corrupt and shallow for the deeper solutions. You are, my friend—dare I say it—another Left-Conservative!

Regardless: You might be the last of the Mohicans who believes literature to be chief among the instruments for such an evolution in the state. Believes that literature holds the key to the deepest interior changes, to that revolution of consciousness. A good reason for your innovations, your technical and topical courage. The whole poetic tradition was at stake. Just as democracy was at stake. The critic Leslie Fiedler said of you that as a literary pioneer you are as offensive as any disturber of received ideas, as upsetting as Copernicus or Darwin, Nietzsche or Marx or Freud. Nowhere more innovative on this American soil than in your use of erotic imagery, the erotic being the other side of the spiritual coin. [*Quoting from Whitman's "Song of Myself"*]

"I believe in you my soul, the other I am must not abase itself to you,
And you must not be abased to the other. . . .

I mind how once we lay such a transparent summer morning.
How you settled your head athwart my hips and gently turn'd over upon me,
And parted the shirt from my bosom-bone, and plunged
    your tongue to my bare-stripped heart,
And reached till you felt my beard, and reached till you held my feet. . . ."

WHITMAN

[Picking up the subsequent lines]

"Swiftly arose and spread around me the peace and knowledge
    that pass all the argument of the earth,
And I know that the hand of God is the promise of my own,
And I know that the spirit of God is the brother of my own,
And that all the men ever born are also my brothers, and
    the women my sisters and lovers,
And that a keelson of the creation is love. . . ."

So you see, Norman, I won't argue with this Fiedler fellow. But, yes, we must remember that political dissent must play a role as well. The eager and often inconsiderate appeals of reformers and revolutionists are indispensable to counterbalance the inertness and fossilism making so large a part of human institutions. The latter will always take care of themselves—the danger being that they rapidly tend to ossify *us*. The reformer is to be treated with indulgence and even respect. As circulation to air, so is agitation and a plentiful degree of speculative license to political and moral sanity.

MAILER

Indeed, Walt. But back to literature, a moment. Your verse innovations were with us a long time, in some cases still are. Your lack of pretention. Your use of everyday speech. The exuberant, even joyful, length of your free verse lines, resonating with those internal rhythms (as opposed to tinkling rhymes and conventional rhythms). Rhythm as your fluid instrument. And your invented words. You were part of the revolution in European literature before the Americans even caught on. You have said, "Emerson brought me to a boil." You and Emily Dickinson, who also credits Emerson,

and whose innovations in compression and very different rhythms and lin-
ear emphases or stresses might seem like the opposite of yours; you both,
however, were not taken seriously by America's literary leaders of your day.

WHITMAN

Well, they had to keep their skirts clean, Norman. But even Miss Dickinson
didn't read me because she heard I was scandalous. [*Laughs*]

MAILER

[Quoting some "scandalous" lines]

"She owns the fine house by the rise of the bank,
She hides handsome and richly dressed aft the blinds of the
    window.
Which of the young men does she like the best?
Ah the homeliest of them is beautiful to her.
Where are you off to lady? For I see you,
You splash in the water there, yet stay stock still in your
    room.
Dancing and laughing along the beach came the twenty-nineth
    bather.
The rest did not see her, but she saw them and loved them.
The beards of the young men glistened with wet, it ran
    from their long hair,
Little streams pass'd all over their bodies.
An unseen hand also pass'd over their bodies,
It descended tremblingly from their temples and ribs.
The young men float on their backs, their white bellies
    bulge to the sun, they do not ask who seizes fast to
    them.
They do not know who puffs and declines with pendant
    and bending arch,
They do not think whom they souse with spray."

WHITMAN

[Applauds the recitation in good humor, then adds a few other scandalous lines]

"City of orgies, walks and joys. . . .
As I pass O Manhattan, your frequent and
    swift flash of eyes offering me love,
Offering response to my own—these repay me,
Lovers, continual lovers, only repay me."

MAILER

[Laughs and gives a thumbs-up]

But here's the point, Walt: your faith in literature for democratic progress might seem at best a faith whose temples have long ago collapsed. At worst, the faith of frustrated—even Jeffersonian—idealists.

WHITMAN

The priest departs, the Literatus comes! We cannot dismiss Literature, if we are serious about political transformation. Literature is an element of the machinery and soul of transformation that is too complex to analyze in an interview. One could spend a lifetime writing about the transfiguring sources, or a lifetime creating those sources. You see, Norman, Literature is a *weapon*. An instrument in the service of something larger than itself, not an end. Not for art's sake! In relation to Democracy, Literature has always been an instrument against those who would draw a line against free speech, free printing, free assembly.

Look at the history of Literature. Many superfluities in any epoch to be sure, but across eons the great Literatus has joined with his brother and sister creators to leave for us, if we will but take counsel from it, a literature of wisdom for humanity. And other arts as well, like music, the combiner, nothing more spiritual, nothing more sensuous, a god, yet completely human.

Moreover, it may be that we need authors far higher in grade than any yet known. Sacerdotal, modern, fit to cope with our occasions, permeating the whole mass of American mentality, taste, belief. Sowing a religious and moral character beneath the political. May not the people of our land all know how to read and write, and all possess the right to vote, and yet the main things be entirely lacking? I would suggest at least the possibility that should some two or three really original American poets arise, they would give more compaction and more moral identity (the quality most needed) to these States than all the constitutions, legislative and judicial ties, and all its hitherto political, warlike, or materialistic experiences. The fruition of Democracy, as I've said, resides altogether in the future. But the throes of birth are upon us.

MAILER

I once had a similar faith in great literature. The writers who formed me I honored and, in the innocence of youth, were to me as gods among men. But I'd argue we've moved not closer but further from such a belief as a people, as citizens. And the corporations who own the publishers have belittled the faith. It's no longer merely capital over labor, as we've said, it's capital over *all*, over every being (organic and inorganic), every creative artifact, every artificial structure. And above all, now more than ever, over politics.

WHITMAN

Am I not to be allowed my prophecy? Admitting all the folly and wickedness, is there no hope for change, growth, higher development of Conscience and Consciousness?

MAILER

For the sake of argument, I might grant that we are in a century-long, or two-century-long slough, and in the larger scheme of human Time we still have opportunity for development. For the moment, however, I'm more interested in your ideas about the democratic potential of literature.

——

WHITMAN

Think first of what satisfies the Soul: To take expression, to incarnate, to endow a Literature with grand and archetypal models, to fill with pride and love to the utmost capacity, and to achieve spiritual meanings, and suggest the future.

You have the capacity to see our literary shortcomings, even though most readers of this interview would say: Are we not doing well enough here already? Do not our publishers fatten quicker and deeper? Are there not more presses than in any other country? Many, I say, will come under this delusion—but my purpose is to dispel it. A nation may hold and circulate rivers and oceans of very readable print, journals, magazines, novels, library books, "poetry," etc. Hundreds of volumes brought out here, respectable enough, indeed unsurpassed in smartness and erudition. And yet all the while, the nation, strictly speaking, may possess no Literature at all. I reiterate: all else in the contributions of a nation or an age, through its politics, materials, heroic personalities, military éclat, etc., remains crude, and defers, in any close and thoroughgoing estimate, until vitalized by national, original archetypes in Literature.

MAILER

But to come even close, as a first step, we would have to defeat our culture of best-sellerdom, "page-turners," one of the props of corporate capitalism. These books that dull the mind. I'd argue we do not have, for the most part, literature as dissent—your "weapon"—in the sense you mean it. Not a literature of the soul. The dissenting soul. Nor even a literature that is philosophically disturbing.

WHITMAN

Would you not honor Thomas Paine, Henry Thoreau? But yes, in the rivalry of writers, especially novelists, success is for him or her who strikes the mean flat average, the sensational appetite for stimulus, incident, and so on, and depicts, to the common caliber, sensual, exterior life. To the luckiest, the audiences are limitless and profitable, but they cease presently.

While, this day or any day, to workmen portraying interior or spiritual life, the audiences are limited, and often laggard, but they last forever.

And of course, there are the dandies and ennuyés, dapper little gentlemen from abroad, who flood us with their thin sentiment of parlors, parasols, piano-songs, tinkling rhymes, chasing one aborted conceit after another. And what was called the Drama of the United States in my time was on a par with the questions of ornamental confectionery at public dinners, or the arrangement of curtains and hangings in a ballroom, nor more, nor less. On a par with the copious dribble, causing tender spasms in the coteries, either of our little- or well-known rhymesters, which does not fulfill the needs and august occasions of this land. Whereas America needs a poetry that is bold, modern, and as all-surrounding and kosmical as she is herself. Like you, I find the first sign of proportionate, native, imaginative Soul (the other name for Literature), and first-class works to match, is so far largely wanting. But we must not despair.

The great Literatuses will be known, among the rest, by cheerful simplicity, adherence to natural standards, limitless faith in God, reverence, and by the absence of doubt, ennui, burlesque, persiflage, or any strained and temporary fashion.

MAILER

"Tender Spasms in the Coteries," a title I should have used for an essay! Or a book, Walt.

[Laughs along with Whitman, then flips to a page in his notebook]

You wrote in more detail of this concept of literature in your 1855 "Preface" to *Leaves*. The idea of the Kosmos—of the Poet as lover of the people, the earth, the universe. "Who troubles himself about his ornaments or fluency is lost. This is what you must do: Love the earth and sun and the animals, despise riches, give alms to everyone who asks, stand up for the stupid and crazy, devote your income and labor to others, hate tyrants, argue not concerning God, have patience and indulgence toward the people, take off your hat to nothing known or unknown or to any man or number of men, go freely with powerful uneducated persons and with the young and with the mothers of families . . . re-examine all you have been told at school or church or in any book, dismiss whatever insults your soul, and your very flesh shall be a great poem." I've put it this way, with help from Aquinas and Hemingway, that we must trust the authority of our senses. Therein lies an ethic, a connection to the Creator, by freeing ourselves of the maxims and injunctions other people have put into us from childhood.

Let's pursue the point further. When you speak of the Personality of the poet, you also remind me of something Milton wrote: "Books are not absolutely dead things, but do contain a potency of life in them to be as active as that soul whose progeny they are; nay, they do preserve as in a vial the purest efficacy and extraction of that living intellect that bred them." Yet I don't know if you can imagine the response that your faith in the dissenting soul, in the artist's—this Literatus's—unchained imagination, would receive in my time.

WHITMAN

In that regard, not much has changed, Norman. Not yet. Our great journey, however, continues. The process so far is indirect and peculiar and, though it may be suggested, cannot be defined. Observing, rapport, and with intuition, the shows and forms presented by Nature, the sensuous luxuriance, the beautiful in living men and women, the actual play of passions, in history and in life—out of these the poet, the esthetic worker in any field projects them, their analogies, by curious removes, indirections, in Literature and art. (No useless attempt to repeat the material creation by daguerreotyping the exact likeness by mortal mental means, but through the magic of genius.) This is the image-making faculty, coping with material creation: this alone can breathe into Literature and art the breath of life and endow it with Identity. Milton's idea that books grow out of Personality.

The true question to ask respecting any book is "Has it helped any human Soul?" This is the hint not only of any great Literatus, his book, but of every great artist. The rest are the careless criticisms of a day, these endless and wordy chatterers. The highest, widest aim of Democratic Literature may well be to bring forth and strengthen this sense in individuals and society.

MAILER

Soul, soul, and yet more soul. The dissident living soul, the primary nutri-ent of democracy, you say! The collection of individual souls—Identities—creating a democratic aggregate, a living—it is not too much to say a spiritual—society. You somewhere called it "compound individuality."

Lawrence, by the way, saw this in you too, that your very definition of democracy was "the recognition of souls"—which soul he also called the "under-consciousness"—as we pass the other wayfarers along the open road of our actual living. Soul and body are one as we travel the common way. Democracy arises out of the *integrity* of our deepest selves, our souls. Though Lawrence feared you might confuse "merging" with "contact," los-ing your soul's integrity as you, we, give in to the impulse to merge with all the fellow travelers, he ultimately decided you offered nonetheless "a great new doctrine of life, the morality of actual living." A new basis for democ-racy as the recognition of the soul-integrity in others. Gone was the idea of the old obsessive morality—the *salvation* of the soul. The soul and flesh are held together in actual living.

It is a fine ideal, Walt, to rise out of such base materials!

WHITMAN

I too at times despair. But then another turn and hope embraces me once again. But one instance: I have stood by the bedside of a Pennsylvania sol-dier who lay conscious of quick approaching death, yet perfectly calm; and with a noble, spiritual manner the veteran surgeon, turning aside, said to me that though he had witnessed many, many deaths of soldiers at Bull Run, Antietam, Fredericksburg, etc., he had not seen yet the first case of man or boy who met the approach of dissolution with cowardly qualms or terror. The doctor, the nurse, attending, but no friend or relative nearby. What have we here if not, towering above all talk and argument, the plen-tifully supplied, last-needed proof of Democracy in its Personalities? So, Democracy, the leveler, is joined with another principle, equally unyield-ing, the principle of Individuality. Of Identity. Personality. The Literature, Songs, Esthetics of a country are of importance principally because they furnish the materials and suggestions of Personality for the women and men of that country, whether the Democracy of that country is embryonic, as is ours, or more advanced.

MAILER

So you see the single solitary soul, this individual consciousness, this Identity, as you put it, as the yet undernourished source of any democratic society. You, the poet, are the mere instigator. But there must by many instigators over time, if there is to be any, what you call, "fruition"?

WHITMAN

My work, my whole project, is but an exploration. I must do the best I can, leaving it to those who come after me to do much better. The service, if any, must be merely to break a sort of first path or track. The real gist of Democracy still sleeps, quite unawakened. Its history has yet to be enacted. Democracy is a sort of younger brother of another great and often-used word, Nature, whose history is also unwritten. But it is also good to reduce the whole matter, as I have, to the consideration of a single self, a man, or woman, to one single solitary Soul, a full consciousness. Your Identity for you, and mine for me. Let thereby creeds, conventions fall away and become of no account before this single idea.

This is the lesson of Nature, is it not? The quality of Being, in the object's self, is according to its own central idea and purpose, and of growing therefrom—not by criticism, by any other standards and adjustments to standards. Yes, a full man wisely gathers, culls, absorbs. But if engaged disproportionately in others, he slights or overlays the precious idiosyncrasy and special nativity and intention that he is, the man's self, the main thing; he is then a failure, however general his cultivation or erudition.

And provision for a little healthy rudeness, savage virtue, justification of what one has in one's self, whatever it is, is demanded. Negative qualities, even deficiencies, would be a relief amid this more and more complex, more and more artificialized, state of society.

MAILER

A fucking little healthy rudeness is itself savage virtue. I see Lawrence as another prophet who suffered at the hands of censors, or what he called "the censor morons." I also think of him as a brother-in-arms against what you've called "Feudalism" of any kind.

Technically, of course, we've had capitalism, not feudalism, by and large since the Renaissance or thereabouts as markets began to break down the ancient order. But I think you are getting at the similarity in hierarchies and in the crass exploitations. We might have skipped the vassals of the old system and substituted capital for land, but one might argue that we have our Executive (echoing the Crown) and his oligarchs (our substitute for nobility) still exploiting the peasantry (or labor, and all the rest of us). The same might be said of the state capitalisms of communism or fascism. So, to my mind you are talking of any devolution of the state that would crush the human spirit, that would mechanize and regiment human beings, that would break us. And break the prophets, the seers, the great Literatuses, as you call them.

Well, one's ego-strength is a bulwark against such forces. I once defined ego as the necessary reservoir of confidence sufficient to keep striving. Call it ego-endurance. Can such ego-endurance help to redirect America? Expose our social taboos and conventions for the artificial falsehoods they are? You wrote, "I believe in the flesh and the appetites. Seeing hearing, feeling are miracles . . ." Like you, Lawrence saw love (including Eros) as one of the great opponents of regimentation.

WHITMAN

Yes. Good for Mr. Lawrence. Even our lovers must be comrades. Wives, husbands, fathers, mothers: we can't stay together, feel satisfied, grow bigger, on any other basis. Love will always take care of itself; it does not need censors, monitors, guardians. It does not need the state.

[Quoting himself sonorously]

"Through me forbidden voices,
Voices of sexes and lusts, voices veil'd and I remove the veil'
Voices indecent by me clarified and transfigured."

———

MAILER

And love certainly does not need state oppression to crush whatever the state deems "obscene," any more than we need state violence to crush people's dissent or trumped-up "enemies" of the state.

WHITMAN

I've always said I'd rather cause the birth of one than the death of twenty!

MAILER

A noble doctrine! [*Laughs*] So, Walt, we are agreed on this, at least: whatever crushes the integrity of the soul crushes democracy as well. [*Flips to his notes again*]

Lawrence too could see mechanization invading the province of love, of emotion, of the vital center. He knew how machinery, technology atrophies our senses; it "is the great neuter; it is the eunuch of eunuchs." He said that "we do not know what we lose by all our labor-saving appliances. Of the two evils, it would be much the lesser to lose all machinery, every bit, rather than to have, as we have, hopelessly too much." He was prophetic in foretelling how technology—like any instrument of convenience—can also become the instrument of oppression. As I've said many times, technology at a certain level of development, its most deadening manifestations stands between us and life, desensitizes us, dulls the senses. The more power the less pleasure, and the more opportunity for oppression. Anyway, you can imagine how Lawrence—his novels, his poems, his paintings—became a danger to the state. He paid for it, especially for the taboos he confronted openly.

WHITMAN

His paintings?

MAILER

Part of his larger revolutionary project. Lawrence saw his paintings too, in his time, as a confrontation with our "terror of the sexual life," our "abhorrence of the procreative act." He wanted his visual art, as well, to counter our repression of the instinctual and intuitive life, repressed for the sake of our spiritual-mental consciousness alone. This emphasis on the optical and cerebral, Lawrence believed, had atrophied our intuitive-instinctual powers, powers that are the source of "that magic awareness we call art." Had stifled wholeness of imagination and consciousness. And our misplaced emphasis, he added, had led to our "bourgeois psychology"—a psychology enslaved by industrialism—that engendered a morality where bodily existence became evil. William Blake, was the exception in Britain and America, to his mind, and Cezanne in France (if to a lesser degree than Blake). Cezanne was heroic, however, *not* for his achievement but for his *struggle*—his sacrifices, his honesty with himself, his own revolution in consciousness. So too with Lawrence.

So too with you, Walt?

WHITMAN

So with you too, Norman?

MAILER

Maybe that's for others to say. But the critics keep missing this: the significance of the author's or painter's *struggle* (his embattled evolution beyond his time, beyond his society's repressions) over the assessment only of his achievement. Or worse, the assessment only of his ideological deficiency.

WHITMAN

So Mr. Lawrence knew that the function of the writer is to shake up the latent forces in all men, shake them up into life. To get in touch with the very deepest sources of life. Tolstoy's *The Kreuzer Sonata* opened my eyes, made me feel we had a master with us, as great as any. But I was astonished by the blatherskites who attempted to suppress it as indecent. It is incredible, it is stupid, foolish to the last degree.

But put that instance aside. I want the utmost freedom—even the utmost license—rather than any censorship; censorship is always ignorant, always bad. I've suffered enough from the censors. I'd dismiss all monitors, guardians, without any ceremony whatsoever. All this fear of indecency, all this noise about purity and sex and the social order and Comstockism in particular and general is nasty—too nasty to make any compromise with. The dirtiest book in all the world is the expurgated book. We shrink from the realities of our bodily life—something to be kept in the dark and lied about instead of being avowed and gloried in. I have heard nothing but expurgate, expurgate, expurgate from the day I started. It is damnable and vulgar. The body is the other side of the soul. But, because of your Mr. Lawrence and others, the time will come when the whole affair of sex—copulation and reproduction—will be treated with the respect to which it is entitled. Sex is the root of it all, the coming together of men and women."

MAILER

On that note, allow me to give you a copy of my "Bodily Function Blues."

[As he pulls out a sheet of paper and hands it over to Whitman, Mailer sings a few bars in his imitation southern drawl.]

"Ohhh . . . Ah can't piss
Ah can't urinate
Ah can't bleed
Ah can't even menstruate
Ah can't salivate Ah can't talk.
Ah can't elucidate Ah can't eat. . . ."

And so on. Anyway, to the point: you paid a price for that belief in sex, in the body, in your writings. So, we are talking, at bottom, about courage in the writer.

WHITMAN

With *Leaves of Grass,* a work of iconoclasm in its art and its subject matter, I believe now that "price" was an advantage, the book's stormy early life. Nothing could make up for the loss of this price—it was a priceless privilege. Ease, comfort, acceptation, would have ruined me.

MAILER

Early success damned near ruined me!

WHITMAN

But you say you fought your way back by first plumbing your own depths. That too is courage. You see, *Leaves* is ultimately a book of faith. And it all goes back to my faith in the future. Mankind is in process of being; woman's and man's justification is not in themselves today but yet to come, something ahead. And I might add that *Leaves* is essentially a woman's book: the women do not know it, but every now and then a woman shows she knows it, its cry of the right and wrong of the woman sex, of the facts of creation first of all.

MAILER

Of the wronging of women, I said in one of my books that redress is overdue. I took the subject up, in part through the lens of Lawrence's examination where Western Civilization had ended up. But I've truly been misunderstood because I challenged not women's suffrage, not whole and equal political and economic rights for women, but instead the mechanization of sex, love, orgasm, emotion, and the technologizing of the womb, of biological reproduction, and, yes, even the misandry that too often followed from those tendencies in the woman's movement in the 1970s. Then the tendentious literary criticism! The lack of fair play, of fidelity to the literary material, and that lack of understanding of the writer's lifelong struggle. It all seemed to be adding up to the technological, totalitarian desexualizing of relations between the male and female. The very opposite of Lawrence, who was being censured, denounced, but who in fact saw sexual love as the salvation of men and women against the regimentations and corruptions of civilization. Artificial insemination—I'll plant my flag here—is not the perfect equal of any great fuck.

WHITMAN

But you buffooned your compunctions in public, let your demons do the talking?

MAILER

Well, some of my daughters tell me it is painful to watch me in the clips!

WHITMAN

Should you have reached out? Could it be the women were part of that revolution you yourself sought, but you misconstrued their true potential? Only combative, never collaborative? Hadn't you all wished to overturn the hierarchies, the systems you railed against?

MAILER

Well, let's say I baited them too often in public. Those who would censor men, who quoted men out of context and out of order, those who worshipped at the altar of technological solutions to ancient contentions, polarities, dualities. Those who were introducing a new kind of prudery even after all the battles had been fought, often by men, to deliver us from the long medieval night of Victorian sex, with its perversions, hypocrisies, and brothel dispensations. Those were parlous times. I leapt in. They didn't call me Stormin' Norman in those days for too little!

WHITMAN

You could be your own worst enemy. [*Laughs*]

MAILER

I have more than once gone on record to say that I don't expect people to accept all my ideas, but I want them to respond to them, challenge them, absorb them, take them a step further and make them evolve or improve on them. These are steps on a journey.

WHITMAN

Indeed, Norman. The quality shared by the greatest men—Emerson, Darwin—is not to be too damned sure about anything.

MAILER

I too have been on a journey to explore the potential sources (you call them "latent forces") for the development of the individual, the soul, the deeper conscience of full consciousness, even the chastening of brutal politics with democratic impulses and inspirations. But as you say, it's all deeper than mere politics, or than politics separated from soul and the full development of the individual, uncrushed by society. One of the great difficulties is knowing whether one's conscience is operating for the good, or, to put it in other terms, for God or the Devil.

WHITMAN

Let me address two points you raise before we talk of Gods and Devils. First, yes, one's egotism carries one a great way toward enduring.

MAILER

Ah, one's egotism. Yes, but there's a dangerous line to walk—one might remain strong, one might be brilliant, but there's that self-defeating bluster, those worst impulses flashing forth like one's Mr. Hyde, that one might do better to watch for. But I've always wondered why egotism everywhere—in politicians, in Wall Street operators, in CEOs, in generals, in celebrities, in academics, and so on—is tolerated or even expected. But let the writer reveal egotism and he or she somehow becomes a subhuman fraud.

WHITMAN

Like you, I had to adjust myself to the negative condition, to opposition, denunciation, suspicion.

Second point: have you read my poem "The Sleepers"? Find there my own sense of something below mere consciousness, below our waking state—

MAILER

I know the poem, yes. Something there you offer as sub-consciousness as a condition of being too.

WHITMAN

[Holds up his hand to finish his points]

But let me say that I am aware that our Conscience, or the idea of Conscience, of intense moral right, and in its name and strained construction, the worst fanaticisms, wars, persecutions, murders and so on have yet, in all lands, been broached, and have come to their devilish fruition. One corrective should be that in response, side by side, with the unflagging stimulation of the elements of Religion and Conscience must henceforth move with equal sway, Science, absolute reason, and the general proportionate development of the whole man. These scientific facts, deductions, are divine too—precious counted parts of moral civilization, and, with physical health, indispensable to it, to prevent fanaticism. For abstract religion is easily led astray.

MAILER

Or any abstract idealism. And I've said the same myself about Fundamentalisms.

———

WHITMAN

And as I say, in the Prophetic Literature of these United States, Nature, not abstraction, but the true idea of Nature, long absent, must, above all, become fully restored, enlarged, and must furnish the pervading atmosphere to poems and the test of all high literary and esthetic compositions. I do not mean the smooth walks, trimmed hedges, butterflies, poesies, and nightingales of the English poets, but the whole Orb, with its geologic history, the cosmos, carrying fire and snow, that rolls through the illimitable areas. And that mankind comprehending these, has, in towering super-addition, the Moral and Spiritual Consciences, indicating his destination beyond the ostensible, the mortal.

And think, moreover, that Democracy, biding its time, ponders its own ideals, not of Literature and Art only—not of men only, but of women. The idea of the women. The idea of the women of America (extricated from this daze, this fossil and unhealthy air which hangs over the word Lady), developed, raised to become the robust equals, workers, and, it may be, even practical and political deciders with men—greater than man, we may admit, through their divine maternity, always their towering, emblematical attribute—but great, at any rate as man, in all departments, as George Eliot and George Sand have demonstrated in the arts. Or, rather, capable of being so, soon as they realize it.

I can think of many examples, but I will offer but one here—of a woman, who, from taste and necessity, has gone into practical affairs, carries on a mechanical business, partly works at it herself, dashes out more and more into real hardy life, is not abashed by the coarseness of the contact, knows how to be firm and silent at the same time, holds her own with unvarying coolness and decorum, and will compare, any day, with superior carpenters, farmers, and even boatmen and drivers. For all that, she has not lost the charm of the womanly nature but preserves and bears it fully, though through such rugged presentation.

So you see, what I have called that Individuality—broad enough to every farmer and mechanic—to the female equally to the male—that towering Selfhood is the Personality of mortal life possessing, nonetheless, ideas of the Infinite, the Spiritual.

MAILER

Well then, Walt, you place your hopes in a certain species of true democracy, or to be more exact, democratic republic. It is a faith I'm not ready to accede to. Not entirely yet. Though of course theology can be political. Jesus was political, come to that. So, your democracy is of your "Individual" and the aggregation of individuals, all right, but of the individual soul, a great democratic current of souls carrying a welter of science, of fact, and of a true democracy's restraint of capital, of the raw, even predatory, impulses of human greed and unchecked capital. As if democracy were a great riverine ecosystem with all these elements in the current. A current that liberates the individual for growth (of full consciousness, of spiritual and aesthetic growth). And it is organic, to continue our riverine metaphor, neither deterministic, nor materialistic. More like a living system of both spiritual and material reality guiding the individual (who can be both anarchic and communitarian) and the state. Will you be charged with putting your faith in the never-was, the never-will be, the nowhere of Utopianism?

WHITMAN

Has any promulgated Utopia ever contained all that you just described, Norman?

MAILER

But you place extraordinary faith in the potential of human beings to transcend ancient follies, the ancient idiocies of history, and the monstrosities of modern history, including humanity's –what shall we call it?—*aboriginal need* for the "Leader" (political, religious, or whatever) to tell us how to live, what to believe and do. The other side of that human duality.

WHITMAN

Say, rather, that my dream of democracy evolving to the level I've described is both an advance of the *potential* within humanity and a check on humanity's more mephitic impulses. The potential I've propounded, its many elements, its People and Personality, I do argue, exists. Can we, will we, evolve together, as it were, our governing system and ourselves to a new level, at least as new as the opportunity given us by our own Revolution, or I should say by the first phase of our Democratic Revolution. That Revolution also grows and evolves, corrects its substantial errors, or it can. Our living Revolution is not determined to evolve or to devolve. There will be back-slidings, disastrous defeats, but there will be advances, victories as well. And victories born of defeats. And we have wisdom to guide us. So long as we consult that wisdom, and so long as we don't abrogate our Free Will.

MAILER

So long as our all-too-human tendency to abrogate free will to oppressive systems or ideologies does not turn out to be so deeply embedded in humanity that any democratic evolution of your description is impossible—either impossible to stabilize or crushed before it can take wing and rise off the ground.

WHITMAN

Listen, there are in me as much as anyone wild growths of poison flowers, and passions of villainy, that must be fought, in defense of virtue. But as to that outcome—the abrogation of Free Will to oppressive systems—only history, or rather Time, will judge. You and I cannot know it, mired as we are, or were, in my time or in yours. The cosmos evolves and wheels on its way. Within that larger Being we all, who live within it, will ultimately choose life or death.

MAILER

God help us, Walt!

WHITMAN

Indeed, Norman. God help us!

———

123

7

TWELFTH ROUND

Mailer on Boyhood, Harvard,
and *Ancient Evenings*

AUTHOR'S NOTE: *This interview with Norman Mailer just before the publication of* Ancient Evenings *(his "big novel" ten years in the making and widely anticipated) was the cover story for the March–April 1983 issue of* Harvard Magazine. *I had published my first book,* Acts of Regeneration, *in 1980 about Mailer's work; based on that book, editor John Bethell (a kind and generous gentleman) gave me the assignment for his magazine.*

Ten years in the writing, *Ancient Evenings* will be published in May. For Norman Mailer, who turned sixty in January, this new book marks an important transitional point. After more than a decade of nonfiction, a big novel—the first of a planned trilogy— brings Mailer back to the literary genre in which he made his name.

Pulitzer Prizes in 1969 and 1980 for *Armies of the Night* and *The Executioner's Song* (not to mention additional awards for these and other books) have affirmed Mailer's standing in contemporary American letters. His public posturing and activist politics have colored his reputation, but two dozen books, three films, a play, and countless articles bear witness to his energy and resourcefulness.

Born in Long Branch, New Jersey, in 1923, Mailer grew up in Brooklyn, graduated from Boys High School, and entered Harvard at sixteen. Although he took his degree with honors in engineering sciences, he was already bent on becoming a writer. In college his output had included more than thirty short stories and two unpublished novels and plays; "The Greatest Thing in the World," written under Professor Robert Gorham Davis, had won *Story Magazine*'s annual award.

Mailer was drafted in 1944. He ultimately served in the Philippines as a headquarters clerk and infantryman. Based on his war experience and published in 1948, his novel *The Naked and the Dead* made him suddenly famous at twenty-five. So began one of the most important, notorious, and mercurial careers in postwar American literature.

Mailer appears to date himself from that 1948 success. (Of an unpublished novel—set in an insane asylum—which he began at Harvard, he later said: "I do not know the young man who wrote this book. I do not like him very much.") Indeed, it would be hard to imagine a more extreme personality shift. The amiable, bright Jewish boy from Brooklyn was to become the ranting, hallucinating, brawling "General Marijuana" of the *Village Voice* in the Fifties. The next decades would bring Mailer's televised invective against the Vietnam War and General Westmoreland, his skirmishes with radical feminists, his wrangles with fellow authors Gore Vidal and William Styron. Thus embattled, the self-appointed Jeremiah got himself in trouble with his literary audience as well as the general public. But it was trouble Mailer wanted. He is nothing if not a disturber of bland uniformity, convention, and complacency—of what he sees as the "cancer," the totalitarianism, the spiritual death of our times.

Yet Mailer today is a gray and courteous eminence. Meeting him—a stoutish, five-foot-eight man who looks at first glance as if he might be vacationing in safari suit from regular stints on "Wall Street Week"—one is taken aback. Can this be the bold excursionist who has struggled with the nature of existentialism, the unconscious, God, and the devil?

The conversation that follows suggests that the appearance does indeed deceive, perhaps as much as Mailer's "media image." It also offers fresh background on the first twenty-five years of Mailer's life, and clues to his current work—about which Mailer has been reticent since the mid-Seventies, when he made his much-publicized million-dollar contract with Little, Brown to complete "a certain big novel."

Talking with Mailer, one sees that the journalist, revolutionary, and holy fool are still alive in the man—but that other, and older, personae have returned. For his capacious personality now seems to accommodate the

———

The author in conversation with Mailer, fall 1982.
Photo by Christopher S. Johnson, from the personal collection of the author.

disciplined worker, the self-effacing novelist, and the scholar. There is even a wink from that earnest young man from Brooklyn who got good grades and went to Harvard to study engineering.

You once said that you started writing at about seven—a long, 300-page story about a trip to Mars. Then you quit. You began again about the time you were at Harvard. If your high-school interests weren't particularly literary, what were they?

I built model airplanes all through high school. I wanted to be an aeronautical engineer—that was my prevailing interest. The books I read in high school were certainly not literary. I wasn't a literary man in any way. My idea of good writers was Jeffrey Farnol, Rafael Sabatini. My favorite book was probably *Captain Blood.*

I'd assumed I'd go to MIT. The only reason I applied to Harvard was that my cousin had gone there. I thought, well, it might be nice. And then, I lived in a very simple part of Brooklyn. It wasn't ethnic on the grand scale. You didn't have to fight your way to the candy store—we didn't have gangs. We were just quiet, middle-class kids. In those days there was so little traffic we used to play touch football and roller hockey in the streets. Just a quiet street with small, what the British call "semi-attached villas," which meant *real* small, two-family homes. And small lawns in front, so small that when you were playing roller hockey, if you body-checked somebody hard they'd go flying across the sidewalk, and you had to go scrambling up a lawn that was banked. If that ever happened to you you'd come out with fire in your eyes and your skates full of dirt.

So street sports and engineering were your early interests?

Right. . . . very conventional. And in my senior year the girls would ask, "Where did you apply to college?" I'd say M.I.T. and it wouldn't register at all. Then I'd say Harvard and they'd look at me, "Whew!" So I thought, well, there must be something wonderful about Harvard.

You've mentioned that rather than the summit of your experience, high school was not a good time. And you felt deprived for thirty years thereafter. Why?

I went to Boys High School in Brooklyn, which is very much a boys' school. I was a year and a half younger than the average student. High school went by in a blur of work and doing one's homework as quickly as possible and getting out in the street to play. And there was no high-school life as such. Later I began to realize that for many people high school was the prime experience of their lives. It was during the dating period and all that. In Brooklyn one went out with dates however one could. I felt straddled between my friends who were my age at home and were two years behind me at school. So I didn't feel I belonged particularly in one life or another. I'd say high school was really the equivalent of college for somebody who was working at a job and going to night school, and was bitter afterwards because he felt he never had any college life.

You've never written about that stage of your life. Is it something you can't deal with in writing?

I've always had the feeling that it doesn't make much sense to write about something when you know that others can write about it at least as well as you can or maybe better. I never felt I had that much to say about my childhood that was so special it was worth recording. It may mean that writers do play games with themselves—it may mean there is something I'm concealing from myself. I find over and over again that I hide what I can write about because it's risky to know that you can write about something. You can plunge into it before you're ready to give it proper commitment. This sounds very odd to people who never write, to see the unconscious as a vast area where military campaigns go on. I think it's the only metaphor that works because I discover over and over again that the unconscious will disclose to me what it chooses and when it chooses to. When I am working on a long book, for instance, I almost never have a thought about it when I'm not working. And I've come to recognize every year that it's highly impractical to think about it because you can lose it. I happen to have one of those memories that's virtually psychopathic in its half-life. I forget half of everything I think unless, in about four seconds, I write it down. It's overspecialization for about thirty or forty years.

You were close to your parents? You felt no sense of needing to break away?

I didn't have a problem trying to break away in the manner that so many writers do. I didn't have to convince my parents that I should be a writer. It often takes up half a young writer's energy. They were soon pleased that I wanted to be a writer. They loved reading my work, as only parents can.

How did you find being at Harvard? Did you feel like an outsider?

Harvard, I think at least in those days, had solved more delicate social situations than any institution that could call itself truly part of the establishment. For instance, my freshman year, I'd say that eighty percent of the people that I was close to were from the same background I was from—they were Jewish, middle class, from small towns, some were from the city.

But we all grouped together very much as young black students would to-day. The difference being that it never occurred to us that we were in an incredibly subtle ghetto. Over the four years at Harvard I don't think I ever felt it once.

Part of this was my innocence. But Myron Kaufmann was a classmate of mine; he wrote a marvelous novel called *Remember Me to God,* and in it the young man is Jewish and he is acutely aware of every social discrimination. That passed blissfully over me. I had no idea at all that I really was very much a part of an out-group; in fact the word didn't exist to me. I had the experience of sitting next to a young man who was dressed in a particular way. I might have sat next to him a whole year. We might have exchanged as much as three lines of conversation such as, "My God isn't old so-and-so stuffy today?" There was that sense that there was this other world, but I think that part of the brilliance of the way Harvard solved that problem was not having fraternities. Fraternities really burn it into you just which little group you belong to because the fraternities all have their status. Everyone in college is aware of it. The Dekes are better than the Upsilons. You are acutely aware of where you belong in that scheme. If you don't get into any fraternity, you're down at the bottom—it breeds such misery.

At Harvard the opposite was done. A few people got into the clubs. Somehow after your first week at Harvard it was clear to you that certain people never get into clubs, and that you were one of them didn't matter. There was a certain scorn for the clubs. Who'd be so sleazy as to get into a club and get three C's and a D and all that? But we never thought of our-selves as being out of it. That was marvelous. That's the way the establish-ment should work. Never got a chance socially speaking, and never ached once. That takes three centuries of careful elaboration of the study of peo-ple's feelings.

Were you aware of anti-Semitism at Harvard?

No. I never felt it directly. The nearest example I could find—I couldn't even say it was anti-Semitism. I remember I went up to Harvard wearing this jacket and pants I bought of my own assistance. My mother didn't know a great deal about all this. . . . I bought a gold and brown jacket and had green and blue vertical striped pants and saddle shoes. I saw my faculty advisor in the engineering department. He was a crusty old man. He didn't think too much of a lot of things, and he immediately told me that I should take a speech course. I said something about wanting to take German and he said, no, you don't need it. And I remember getting just salty enough to say to him, "Well, sir, if I can pick up German in the course of a year or two, I don't see why I can't learn to speak English." He was very aware that I came from Brooklyn. I'd say that was the strongest single example I can think of. If people were anti-Semitic at Harvard in those days, and I'm sure some were, they were incredibly well bred about it. I didn't feel it was something that impinged on me. The way I felt it was only by comparing that comfortable, middle-class world I had been in—somehow I hadn't taken enough things in, it just wasn't a wide enough horizon. There was a tremendous amount to learn.

But it came to you at Harvard that there was an "establishment"? That's a theme that comes up again and again in your work.

In the part of Brooklyn I came from . . . in the public school I went to, even at Boys High, there was no feeling at all of an establishment. But by the time I got to Harvard I had to realize that an establishment was immense, was subtle, did not have a face, you couldn't even feel it particularly. The only way you were aware of it was that people were terribly serious about their education. And in Brooklyn I was always ashamed of being smart— somehow you weren't manly if you were smart. At Harvard it was the other way around. You were ashamed because you were maybe not smart enough. There were always people who were more brilliant than you, and that was admired, vastly admired.

I have to separate the Harvard establishment from other establishments. I'm not sure that you shouldn't have an establishment, that establishment isn't necessary. The question is one of my obsessions, if we define obsession as a matter to which one always returns. And each time one returns to it with a different point of view about it. When we speak about something being obsessive it's because we don't end up with a fixed opinion. We could argue that certain obsessions are filled with hatred, but they are the exact opposite of what I'm saying—in such obsessions one always goes back to hate in the same way. I'm talking about the other kind of obsession, where one can't make up one's mind. I've pondered the question of an establishment all the time. Is it good? Is it bad? Should we have an establishment as such? After all, what you are talking about is the manipulation of people by other people. That's the side which you have to question, the manipulation. Is it finally an absolute evil or a partial evil or a human necessity?

If we accept the idea of an establishment, then no question Harvard has the best establishment I've ever encountered, certainly better than the military establishment, better than the Washington establishment, better than the New York publishing establishment.

What teachers influenced you? You've mentioned Robert Gorham Davis in English A—you became a friend of sorts.

Yes, we're friendly to this day. Theodore Morrison was another who had a certain influence. I remember Dr. [Henry A.] Murray in abnormal psychology. . . . for his geniality, for the charm he brought to a subject normally considered charmless. Robert Hillyer was kind of marvelous. I'm one of the few people who ever took four years of writing courses at Harvard. . . . Hillyer I remember for his exquisite manners. That was probably a crucial part of my education at that point. If you're talking about shockers, the shock was simple. One grew up with rough and ready manners, and you just never measured people by their manners. You measured them by their athletic ability, their loyalties. You considered your parents and their evaluation of people by how much money they made, how good they were as providers. These measures were strong, crude, and serviceable.

At Harvard you ran into a spectrum of manners, and it was as if the manners were the morphology that revealed to you the social pattern behind. In other words, the degree to which one had social imagination, one could begin to conceive whole areas of society by the manners. That's a lifework. After all, it takes a life to know how a third or a half or even a fraction of the country works, socially speaking. But through others' manners you can imagine projections into what these people's lives are really like. It enlivens literature. I think the rich appreciation of literature is difficult without having some sense of the style of the people who go through the books.

In that sense the professors I tend to remember are not necessarily the ones I studied with, but the ones who had manners that were memorable. I never took a course with F. O. Matthiessen, but I heard him give a few lectures, and they were memorable because there was something in his manner that was tragic. He had one of the most grave and dignified manners.

How about students? Any friends that particularly influenced you?

Thirty or forty or fifty, but I think just to name them would distort the reality of it. We influenced each other a lot.

As I think of it, meeting Bowden Broadwater was an extraordinary experience. Because Bowden had more style than anyone I'd ever met. He dominated the *Advocate*, his personality. When I came on as a sophomore, I think he was then a junior or senior—he was Pegasus and he had high style. I remember when I read *Brideshead Revisited,* I kept chuckling as I read it. It wasn't that Bowden looked in any way like Sebastian Flyte or that we were close friends. On the contrary, we were on opposite sides. There were two factions.

Would you say that was the high point of your Harvard years?

Oh, yes. The *Advocate* was probably what I enjoyed most about Harvard. I think it comes through in the article I wrote for *Esquire.*

What was your worst experience at Harvard?

There wasn't anything terribly onerous, nothing that makes me writhe with anger. There were a few silly experiences. Mostly my first year. Going up to Harvard, I managed to go over all the literature that was sent to us. Phillips Brooks House sent something that said when you get here, please drop in and visit us. Somehow I had the idea that the first thing you did when you got to Harvard, before you even went looking for your dorm, was to go to Phillips Brooks House. As I was driving up with my future roommate, Martin Lubin, and his father, I said when we get there, we've got to find Phillips Brooks House. We were looking at the map of the Yard, and I directed the car through traffic, and I went in with Marty. It was deserted, of course. It was Freshman Week, and a few juniors and seniors had come up to work, and there was one fellow there. He was a very tall senior and handsome— handsome as a Princeton man—literally smoking a pipe behind a desk, and he hadn't seen anyone in two hours. I realized I had made an error. I remember looking at him and saying, "Well, we're here." It just changed his day. He had to come up out of whatever he was thinking about . . . probably something pleasant. The moment I said it, all I wanted to do was get out of there. Of course he was feeling he wasn't doing his duty, so he was pulling us in and we were pulling away. Finally, we got out and I was perspiring behind my ears. So that was an embarrassment.

Once we were trying to get into the Old Howard. And they asked us how old we were. The others all said eighteen, and I, without thinking, said seventeen, and I was sixteen then. I thought I had to lie, so I said seventeen, and the guy said you can't get in, you have to be eighteen. I said I'm eighteen, I'm eighteen! I'm a freshman at Harvard; you've got to be eighteen to be a freshman at Harvard. The guy looked at me at the door and said: "All right, kid, go in." And so all through freshman year whenever I would be winning an argument with my roommates, they'd jump up and start waving their identity cards yelling: "I'm eighteen! You've got to be eighteen to go to Harvard!"

And probably the bitterest blow freshman year was going out for crew and working and working at it and realizing at a certain point that far from not making the team, the coach never even looked at me. And I realized why. Someone took me aside and told me, look, you could be good but it wouldn't matter, your arms are too short. You throw off the entire rest of the crew. That experience of working one's manful best each day at those oars and never being looked at by the coach. . . .

As you see, I just don't have memories of real unpleasantness. I doubt if there have been four less painful years of my life.

What happened that you went to Harvard an aspiring aeronautical engineer and came out heading for the Pacific and wanting to write the great American war novel?

I think really the main influence was English A, because we were given *Studs Lonigan* to read. And that turned me on my head because Studs Lonigan grew up in a much tougher environment than I did, but there was still a similarity. He talked the way my friends and I talked in Brooklyn. And I realized you could write about those kinds of experiences and that was almost endlessly exciting. Dos Passos, Hemingway, Fitzgerald I also read in my freshman year. By the time that year was over I wanted to be a writer. It just took another year before I was so certain I wanted to be a writer that I knew I'd never be an engineer.

There wasn't anything in particular that was acting on you from outside, influencing you, changing you? It was a process of self-discovery?

Yes. That is not at all an unnatural development for writers. Certain books stimulate them and make them know that they want to become writers. I did take a course, now that I think of it, with Howard Mumford Jones in American literature that meant a lot. In fact, I still remember one of his phrases. He was talking about Dreiser. Howard Mumford Jones used to talk with great bombast, and I'm not deriding it. People use bombast, and it's dreadful, but he made it great. He said, "You know Dreiser was a great writer, but when it came to style, he was abominable. His style reads like a streetcar wheel with one flat side. It goes KA-BLUNK, KA-BLUNK, KA-BLUNK." He'd walk up and down the classroom doing that and we'd roar. But we'd be interested in Dreiser.

When I think of Harvard I don't think of it really in terms of influences. I think of it more as a matter of nuances and moods and modes, as if everything were connected to everything else. There was a fine filigree to one's stimulation. The art of it was you couldn't trace it out afterwards. Harvard changed me profoundly, but I couldn't say this was the reason or that was the reason. It was all of it.

And after you got out of Harvard?

I went into the Army nine months after I graduated. I think my draft card fell to the back of a file. There is no explanation for it because I should have been drafted after two months. And I didn't go to the draft board to ask because I was working on a novel and kept hoping that I'd have that much more time to finish it.

You mean *Transit to Narcissus*?

Yes. That got written in the nine months before I went into the Army. But then there were two years in the Army and that was a great change. And so was the success of *The Naked and the Dead.* In effect I encountered three sizable shocks during the period from 1939 to 1949. In those ten years [of] my life I was transplanted three times. It was really not a shock of brutality or tragedy. There was nothing designedly cruel about it. It was the kind of shock that a plant would feel if lifted from one bed and put into another.

Are there things that you are aware of that happened to you that would help explain the dramatic change from your studious, disciplined boyhood self to what, starting in the early and mid-Fifties, is your infamous self, the "General Marijuana," the renegade, the ranting critic of American institutions—that self?

We're getting into questions now that I can't answer short of writing a novel. To talk about it in an interview wouldn't work. It would just be confessional. I think the change that took place around '53, '54, '55 was so drastic and so thoroughgoing that we'd really have to pursue it to all the roots I have. Not only the biographical roots, but even, if you will, the karmic roots. I'm a great believer in karma. I do believe that we're not here just one time, and I don't have any highly organized theology behind that—it's just a passing conviction that keeps returning. Karma tends to make more sense than a world conceived without it, because when you think of the incredible elaborations that go into any one human being, it does seem wasteful of the cosmos to send us out just once to learn all those things, and then molder forever in the weeds. It doesn't make as much sense as the idea that we are part of some continual process that uses us over and over again, and indeed uses the universe over and over again. There is some sort of divine collaboration going on. So in that sense, since I believe in it and for me it's psychologically true, it's hard to give an explanation. But if I were to give one, the roots are also karmic. There are arguments that can't be accounted for by one life.

Did the 1949–1950 screenwriter period produce shocks that caused change also?

We're giving a picture here of someone who is not terribly adaptable. My father was a terribly fussy, punctilious man. A marvelous man. A lot more of a gentleman than his son turned out to be. I remember one point when he was unemployed during the Depression and looking for work. He went out every day wearing spats in the heart of the Depression. He had marvelous manners—he came from South Africa, was very English as only a South African can be. I think that probably some of his rigidity is in me. That's why each of these occasions came as a great shock.

Hollywood must have made a pretty big impact, because you were writing *Barbary Shore* there and later *The Deer Park*, and in those books your political vision seems to change. What was it about Hollywood?

Well, it wasn't Hollywood as such. I'm not one of the champions of Los Angeles. It's not a place I'd enjoy living that much. I suppose there are two recurring subjects in my life that just fascinate me over and over again. One of them is what we've already discussed, the establishment. The other is identity. And movies fascinate me inordinately because the question of identity is so vivid in them. Movie stars fascinate me. Their lives are so unlike anyone else's. You could almost postulate they come from another planet. The way of life of the movie star speaks of another order of existence. The lack of connection between a movie star's life and our lives is greater than the points of view we have in common.

Does that work into *The Deer Park* at all?

In *The Deer Park* I'm just beginning to contemplate the problem. Think of the character Lulu Meyers, the movie star. She's my first attempt to deal with that question. Of course I go at it hammer and tongs with Marilyn Monroe. But my Egyptian novel is also a study of identity. You see, I think there have been periods in history when no one has contemplated the problem of identity. Because we weren't necessarily far enough removed from the animals. We reacted to things that impinged upon us in the way a beast does. We fled, we attacked, we ate, we went to sleep. I think generations went by of that sort—and then there were periods where no question was more critical to anyone alive. Certainly in my early years at Harvard the question of my identity was paramount. The most interesting question to many of us in those days was, what do you really think of me? I remember once having a long talk with my roommate Marty Lubin, and I primed him—I wanted to come back with some fish. So I talked for about half an hour, analyzed his character in great detail. He listened, and when I got all done I said, "Marty, what do you think of me?" He paused and then he said, "Ah gee, Norm, you're just a good guy." At which point I was ready to throw him out the window from the fifth floor of Dunster.

Speaking of identity—do you think the notorious publicity, the *People* side, the *Enquirer* side of your identity has hurt the public and critical acceptance of your work?

Well, it certainly hasn't done it any good. . . . I do believe that when people buy a hardcover book these days, to a slight extent it's a sacramental act. Very often the price of the book is such that people are making a choice between that or getting something else. To be crude about it, between the book or getting the baby a pair of new shoes. So you have to respect the author. If the author is somehow unsavory—and I don't see how anyone could run through *People* five times and not be wholly unsavory—then they may not buy your book. And there's a crude notion that if you get a lot of publicity, you sell books. Nothing could be more untrue. The authors who sell well, that is the good authors who sell well, get very little personal publicity. We don't read much about Saul Bellow, John Updike. We didn't used to read much about John Cheever. . . . But my image can't be changed. So I've just said the hell with it. I'll go ahead and do what I want to do. I don't think there is any way I could change that media point of view about me because of the mechanics of the media. When they run a story about somebody, they go to the clips. There's no way I'm going to get those clips out of all the media organs.

Let's talk about artistic identity. I see an apparent change toward more self-effacement in your writing, in narrative technique, in the last five years. Do you see a new maturity in your writing?

Maturity comes of its own accord. You don't ever say to yourself, well, now I'm going to be more mature. You get older, so your point of view shifts and compromise takes on a bit more luster. A fixed point of view begins to seem harsh. The result is greater maturity in the writing. But I may well go back to writing in the first person. I don't have any feeling about it as such. I just don't like to be bored when I'm writing. I often think by now I have much in common with a dentist who's been working for forty years. I'm sure he looks for a new way to make a hole in a tooth. Because otherwise he'd go mad.

It's interesting that the two books that you got the Pulitzer Prize for, *Armies* and *Executioner's Song*, are two extremes—the presentation of the self on the one hand, and the reduction of self on the other. So the reaction has been positive to either side of your artistic identity.

Well, I think they are also two of the best books I've written. If I had five favorite books those would be two of them. I don't think there was any larger point of view in the choice of those two. I think it just happened that *Armies of the Night* was a pretty good book, and it came along in a year when let's say the Pulitzer Committee was sympathetic to that sort of book. *The Executioner's Song*, in its period, probably, well . . . that sentence finishes itself.

In Joseph Elroy's writing class at Columbia, you were talking about *Why Are We in Vietnam?* And you said that if there are any forces in the cosmos that "step in and give a writer a helping hand, I got it right there." Do you find there are such moments of inspiration?

I can lay out a speculation for you.

All right, lay out a speculation.

If a god or a devil or some demiurge is looking for a writer or has need of one . . . or an angel or an ogre or whatever . . . if there's anything up there or out there or down there that is looking for an agent to express its notion of things, then, of course, why wouldn't they visit us in our sleep? Why wouldn't we serve as a transmission belt? Just in the same sense, although this is gross, that a coach might look for a wide receiver who really has great speed of foot because he has designed some very long passes via a quarterback with a particularly powerful arm. So it might be that your own abilities would be one of the factors behind the ogre's choice of you. That's a *possibility*. The only book I truly felt that on was *Why Are We in Vietnam?*

Did it play any role in the Egyptian novel?

No, that was just hard work, every step of the way.

Do you have any desire at this point in your life to nurture another side of yourself?

If my eyes hold up, I think I would like to start reading seriously again. There have been years when I've had a great deal of eyestrain and I couldn't read as much as I wanted to. And then there were years when I didn't feel like reading. I was too unsettled to read. I think twenty years went by where I haven't been reading as much as I've wanted to read.

Do you see any young writers coming up that you admire? Any who might take the place you've talked about so many times, and maybe at one time tried to fill yourself, as "the champ"?

I have a confession to make. In the course of not reading enough in the last twenty years, I've not read the young writers. I've read them hardly at all. I remember when I came along, I thought, oh boy, now I'll be able to talk to Hemingway and Dos Passos, Farrell, all the writers I care about. They'll read my book and we'll be able to talk about it. My dreams will be realized. But I never met Dos Passos or Hemingway. I met Farrell once for lunch. I never met J. P. Marquand or Steinbeck. I sent Hemingway *The Deer Park* but it came back marked "Addressee unknown." I always felt he gave it to somebody at the post office to stamp it that way and send it back. It seemed to me that would be his sense of humor. At any rate I corresponded with Hemingway ten years after *The Naked and the Dead* came out. At the time I was shocked that older authors didn't read younger authors. And I didn't understand it. I was furious. And I'm sure young authors feel that way now. You know: Why doesn't Mailer read me? I grew up reading him and he influenced me in part and he owes it to me to read me. Why doesn't he? The reason is simple. I know now why they weren't reading me, and I know that because I don't read the young authors. One gets locked into one's own continuing concerns. I haven't used any prize-fighting images up till now, so I guess I had better use one. Whether you're fighting for a championship or not, you're fighting a fifteen-round fight. And by the time you reach your sixties, you feel as if you're in the twelfth round and you're battered. I don't say this self-pityingly—you're just not as good as you used to be in an awful lot of ways. . . . And your powers to protect yourself from distraction are much smaller. You really have to concentrate on those last few rounds. And so there's much less loose generosity in you. . . . You tend to isolate yourself because the odds that a young writer would come along and write something that can teach you something is not likely, although it might delight you, and you might say, gee, what talent. . . .

I've seen young writers that I think are good, some are damn good, and there seems to be more and more felicity all the time. And technique gets more and more elaborated. But I can't think offhand of any young writers who are philosophically disturbing at this point.

Czeslaw Milosz, in *Bells in Winter,* writes about poetic inspiration as if the poet were a living room with its doors wide open, visitors come and go—all he can hope for is that the visitors are forces of good rather than evil.

I think to the degree that you dare the prevailing winds you set yourself up for some incredible gusts.

It may be that part of remaining a writer is to learn how to expose yourself less and less over the years and ring yourself around more and more with various protections. The price of that, of course, is that inspiration enters the door much less often. But at the same time you can carry out your projects. It seems to me that if there is any lesson I can draw from my working, it is that it has taken me close to forty years to learn to write long books. *The Naked and the Dead* came early and that was to a certain extent a gift. I was a simple young man, and I didn't understand the difficulties. If I had known the difficulties, I wouldn't have gotten into it. It would have taken me ten years.

You said in 1981 that things are sinister but not in the way you used to think they were sinister. What did you mean by that?

In the Sixties I used to see it as the FBI, the CIA being sinister. I had a sort of paranoid vision of the invisible government. Now I suppose it has moved over to the idea that such things as television and plastics are probably doing us much more harm and getting us much closer to totalitarianism than the FBI or the CIA ever would.

What's the force behind that?

Well, there you get into dreamland, don't you? I sometimes think that there is a malign force loose in the universe that is the social equivalent of cancer, and it's plastic. It infiltrates everything. It's metastasis. It gets into every single pore of productive life. I mean there won't be anything that isn't made of plastic before long. They'll be paving the roads with plastic before they're done. Our bodies, our skeletons, will be replaced with plastic. It's some absolute vanity. It's human vanity that I might assume is devil inspired, but it doesn't have to be. It could come right out of man. . . .

On the one hand we, all of us, consciously or unconsciously, contain an adoration of the universe. We also have this great animus toward the universe. It's larger than we are and that's intolerable to us. The ego, or the twentieth-century manifestation of it, flames up in us. We have to do something to that universe. We have to *score* it. We have to literally score on it, and plastic is a wonderful way to do that because we create something that the universe can't digest. We literally make those carbon chains, these protein chains, that are put together in a way that they just won't break down—"non-biodegradable"—that marvelous little new word.

The artifacts of this civilization will go on forever.

They'll go on forever, some of us hope and some of us don't hope. But those who do are capturing the world. You say, well, where does it all come from? What's the origin of it? And then, of course, one's past philosophy runs out in outer speculation. . . .

But I do think that plastic tends to deaden people. It deadens their nerve ends. And when the nerve ends are dead, the mind is much more susceptible to manipulation. Because, finally, the senses are always our objective correction against having our minds manipulated too far in a direction that's not natural.

So plastic becomes an effect as well as a cause?

Well, put it this way. If you wanted to convince someone of something that would be very hard for him to swallow, wouldn't it be a good idea to half anesthetize him first? And plastic does that. It just deadens us. Now we get it from infancy on. I think one of the reasons cocaine is so widespread now is that people's nerve endings are so deadened they need something to absolutely jack up those nerve ends. So that's one thing. And of course television is another. It's as if a great dragon called entropy has come into aesthetics. And television is the final reduction of all art into fifteen-minute slugs of pap. The natural tendency of television is to reduce all entertainment to the level of a commercial. When the commercial is as interesting as the television, then you've got perfect television. . . .

Robert Frost once said there was something immodest in a man who believes that he is about to go down—or that we are about to go down— before the worst forces ever marshalled against us in the universe. In your work the point seems to be that we may very well be going down before just such forces.

Well, I never said Robert Frost was going to approve of me.

But do you think we may be at such a crisis?

I don't think I'm the only one who thinks that. An awful lot of people are worried. . . . The world is now going through an apocalyptic time—I think the Eighties are going to be an incredible decade, with more surrealistic, fantastic, incredible change even than in the Sixties. . . . There are certain signs that we are in a period that's not like other periods. One of them, and I think this is incredible, is that in the last twenty years or certainly in the last ten years, we've come to a point in this country where people no longer believe the president knows the answers. I think part of Reagan's vast popularity in the media is because he's probably the most relaxed president we've had since Lord knows when. Maybe there was never a president as relaxed as Ronald Reagan. So people feel, well, he seems secure. Maybe he does know the answers. You know there's nothing more disconcerting to the average American than the thought that the president doesn't know the answers, doesn't really know where we're going.

Maybe that's why he is so relaxed, because he knows he doesn't know.

That could well be. Maybe you've come up with the first explanation of Ronald Reagan that makes sense. It makes him rather a nice man. There is this humility before the imponderables that is a mark of grace.

———————

Let's turn to the work you've been doing recently—your Egyptian novel, *Ancient Evenings*. Do you feel good about the completed work at this point? You announced the book as early as 1972, in *Existential Errands*, so it's been a long, probably difficult road.

If I say I feel good about it, it's like saying my child is wonderful. It's not seemly. I will say it's the most ambitious book I've ever worked on. It's by far the most unusual work I've done, and it's out of category. I can't think of any other novel that's remotely like it. . . . My hope is that it's very good indeed. But how good I don't have a clue. I think when it comes out it will be the usual story. I hope it will get some wonderful reviews, and I'm sure it will get some terrible reviews.

———

If I were an unknown author, the book could be read a little more easily. But the trouble is everybody is going to be reading it and saying, "How the devil does Norman Mailer get himself up to start writing about Egyptian pharaohs? I mean that's really going too far." But it has nothing to do with the fact that that's my name. I'm an author. I have a right to imagine a work, and to write a work of the imagination. If I had any name but my own, people could read the book without too much suffering.

If it is indeed good in the artistic sense, maybe it would not have been published. It's not a blockbuster, a bestseller sort of book.

I certainly think it's good enough that no matter who had written it, it would have been published. And I think it's good enough that no matter who had written it, it would have received attention. Because if you spend ten years writing a book it should be good. Spending ten years on a book is like being married to someone for ten years. You wouldn't want to say at the end of those ten years that half of the time was worthless.

There were a lot of expectations, and at times earlier on you seemed to feed those expectations—that this would be your masterpiece. If that was ever the goal, did the process of writing the book change the goal?

Well, it deepened. It started as an excursion into Egypt. I was going to dip into Egypt for a chapter or two, then get out, move on to Greece and Rome, then the Middle Ages. I was thinking a sort of picaresque novel. That was in the first half year of working on it. But I began to realize at the end of that half year that I was in Egypt for the long haul. So I started studying, and I've learned about ancient Egypt these ten years.

Was there any fear of the risk? You've used the word risk yourself several times.

Well, there is always fear in writing a book. If I had tried to write the book in a year, the fear would have been so great it couldn't have been written. But over ten years, you can carry the fear. *Writing* a book is the fear. That's why there are many more people who can write well than who do.

And there are other reasons for it. Some people can't take the meanness of the occupation. There's nothing very attractive about going into a room by yourself every day and looking at a piece of paper and making scratch marks on it. Doing that day after day, year after year, decade after decade, is punishing through the very monotony of the physical process. . . . Just the act of writing as a physical act is less interesting than painting. I never feel sorry for painters. I feel sorry for writers.

Obviously the emoluments of a profession and the spiritual satisfactions are quite different from the mean daily details of the work. In that mean sense, writing is not a comfortable or attractive profession day to day. Then you add to it the fear. There is always fear in writing. Most people take pride in the fears they can endure. It's obvious that you can't be a professional writer for as many years as I have been without taking a certain pride that I can endure those fears. I would say that writing is like all occupations that have some real element of risk. You really don't want to write a book in which you're not taking on some risk . . . especially a long book. You can write a book quickly in two months, six months, or a year in which the risks are minimal. But to do a long book, you would want to take risks. Why not? How dignify it if large risks aren't being taken? And I will say that I've taken more risks with the Egyptian novel than any book I've ever written. It's the most, dare I say it, audacious of the books I've done.

You've said all we can ever know is whether we have worked as hard as we can. Do you believe you've done that on this book?

Yes. I think I've used up every bit of inspiration I've had on this book. If the book is not good enough, then I'm not good enough. I feel that kind of peace about it.

Did it take you places you have never been before. Creating new ideas?

Yes. It also gave me an understanding of certain things. I think people are going to be immensely confused by the book. They are going to say, why did Mailer write it? What is he saying that means something to him? The man we know. What is in this?

Well, I think I've come to an understanding of the wealthy I've never had before, dealing with Egypt, its gold, and its pharaohs. . . . There's that marvelous remark of Fitzgerald's that the rich are not like you and me, and Hemingway's answer, which was much applauded, but which I've always thought churlish, you know, yeah, they have more money, and everybody roars like crazy. The fact of the matter is that Fitzgerald was trying to say something, and Hemingway was trying to keep him from saying it. The very rich are not like you and me. Just as movie stars are not like you and me. In fact the very rich and movie stars have much in common. They no longer have a trustworthy relation to the society around them. In the most umbilical sense, they can't trust anyone.

That' a good partial answer to my next question. Why Egypt? You've mentioned elsewhere that the beginning of scientific technique is a perversion of primitive magic, and you've also said that we went astray when we separated ourselves from "the dire discipline of magic," which might enable us to communicate with the cosmos. Is Egypt your subject because it represents a turning point from primitive dread, from magic, toward technology and the abuses of technology?

I don't know enough about history to be able to answer that, and I don't know if that's the point. I don't have a clue. Egypt was one of the places—I think it was definitely one of the places where magic was being converted into social equivalence, in effect used as an exchange.

That's what interested you, at least in part?

What interested me was that I made one assumption that certain people will argue with and others will find natural. The assumption is that the Egyptians had minds that are easily as complex and interesting as our minds. They had an intellectual discipline that was highly unscientific from our point of view. But I suspect no farther off the mark than ours. Now these are assumptions. So the book has an immense preoccupation with magic as such. I tend to end up writing the best novel on subjects no other good writer has ever written about. I can name a number of subjects that I've written the best work on, where there's no competition, a subject no other writer would tackle. For instance, I'd say I've written the best biography of a movie star that's ever been written—*Marilyn*. Again there's no competition. I've written the best book about a heavyweight prize fighter that's ever been written, *The Fight*. Again, no competition. Now I think I've written the best novel about magic that's ever been written. But where are the others who have been writing about it? I don't know of a serious writer who's devoted himself to writing about magic. I mean, Aleister Crowley has written a novel about magic. Dion Fortune has written about magic. Other people have written magical novels, but they are not writers who are highly regarded. But I will say once again, that I've taken a field—I'm a bully— where there's no competition.

Are you writing about the rich? What we know of Egypt is mostly the testament of the rich, isn't it?

Yes. Of course, that's always your problem. There are very few characters in the novel who are not well born. Most of them are nobles of the highest rank.

Do you think that these people whom you are writing about, that in some way God's will was not kept from them? That they had a sense of what God's will was? Unlike as you've said, we may have lost touch with whatever God's will might be?

One has to keep reminding oneself that this is before the Judeo-Christian era. We're dealing with pagans. The pagan mind is fascinating, but I found while I was writing the book that when I went through it I had to keep making certain that there wasn't a single Judeo-Christian idea in it. Actually I think the Egyptians had a tremendous influence over the Hebrews. Much of the Old Testament you find in Egyptian prayers. Some of it's startling. The early pages of Genesis, the first page of Genesis could be taken from certain prayers to Ammon and the ways in which he created the universe.

Is it safe to look at Hebrew culture as a competing minor culture at the time?

It wasn't even quite a minor culture at the time. They were still a race of tribes and barbarians. They weren't taken seriously. Not at this period.

147

Later they were. This is 1100 B.C. In fact, Moses appears in my book for about a page. He's seen as some sort of guerrilla who kills some Egyptian guards and takes the Hebrews to a certain town with him across the desert to escape. The idea is to immerse yourself in another point of view when you are writing. Because when you do, a lot of things come to you.

You said you wished nothing in the book to be contemporary. In what sense is there a connection between ancient Egypt and today? In other words, what's in it for modern readers?

Well, I've failed if we start reading the book that way. And I think that's going to be one of the difficulties for people, because most historical novels perform a service or pretend to teach us something about today. And I will have failed if that's the way people react to my book.

The attraction then is not that there is a connection—the attraction is the lack of connection?

The lack of connection. I want people to realize, my God, there are wholly different points of view that can be as interesting as our own. In other words, probably a social evening in Egypt—and this is one of the reasons I ended up calling the book *Ancient Evenings*—in that period three thousand years ago was as interesting as an evening in New York today. Not more interesting, necessarily, but as interesting . . . for altogether different reasons.

Not much happens in the sense of action, I believe you've said, in the sense of a typical wide-canvas, panoramic, historical novel.

Well, no, a lot does happen, but it doesn't happen immediately. The book certainly has the most complete architecture of any book I've written. It's in seven parts. Each of its parts, I would say, has a separate existence. The book continues from part to part, most definitely. But the nature of the book discloses itself part by part. When you've read part one and part two, you won't have any clue at all what part six and seven are going to be like. It's as if the book moves in a spiral.

You've said you're planning a trilogy. Will the other books be ten-year projects?

My hope is to do the next two books in three or four years each. If they each take ten years, I'd be celebrating my eightieth birthday.

My last question—people criticize you for presenting your existence, your life, your work, in a way that seems you want other people to believe as you do or be like you or live like you. How do you respond to that criticism?

I think I'm truly misunderstood there. I'm right and I'm wrong so often, so many times of the day, that I have no interest in having people think the way I think. What I'm interested in is that however people think they get better at it. That's what's important about one's work. In the work of good authors, if a book is good enough, you cannot predict how people are going to react to it. You shouldn't be able to. If it's good enough, it means it's not manipulative. If it's not manipulative, everybody sort of goes off in a different direction. One of my favorite remarks is that it's not that I'm for the cops and not that I'm for the crooks, but that I'm for the cops getting better and the crooks getting better. I have a notion of society as an oven where some fabulous dishes are being cooked, and in order for the banquet to take place, every ingredient has to be in it.

I don't think it's an accident that I'm a novelist. Novelists have a wicked point of view—wicked as opposed to evil. They are interested in upping the ante. They're interested in more happening, not less. One of the reasons that I detest television is that it reduces our possibilities. Television was welcomed as something that would help us understand the world. But I think, quite the contrary, it takes away from us any possibility of ever comprehending the world because it deadens our senses and because it gives us false notions, periodically, systematically, and intensively.

So presenting your ideas with force is a way of saying these are my beliefs and this is my life and they are meant to stimulate you into whatever it is that will be your ideas and your life.

Yes. Once Ralph Ellison and I were out in Iowa together many years ago, back in 1959, and we worked like crazy. We had a lively audience, and the symposium went on for three or four days, for *Esquire*. At the end of it, it suddenly seemed a little absurd to me that we really worked that hard, got in so many arguments with students, talked back and forth, and even argued with each other as lively as hell. But when it was over, there was a little bit of sadness that something that had been truly exceptional was over. So I said to him, "Why the hell did we do it?" He said, "Ah, shit, man, we're expendable." I've always loved that remark. Because in a certain sense one's ideas are expendable. If the best of my ideas succeed in changing the mind of someone who's more intelligent than myself, then that's fine. I'm a great believer in the idea that if you advance an idea as far as you can and it's overtaken by someone who argues the opposite of you, in effect you've improved your enemy's mind. Then someone will come along on your side who will take your enemy's improvement of your idea and convert it back again. I'm nothing if not a believer in the dialectic. And to that extent one does the best one can. And that's the end of it. The thought of everyone thinking the way I do is as bad as any other form of totalitarianism.

8

ERNEST AND NORMAN

A Dramatic Dialogue in Two Acts

AUTHOR'S NOTE: *This dialogue was performed at the Hemingway-Mailer Conference in Sarasota, Florida, 6 November 2009.*

PRELUDE

Out of murky fog a figure emerges, searching, as if for some clue to where he is or how he has come to be here. We hear Miles Davis playing "So What?" As light gradually increases on the wandering figure, we begin to discern someone who looks not unlike Norman Mailer at about 50. He keeps turning slowly, looking into the surrounding obscurity.

Shortly, another figure barely emerges in the near distance.

MAILER

Whatever thing you are, guide me. Tell me where I am.

SHADE

Though I once was a man, I'm now a soul among souls.

MAILER

[Squinting, putting on his glasses, as the shade emerges more clearly]

That fountain of pure speech? How I poured out an apprenticeship on your lines.

The figure of Ernest Hemingway has fully revealed itself by now: a man in his forties, hale, in his prime.

MAILER

What beasts have followed me here? I hear and smell their breathing wherever I turn.

HEMINGWAY

Don't fear these beasts. We cannot slay them. Follow me, instead. I'll lead you to the eternal place, so long the object of your speculations. And to your rest. This way.

MAILER

My rest?

A Greyhound emerges and leads the men off into the fog, Mailer some five paces behind Hemingway.

———

ACT I

The men approach a wide river. The Greyhound sits down between two lawn chairs turned sideways to partially face one another. We notice now that both men are wearing bathing suits, overhanging khaki safari shirts, and sandals.

———

MAILER

What river is this?

HEMINGWAY

The river all must travel. Await the boatman. [*Gestures*] Sit here. You've wanted to talk?

MAILER

I did my part. [*The men seat themselves on opposing chairs.*] I sent my book. And Plimpton tried to arrange a meeting.

HEMINGWAY

We'll have plenty of time. [*Reaching out to shake Mailer's hand*] Just to be clear, I didn't receive it. That *Deer Park* you sent. Read it later.

MAILER

I wanted to live within your discipline. Cultivate one's manhood. I was desperate for good words of the book, during a time when my nerve was failing me, and I was coming out of a five-year depression.

HEMINGWAY

"Because finally after all these
years I am deeply curious to know
what you think of this."

MAILER

You remember my note?

HEMINGWAY

One eventually remembers everything. You published it, after all, in *Adver-tisements for Myself.*

MAILER

"But if you do not answer, or if you
answer with the kind of crap you
use to answer unprofessional writers,
sycophants, brown-nosers, etc., then
fuck you, and I will never attempt
to communicate with you again."

HEMINGWAY

[*Laughs*] Your own worst enemy.

MAILER

I was young, unformed. Confused by failure and self-doubt after stupen-dous success. I liked the novel and didn't like it. Feared I had somehow missed the boat with it. I had to find my courage, physical and mental cour-age, as I had as a rifleman in the Army. And I had to find my way past my intellectual barriers through the doors of my unconscious.

HEMINGWAY

S.O.P. Mary sent everything back, unopened, unless it came by way of a trusted friend. Three worst enemies of getting serious work done: the tele-phone, visitors, and those packages out of nowhere. Learned that lesson in the Key West years.

MAILER

You knew of me?

HEMINGWAY

Everyone did. *Naked and the Dead.* Selling like Daiquiris in hell!

MAILER

I was famous too soon. You read it?

HEMINGWAY

Didn't much care for it.

MAILER

You don't like war stories?

HEMINGWAY

I thought you faked a lot of it. Probably hadn't seen much combat. War, when you've really seen it, is the best subject because it groups the maximum of material and speeds up the action and brings out all sorts of stuff that normally you have to wait a lifetime to get.

MAILER

I was in a platoon in the Pacific theater. I don't have to tell you combat is not just fire fights tallied. Combat is patrols in hostile territory, day after day. Sweat, monsoons, disease, fear, festering corpses, boredom, taking and returning fire from time to time. Hard labor, miles of it, uphill and down, and mucking through rice paddies. Fatigue, danger, despair. I had more direct experience of combat before *Naked* than you before *A Farewell to Arms.*

HEMINGWAY

Couldn't tell from your book.

MAILER

Read "The Dead Gook." It's all in there.

HEMINGWAY

Send me a copy.

MAILER

Fuck you.

HEMINGWAY

And the pastiche put me off. Dos, Farrell, Dreiser. The whole crowd.

MAILER

So why not tell me? Maybe I'd have learned something.

HEMINGWAY

You're riding high. Wunderkind and all that crap, but still learning your craft. Why should I be the nay-sayer? They'll destroy a good writer soon enough, without me. A writer has to be as tight about money as a hog's ass in fly time. It's only by hazard that he makes money. *Si Dos y la Puta Hostia quieren.* Then a writer increases his standard of living and he is caught. He has to write to keep up his establishments, his wives, and so on, and he writes slop. Slop not on purpose but because it is hurried, or because there is no water in the well, or because he is ambitious. Then, once you have betrayed yourself, you justify it and you get more slop.

Or else you read the critics. Criticism is shit. These people paid to have attitudes toward things, the camp followers and eunuchs of literature. These veal brains hang attributes on you that when they don't find said attributes in your work accuse you of sailing under false colors. Look at the condescending phony intellectuality passing as criticism in the *New Yorker*. Most critics are so anxious to fit the new orthodoxies that they are obsessed with their own schisms. The good ones, the ones writers can learn from like Berenson or Ivan Kashkeen, my Russian translator, are all too rare.

MAILER

I always thought the critic had a moral requirement: he owes it to his audience and to the book to separate the book's ideas from his own.

HEMINGWAY

But you read most criticism of your work and you learn nothing, only that they have a thesis to grind or that soon there will be no writers, only critics. I like the slogan in Madrid during the fascist bombing and shelling: "Respect anything you do not understand. It may be a work of art." Anyway, if you believe the critics when they say you are great then you must believe them when they say you are rotten, and you lose confidence.

MAILER

So you were doing me a favor.

HEMINGWAY

Look, I never spoke publicly about my opinion of the novel. All that would do is piss you off. You're pissed now. Same goes for *Deer Park*, once I read it. You really blew the whistle on yourself there.

MAILER

Still, I must have done something in *The Deer Park* to get that many people upset—all through the tragicomedy of trying to get it published and later as displayed by many of the reviewers. Don't tell me you never spoke your opinion to anyone.

HEMINGWAY

Friends only and off the record. And later that one letter to you.

MAILER

Then why'd you tell your son Gregory I was probably the best postwar writer?

HEMINGWAY

My opinion altered and you continued to write.

MAILER

I liked Gregory. Met him through his third wife, Valerie, who knew my fourth wife, Beverly Bentley, from their time together running with your crowd in Spain that "dangerous summer" of '59. I wrote the Preface to Gregory's memoir of living with you and was astonished to see you'd said I was the best of the lot, and then you added: "He's a psycho, but the psycho part is the most interesting thing about him."

HEMINGWAY

[Using a phony British accent]

Spot on there, Old Boy!

MAILER

If you weren't psycho by then you weren't paying attention.

HEMINGWAY

I rest my case. *Advertisements for Myself* caught my attention first: that ragtag assembly of your rewrites, second thoughts, and ramblings shot through with occasional brilliance.

You wrote too much and you talked too much, even on paper. You didn't realize when your stuff smelled of the lamp. Anyway, look Norman, it doesn't matter anymore.

MAILER

It always matters. Posterity matters. No one believes that more than you.

HEMINGWAY

Nobody cares what I *thought.*

MAILER

Feeling sorry for yourself.

HEMINGWAY

Sorry for all of us.

MAILER

Not around to defend yourself.

HEMINGWAY

You shouldn't have to defend yourself, even when you're still around. You don't have to smile and take it up the ass. But writing to the *Times,* correcting some obscure academic with an axe to grind, answering snotty letters: that's a chump's game. Better to keep the little pricks beneath your notice.

What you write is not immediately discernable, and that, as I said in my note to Sweden, is sometimes fortunate. You'll either endure or be forgotten by what is finally discerned about your work and the degree of alchemy you possess. If you grow in public stature when alive, your work deteriorates. Yet all you have is your lonely work facing eternity, or the lack of it, each day.

———

MAILER

Took me some time to figure that out. After *Advertisements for Myself* when I'd gotten a few things off my chest. I pretty much started over.

HEMINGWAY

Took me some time too.

MAILER

Where you think I learned to make my life good copy? You started advertisements for yourself all the way back to your Pamplona stories for the *Toronto Star Weekly*. You were the grand master. You worked to make your personality enrich and sell your books, and I took a page out of your book.

HEMINGWAY

Not if it's fool's copy.

MAILER

Even Holy Fools?

HEMINGWAY

You're shitting yourself again. You think you're exploiting the press but they're exploiting you as much or more. You have to hold your purity of line through maximum of exposure. [*Pauses*] Look, Norman, you had a couple of good books. That's enough for anyone. Scott had one. No one had more talent or wasted it more. Scott's the great tragedy of talent in our bloody generation. Only Faulkner could come close in sheer talent, and nobody could write half whore and half straight like wild Bill.

But you're not in competition with your contemporaries; you are competing with the clock, which keeps ticking. Forget success when you are alive: that's my advice to writers. Go for success after you're dead.

MAILER

You didn't try to pump your reputation after the first war?

HEMINGWAY

Before I became a serious writer I did what any kid home from the front might do. And I paid for it. But later I took much effort with Scribner's and the movie people to put the focus on the writing and off my personal life or any phony hero they wanted to make me. I told them I was no football hero and was only a minor camp follower attached to the Italian infantry whose Italian decorations were only because I was an American attached to their army. And that any sane person knows that writers do not knock down middleweight champs, unless the writer's name is Gene Tunney. I specifically told the boys not to build me into a glamorous personality like Floyd Gibbons or Tom Mix's horse Tony. But as I went on to lead my private life with my own private adventures, the boys wouldn't leave me alone and kept up the bullshit. Your legend grows like barnacles on the bottom of a ship—and is less useful. If a book is any good they won't forget you. If it isn't, why should you want people to remember you for your extracurricular activities? You just have to go ahead and write the fucking books, burning the lamp less, discovering life more.

MAILER

So you think I wrote a couple of good books?

HEMINGWAY

Sure.

MAILER

You're not saying.

HEMINGWAY

I never went in for explaining myself. I go in for it even less now.

MAILER

[Looking around]

Where the Hell are we? Somewhere between *The Inferno* and the *Book of the Dead?*

HEMINGWAY

Close enough.

MAILER

You're not going to tell me anything. No warnings.

HEMINGWAY

An existentialist's dream. [*He stares at the river, as if expecting something.*] You'll learn.

MAILER

Someone coming?

HEMINGWAY

May be a long wait.

A tall, slim woman in a long, black close-fitting dress appears, carrying a bottle of Black and White Scotch and two glasses. Behind her, his head about the height of her tempting rump, an apelike figure, a simian gargoyle, carries a small plastic folding table. She holds the liquor bottle and two glasses up between Hemingway and Mailer while the gargoyle shoos away the Greyhound, snaps open the little table, and sets it up directly between the men. The woman places the bottle and glasses on the plastic table. Then they turn and disappear.

MAILER

You fucking her?

HEMINGWAY

That's over. Get used to it. No more Mr. Scrooby.

MAILER

No Don Juan in Hell?

HEMINGWAY

You had your chances.

MAILER

Ah, your Beatrice.

HEMINGWAY

I always betrayed my Beatrice.

MAILER

Join the club. *[Laughs]* You loved pussy too much.

HEMINGWAY

Coming from you that's absurd. Anyway, you're about to find many who loved pussy too much.

———

MAILER

No women who loved cock too much?

HEMINGWAY

You don't think the numbers are disproportionate?

MAILER

Not in my experience.

HEMINGWAY

You and Sinatra.

Hemingway picks the bottle of Scotch off the table and pours them both a double shot. From his shirt pocket he pulls two Cuban cigars, hands one to Mailer, and then lights his own with a long match and offers the flame to Mailer. Mailer refuses the light but sticks the cheroot in his mouth as if testing the feel of it. The two men sit and sip appreciatively, Hemingway puffing.

HEMINGWAY

[Holding up his glass and turning it slowly]

I've drunk since I was fifteen and few things have given me more pleasure. When you've worked hard all day with your head and know you must work again the next day, what else can change your ideas and make them run on a different plane than whiskey? Or what better way to make boring people bearable.

MAILER

We're all rummies at heart. And we're all prison mates.

HEMINGWAY

Modern life, too, is often a mechanical oppression, and liquor is the only mechanized relief.

MAILER

Or one drug or another.

HEMINGWAY

I didn't take other drugs.

MAILER

[Holding his glass up to Hemingway]

Booze is best. [*Sips appreciatively*] You know, when your life's over you can't help looking back on it, just as you can't help wondering what's next. [*Pauses*] Who weighs my heart against the feather of truth?

HEMINGWAY

No one. You'll weigh your own heart soon enough.

More silence and sipping. More Hemingway puffing.

MAILER

Maybe ignoring me you did me a favor, Ernest. [*Blows a contemplative imaginary smoke ring*] But I spoke well of you, mostly.

HEMINGWAY

When you were in the mood. [*Quoting in a mock-Mailer voice*] "Hemingway's suicide left Mailer wedded to horror. . . . the death would put a secret cheer into every bureaucrat's heart for they would be stronger now. . . . Hemingway constituted the walls of the fort; Hemingway had given the power to believe you could still shout down the corridor of the hospital, live next to the breath of the beast, accept your portion of dread each day. Now the greatest living romantic was dead. Dread was loose. The giant had not paid his dues and something awful was in the air."

MAILER

John Gardner once remarked that a father who commits suicide condemns his son to dread, to suicidal dreams and desires. There's your father, your brother Leicester, you. Gregory—

HEMINGWAY

What made it worse was my father was the one I cared about. He caused me to suffer the Black Ass, but I gained more tolerance. By my fortieth birthday I had argued myself out of it so often I understood why he did it. I've always said it's a bad example for the children. But you wasted too much juice on theories like that. Norman the Grand Speculator.

MAILER

That *was* my juice.

HEMINGWAY

I never liked to repeat myself.

MAILER

Gregory saw your suicide as an act of courage, but he had to live with it the rest of his life, a life ruined in other ways.

HEMINGWAY

Gregory! Gig was the son I had the most difficulty with.

MAILER´

As I had with my son Stephen. Stephen, who was all soft smiles and chuckles and fun as an infant! But all that is too painful to go into now.

HEMINGWAY

Only wrote me when he was in trouble, like when his wife left him. I never worried how Bumby or Patrick would turn out. But Gig I had to worry about. Part of it was loss of control over him, the youngest, after the divorce with Pauline. Gig had the biggest dark side in the family except for me, and he kept it so concealed you thought maybe it would back up on him. He was a champion at just about anything he tried—shooting, riding, playing by himself or competing with others. Great shooter from the age of nine. A cold athlete without nerves, a real Indian boy (Northern Cheyenne) with the talents and the defects. As with the others, I tried to teach him everything I knew. Nonetheless, we all have to figure out how to live our own lives and die our own deaths.

MAILER

I had to admire your lifelong struggle with your own cowardice and against your secret lust to suicide, spending your nights wrestling with the gods. You carried a weight of anxiety day to day that would have suffocated a lesser man. You were brave by an act of will, not by a grace of nature. Perhaps you and Marilyn Monroe had that in common.

HEMINGWAY

Don't confuse your own imagination with others. A writer makes something from invention that is not a representation but a whole new thing truer than anything true and alive, and you make it alive, and if you make it well enough, you give it immortality.

MAILER

But every writer has to find for himself what makes it work. Sometimes speculations and obsessions germinate the good work.

HEMINGWAY

Better to keep most of it to yourself, then. The better the writers the less they will speak—and write—about what they are thinking, have written, or plan to write. Joyce was a very great writer, and he would explain what he was doing only to jerks. Other writers that he respected were supposed to be able to know what he was doing by reading it.

MAILER

I admitted your generation of writers is much more impressive than my own. But where is the great work one of you might have pulled off after the war, in the fifties, I mean? All your best is before. And you ended like so many of the Americans proselytizing for the American Century. You ended with windy writing.

HEMINGWAY

The Old Man and the Sea?

MAILER

At the time I thought the prose was affected and too much Hemingway the Fisherman rather than the Cuban fisherman. Your writing grew more narcissistic from *To Have and Have Not* onwards, violating the hermetic logic of your characters.

HEMINGWAY

You should talk! Me a narcissistic writer who imposes himself on his characters? Physician, heal thyself! Listen, that was the prose I had been working for all my life, prose that should read easily and simply and seem short and yet have all the dimensions of the visible world and the world of man's spirit. But it's not for you to assess your own success or lack of it truly at the end of your life. Time will take care of that.

As for your generation, Algren might have been the best, finally. It seemed nobody wanted to serve an apprenticeship and learn their trade anymore—the immutable laws of prose writing—and all you Brooklyn Tolstoys wanted to be champion without ever having a fight.

MAILER

Not like you to be glib, Ernest, and show your ignorance. I'd probably written a million words before my first novel was published, worked at it like a galley slave.

HEMINGWAY

News to me. Look, Norman, we've had many skilled now dead writers in America. Many with rhetoric who find in others something to write about, but without sufficient experience of their own. Melville was the exception because he had rhetoric and experience but is praised falsely for his rhetoric. And other deads who wrote like English colonials and men of letters—Emerson, Hawthorne, Whittier and company. Our classic writers did not know a new classic bears no resemblance to preceding classics. You can steal from a classic but not derive from or resemble a classic. But too many of these respectable gentlemen wrote as if they didn't have bodies. Nor the language people speak. Our best were Twain and Crane.

MAILER

I used to think *An American Dream* was the first novel since *The Sun Also Rises* with anything new in it.

HEMINGWAY

We were both sweating it out. Still, no one should write merely to save his soul, or to make money, or to receive praise, or to blame or attack others. And what difference does it make if you live in a picturesque little outhouse surrounded by 300 feeble-minded goats and your faithful black dog. The question is: Can you write? But, yes, no one in your generation, whatever their gifts, produced the truly great work either.

MAILER

Maybe it was way too late for that—even then. You were awfully hard on your fellow writers though, petty and vindictive. By the way, I saw Scott on the way in. He tells me his dong's longer than yours. Jesus, Ernest, in the end you were afraid even to grant most of them their successes. It got to be unseemly, unworthy of you.

HEMINGWAY

You talk like an innocent! Are you shitting me or yourself now? My old friend Philip Percival said it: "We have very primitive emotions. It's impossible not to be competitive. Spoils everything though."

Just don't start feeling sorry for yourself, or about how you wrote and lived. Too damned late for that. And you can never control what other people think of you. Dear Old Lillian Ross. She said it so I didn't have to. Some people didn't like the way I talked, didn't like my freedom, my joshing, my wasting time at boxing matches, talking to friends, celebrating with champagne and caviar completion of a book. They just didn't like Hemingway. Wanted me to be somebody else—probably themselves.

MAILER

[*Laughs*] Instead, maybe in the fifties you should have been President. I nominated you.

HEMINGWAY

I read about it. Lot of good that would have done.

MAILER

Who knows? History takes an interesting turn. That was '56 on the Democratic ticket, against Eisenhower. No one else had a shot. You had the charm before Kennedy. By *then* you had the virtue of an interesting war record, a man of more physical courage than most. You were inclined to speak simply and freshly, opposed to the turgidities of the Kefauvers and Stevensons.

HEMINGWAY

True, I could never have voted for any of those guys, especially with Nixon and his record waiting in the wings for Ike to die, which was looking likely by then. I'd have needed another Eugene Debs, an honest man and in jail, who I once voted for. The only one.

MAILER

You had one fine additional asset: no taint of a previous political life.

HEMINGWAY

Another fool's errand. A writer is a Gypsy, owing no allegiance to any government, and a good writer never likes the government he lives under. His hand should always be against it and its hand will always be against him. The minute you know any bureaucracy well enough you will hate it because the minute it passes a certain size it is unjust. That's why a true work of art endures forever, no matter what its politics. All I care for is liberty. First I have to take care of myself and my work; then I care for my family; then I would help my neighbor.

MAILER

So you're an anarchist! Well, they called me a fool running for President in my own mind and running for Mayor of New York for real. But like the writing style you formed after the First World War, timing was everything. After the second war, the time was right for a Hemingway presidency. I think you might have beaten old Ike for that second term.

HEMINGWAY

Timing is a thing you don't plan. You write the way you can to capture best the sense of being alive you are after, and if the time is right for what you are doing then you get lucky.

MAILER

That's what happened to me with *Naked*, telling some of the hard truths about being a soldier, being in the Army, the enigmas of leadership, some of the frightening reaches of men's souls. Jim Jones got the same luck, and did it even better than I did because he had a less-educated raw power to his structures and his prose.

HEMINGWAY

Jones was a whiner and a fuckup. A sneering permanent KP boy.

MAILER

You were much too unfair to him. Jones had great charm and tremendous animal magnetism—a most peculiar mixture of Warden and Prewitt, very complex, noisy, crude, affectionate, amazing in his naïveté and his shrewdness and insight. Loved life instinctively. Very exciting to be around. But all that's another story.

ERNEST AND NORMAN

HEMINGWAY

Sic transit hijo de puta.

MAILER

Point is, if you came along with the style you forged earlier in, say, the 1970s or '80s you wouldn't have had the impact you did. Moods changed, history changed, and technology had profoundly altered people's senses and acuities. When you did come along you moved people profoundly, and a writer could still affect things in the world, alter consciousness maybe, if he was that good. Just after the Second World War, or maybe even just before, time ran out for writers who wanted to be major figures, wanted to alter consciousness.

HEMINGWAY

That might be too ambitious in any time. But as I've said before, my style wasn't so much a calculated effort to change consciousness as it was to try to make something that had not heretofore been made, not a "style" at all, which is a term for amateurs. But my awkwardness in making a new thing is what others call my style.

Trying for a fourth or fifth dimension to prose, seeing how far you could take it, is the hardest writing, harder than poetry. Prose that has never been written, but without tricks or cheating. Writing well is the hardest thing to do but makes you happier than anything else when you are doing it. Of course, you are likely to fail. But you must have a conception of what it can be and an absolute conscience to prevent faking. Then you must be intelligent and disinterested and above all survive, because time is so short to get the work done.

So I did have the ambition to try to write something of permanent value. Also, I believed it very important for the language to restore its life that they bleed out of it. Those writers who do not last are always more beloved since no one has seen them in their long, dull, unrelenting no-quarter-given-and-no-quarter-received fights you make to do something as you believe it should be done before you die.

MAILER

Your books did alter both the style of others and the sense of mood in your time. When you do that, you test the conscience of a people as well. When at your best, that is.

HEMINGWAY

Tolstoy, Stendhal, Dostoevsky: writers are forged in injustice as a sword is forged. And the forging is a necessary shock to cut the flow of words and give them a sense of proportion. No unit larger than a village can function justly. Large organizations and countries are badly managed and run by human beings. I care nothing for the state. I'll offer a generalization, which I always hated to do, but at no cost now. A writer without a sense of justice and injustice would be better off editing the yearbook of a school for exceptional children than writing novels. All great writers have that radar.

MAILER

That built-in, shockproof shit detector.

HEMINGWAY

You see, generalizations are easy if they are sufficiently obvious.

MAILER

Which is different from a political writer, unless he sees politics not as politics but as a part of everything else in life. I wrote because I wanted the bastards to itch. I was saying "I hope I make you uncomfortable to death."

HEMINGWAY

Injustice is the normal state of life. But none of what we are talking about is a writer's "style."

MAILER

I never tried to diminish your gifts, but I always thought you made a virtue of a weakness—what good writer does not?—when you wrote in a way that suggested you were incapable of writing a long complex sentence with a lot of architecture in the syntax. So your short declarative sentences and your long run-on sentences with a lot of conjunctions suggested your natural strength, even as Faulkner's sentences suggested his incapacity for writing simply.

HEMINGWAY

Once you finally discover your strength you use it to make something of value beyond the moment.

MAILER

I always thought that you and Fitzgerald created experiences through your books. The sensuous evocation of things. Much closer to poetry in effect on the reader. You come away with a new experience in your gut that you remember, as if it were a part of your own life. Rather than a sense of an intellectual or philosophical adventure or experience.

HEMINGWAY

Scott, for all his flaws, was important to me early on when I was learning to write that first novel.

MAILER

You treated Scott badly, but you were both important imaginative figures in my life when I was young. Wolfe too, for the same reason, but with his own completely different approach to laying out language on the page.

HEMINGWAY

What people felt about our writing back then, well, let's say that's by-product, the by-product of what you try to do with your talent, as you forge your talent into something new and, if you get lucky, something that will last. If it lasts, it is because, yes, like all good books you've created an experience the reader feels happened to him and now belongs to him.

MAILER

I think it's also part of forging your identity, not just as a writer but as a man, as a human being.

HEMINGWAY

If you are a real writer, your identity is in everything you do as that writer. The man and the writing keep changing one another toward firmer identity. Scott died in himself around the age of thirty or thirty-five and his creative powers died somewhat later. Suffered much in his marriage and from depression—The Artist's Reward. And he threw too much of his juice into those *Post* stories, judging a paragraph by not how honest it was but by how much money he could make. Let me put it this way, the person and the writing work together to make oneself stronger or weaker, better or worse, more honest or less honest.

MAILER

Well, Ernest, I think I can say I certainly used more personas, identities, than you ever did, had a quiver of styles and modalities to your one. But I've always thought that you were forging your identity every day of your life—both in the life and in the writing—and that seems to be what you're saying. I think most artists have that problem. And if you have been wounded in any way, the identity must grow out of and beyond that wound.

HEMINGWAY

I came from the Midwest, had a mother with very strong ideas about who I should be, and had my struggles, lessons, and serious wounds along the way. We are all bitched from the start, and you have to hurt like hell before you can write seriously.

You came out of Brooklyn, Norman, a smart, scrawny little kid placed ahead of your peers in school and so mixed in with the bigger kids, the more mature kids, and had to try to hold your own, and to retreat into your own world. Your war changed you as my wars changed me. You came out of the Pacific theater no longer the good Mama's boy, the little kid in the class, the brainy little Jewish boy at Harvard. Once you had your shot at fame it changed you. Then your failures wounded and changed you more. You got the shit scared out of you as a writer, Norman, and started getting belligerent. You even did Hemingway manqué for a time. Belligerence is not necessarily a bad thing for a writer. But you've got to put it deep into the work. The rest is posing.

MAILER

You never posed, Ernest? As you've said yourself, an unhappy childhood is the best training for a writer. But look, again, everything had changed for a writer in America by the sixties and seventies.

HEMINGWAY

You think the posturing was necessary to your writing?

MAILER

It was more experimenting, in the laboratory of myself. That got me up and moving in the morning. For years I had to get my guts up every day so I could do the writing, no matter how bad things might be for me or for writers in our time and place. No matter how hard the shits were trying to kill us.

HEMINGWAY

You wasted a lot of time poking the shits in the eye on TV, in public, and in the writing.

MAILER

As if you never wasted time. We all waste time that we regret when we have little or no more time.

HEMINGWAY

You have to live so that when you die you know you did everything you could do about your work and enjoyment of your life up to that moment, reconciling the two, which is very difficult.

From deep in the murk along the wide river a muffled sound like that of an oar bumping a boat catches both men's attention. Hemingway gets up, walks to the shoreline of the beach and, cupping his hand over his eyes, peers into the river's obscurity. Mailer remains seated, pours himself another two fingers of Scotch, and watches Hemingway on the beach.

MAILER

Anything?

Hemingway continues to peer out into the murk. Cups both ears toward the river. Finally, he turns and walks back up the beach to his chair.

HEMINGWAY

Nothing. Yet.

MAILER

[Pouring Hemingway another drink]

Well, then better have another, Ernest.

Fade to darkness as the two men raise their glasses toward one another.

ACT II

Mailer is standing up to his shins in the foggy river water while Hemingway remains seated. Bright light shines on the beach, giving a sense of atmospheric warmth along the sand. Hemingway now sits under an opened large beach umbrella by the table between their chairs. Both glasses have been drained. The bottle of Scotch still stands, half full, on the small plastic table.

MAILER

The water's perfect. If I didn't know any better, I'd go for a swim.

HEMINGWAY

Swim if you want. Better not let your head under.

MAILER

[Turning back toward Hemingway and slowly walking up the beach toward the chairs]

I'd have to be a lot drunker than I am now. [*Laughs*]

HEMINGWAY

Shouldn't be much longer. [Pours them each two more fingers]

MAILER

[Wistfully]

I'll miss the women.

HEMINGWAY

Maybe the women won't miss us.

MAILER

[Sitting down]

Without loving, without fucking, it's going to be a strange trip indeed.

HEMINGWAY

You get over it. Maybe we have some dues to pay.

MAILER

Gives you a little perspective, finally? Karma coming home to roost? I don't believe either of us was easy on the people we lived with—and the dull pomade of marriage tests everyone who marries. [*Looks directly at Hemingway*] Still, how can you be a misogynist and have loved four wives?

HEMINGWAY

Or your six wives and raised your five daughters? [*He slides Mailer a look.*] Saying nothing of the quick affairs. Pauline used to say, "I don't mind Ernest falling in love, but why does he always have to marry the girl when he does?"

MAILER

[*Laughs*] Maybe it's generational. Our generations.

HEMINGWAY

Well, I loved Hadley all my life and tried my best financially and otherwise to provide for her and Bumby. That failure was my fault. My guilt created my Hell. Even with Pauline some kind of gentleness set in again during after-divorce relations and feelings, mitigating our version of that great unending battle between men and women.

MAILER

Maybe you never get back what you once had with your first wife, and you carry around a lot of accusing self-pity when you look back on the damage you've done. To all your wives. Lawrence was right. There is a harshness between men and women. Maybe nigh on to impossible to transcend, for most mortals.

HEMINGWAY

I started early in my books exploring women's alienation from men and men from women. And what the absence of any feminine influence does to men.

MAILER

Being married tests everything you have: Can you both go the fifteen rounds? You're certainly not alone if you can't.

HEMINGWAY

Harder if the woman you are in love with is stronger than you are. And since writing and love making are run by the same motor you have to strug-gle to balance loving and writing.

MAILER

[After musing a few moments]

If you look back on it, you see we both loved, and married, strong women. All with their own ambition and determination.

———

HEMINGWAY

Yet for all the adventure and good you bring to them, if you're often as not a sonofabitch to live with, you can't expect it to last.

MAILER

We're all sonsofbitches and bitches to live with.

HEMINGWAY

Card-carrying members. But while you love someone, truly, it is only in their pleasure that you are happy.

MAILER

Love gives force to one another's courage, and to the life within both of you. More afterlife perspective.

HEMINGWAY

Mary, who I loved, was determined to be the last Mrs. Hemingway, and suffered on that marital cross. In our later years she came to me and said: "Your insults and insolences to me hurt me, as you surely know. But in spite of them I love you, and I love this place, and I love *Pilar* and our life as we have it here normally. So, try as you might to goad me to leave it and you, you're not going to succeed. Are you hearing me? Because I think it would be bad and disorienting for you as well as me. Okay, that's it. No matter what you say or do—short of killing me, which would be messy—I'm going to stay here and run your house and your Finca until the day you come here, *sober*, in the morning, and tell me truthfully and straight that you want me to leave."

You're easily blinded to her suffering when you're in the middle of that emotional catastrophe a marriage is, but in the aftermath it's not easy to be proud of yourself.

MAILER

Especially if your abused body and mind are turning to shit. Norris had the same determination—to be the last Mrs. Mailer. She put up with a lot of my crap. We loved one another anyway. Loved all the children, had found one another finally despite all the betrayals and battles. [*He looks up toward where a sky should be. Lets out a deep breath.*] She was the warm presence and subtle influence who created a domestic climate that not only allowed me to thrive at work but even to love the idea that there is work to do and it is worth doing. All the time doing her own work, too. Enduring her own losses and gains.

HEMINGWAY

Marriage is never all downhill running in powder snow. And once you've made too many cruelties to one another, you cannot erase them. Nobody will ever accuse you or me of lacking ineptitudes and self-destructive flaws.

MAILER

Even those who more or less lionized us. But, yes, it's like living chained to a stunted ape. Who among us is not? Still, we've been misunderstood, you and I. Our names turned unsavory. It got to be awfully hard for people to countenance our human frailty. In fact, they couldn't read the writing without recalling our personal flaws—real or trumped up by our enemies—coloring the work, distorting patience and understanding.

HEMINGWAY

In your case you asked for it. Too many public belly flops. Maybe I had a few too many too, but you never learned to stay off the stage, the TV even. We writers have to take off our Rabbi Suits. You never learned to shut up, and you'll be tarred with your worst psycho-rants for a long time to come.

MAILER

I can wait an eternity now. But look, Ernest, I've said as much myself. And nobody likes to be thought unsavory. Like a bad big review, in practical terms a bad perception of you hurts a professional writer's pocketbook. An unseemly reputation perpetuates, foments, misunderstanding upon misunderstanding. Those misunderstandings you bring on yourself and those others are all too happy to bring on you. It doesn't matter what you do by way of clarifying or testing your speculations further. Fame came to me with my first book, to you by your fourth—at least on the level of losing any control over readers' mythmaking about you, the legend and gossip outweighing the work itself.

I should have known—and maybe I did—when I entered the arena of the women's movement that nobody was going to thank me for pointing out what appeared to be certain technological-totalitarian elements in women's liberation, circa 1970–80. I'd been calling out *men* for precisely the same tendencies on different fronts *for decades*. But that didn't matter, any more than it mattered that I was all in favor of greater political and social freedom for women. I didn't see avenues of greater freedom, however, for men or women through technology, the corporation, and the hierarchies of the corporate state. Instead of the revolution in consciousness I'd been looking for and trying to spark for a long time we were getting a greater and greater absorption of human capital (men, women, and young people) into the Corpstate maw. More death, less life.

HEMINGWAY

Your arguments were too public, too lengthy, and too abstruse. Your own worst enemy, again. And once they decide you're nutty, they don't have confidence in you anymore.

MAILER

Coming from you, Ernest, *that's* absurd. You didn't take the women's movement of your time head on, but by your actions, your machismo, it came to the same thing. Not to mention what they say about the women in your novels.

HEMINGWAY

They always say a lot of shit, but Virginia Woolf, who bitched me in her review of *Men Without Women,* mostly because I was outside of Bloomsbury, also said something worth remembering. "Tell a man that this is a woman's book, or a woman that this is a man's, and we have brought into play sympathies and antipathies which have nothing to do with art. The greatest writers lay no stress upon sex one way or the other." And I often spoke highly of Djuna Barnes, Beryl Markham, and Isak Dinesen. Katherine Anne Porter I couldn't read very much, but I was polite and she bitched me in return. Beryl wrote so marvelously well I was completely ashamed of myself as a writer.

MAILER

I loved the work of Iris Murdoch, Diana Trilling, Joan Didion, among other women, and had many fan letters from women through the 1960s. When your Mary was asked somewhere in the 1970s whether she agreed that men are chauvinist pigs, she answered: "No more than women are chauvinist sows. I'm thankful for almost every man I've known and the mother who produced him."

HEMINGWAY

[Laughs] Mary never suffered fools.

MAILER

But the point is more that the women who took us on, and took Miller and Lawrence on, proved to be unforgiving, unfair, incapable of quoting accurately, and quick to distort the deeds of their adversaries. And they would never admit they tried to eliminate the blind goat-kicking lust from sex.

HEMINGWAY

That's the sort of goddamned phony patriotism ruined a lot of writers. That

———

red and black enthusiasm I sent up in *Torrents of Spring*, the terrible shit about the nobility of any gent belonging to another race than your own. And Gertrude Stein, who I loved and learned from, finally caught her patriot's disease: that nobody was any good who wasn't queer; then that anybody who was queer had to be good; then, third, that anybody who was good must be that way even if they were concealing it. The main thing is you better not disturb their categories. And nothing will disturb their categories more than when you joke about that patriotic crap. Bullshit is bullshit, so why worry about the bullshit?

MAILER

[Raising his glass to Hemingway, smiling broadly, and draining it]

You worry if you're thinking too much about posterity.

HEMINGWAY

One has to learn, finally, to let posterity take care of herself.

Hemingway refills their glasses. Mailer gets up, glass in hand. Walks to the edge of the big river again. Dips his feet back into the subtle current.

MAILER

The sun shines over us, yet fog up river and down. Where's that fucking boatman?

HEMINGWAY

He'll be here soon enough. You wanted to talk, Norman, so we're talking. You and me.

MAILER

Hell of a time to finally sit down and talk.

HEMINGWAY

Best time there is. You said it yourself: you get a little perspective, finally.

MAILER

I'm in the moment, the way I like to be. But I've spent a lifetime speculating about this journey, and I want to engage it. I want to be onto the next leg of the trip. Purgatorio or Inferno. Or the isles of bliss, Paradiso. Or whatever there is to move on to.

HEMINGWAY

Forget *Inferno* and *Paradiso*. Forget *Purgatorio* for that matter. Dante was a great poet, but if you study his life he seems to be one of the worst jerks who ever lived. Maybe a lesson to us all, but don't expect to be wending your way through *La divina commedia*.

MAILER

I never expected to. Always favored Milton to Dante myself. But why not Karma? Some sort of Karmic state of evolution and return?

HEMINGWAY

Forget all of it. You'll arrive where you're going soon enough.

MAILER

Limbo then. Some kind of Limbo? I've written about Limbo, feel as if I know something about it.

HEMINGWAY

You'll see how much you know. [*Laughs*] Maybe we're in one of Santayana's *Dialogues in Limbo*. My Democritus to your Alcibiades?

*Mailer starts to wander up and down the sandy margin of the river,
looking off into the fog one moment, up toward the sun-drenched sky the
next, over to Hemingway seated another; down at the sand at his feet yet
another. One hand on hip, one holding his glass and sipping from time
to time, he turns his head this way and that, peering into the fog still
lying over the river in the near distance. He begins to talk, as if to himself, knowing Hemingway is overhearing him, but in a state of dramatic
soliloquy nonetheless, quoting himself.*

MAILER

Limbo! The telling monotonies of Limbo—those stupors and apathies upon
apathies, the playback of cocktail gabble, the gluttony of red wine taken
on top of white on top of harshly cooked food, the holes in one's memory
plugged by electronic hum, all the stations of the cross of feeling empty
while waiting for subway trains and airline shuttles and waitresses in busy
lunchrooms—yes, all has to be experienced in Limbo as direct punishment.

But enforced immersion in every sensation, episode, glut, glop, and re-
pellent handle of experience (a recapitulative vision of the faces of dig-
ital watches, the smell of pharmacies, the touch of polyester shirts, the
wet wax paper of McDonald's hamburgers, the air of summer traffic jams
and shrieks of jacked-up stereos) is not to scourge you around one eternity before dispatching you to another, but might be instead your own,
each his own, my own, natural field of expiation. No expirations of soul,
no sufferings of damnation, but my own karmic chain of purification of my
own misspent hours before being thrown back into the contest again. [*He
glances toward Hemingway, who remains silent.*]

The standard of Limbo is that time is not to be wasted. All who die are
guilty, in part, and in part all are innocent. For all are judged by one fine
measure: Had they or had they not wasted more of the soul's substance
than was required by the exigencies of their life? Taking into account their
upbringings, the neurotic, psychotic, screwball, timid, stingy, spendthrift,
violent, or fear-filled habits, had they nonetheless wasted time or rather
spent it as wittily, cheerfully, and/or bravely as possible?

HEMINGWAY

[Holding his glass up to Mailer, grinning now]

You can fornicate yourself into that dreadful state of absolute clearheaded-ness that is the nonbeliever's Limbo. Makes you ready to write, to bite the nail once again.

MAILER

[On a roll]

I would have done less damage to my being by going to church or temple once in a while rather than increase the total of my appearances on tele-vision. The House of Limbo is here to bring you face to face with those sins for which there are no tears, even as a husband and wife cannot weep if they lose a potentially heartfelt piece of ass by watching TV all night. I will be asked to meditate at length on those yaws and palls of my life passed through TV, obliged to regard my own wretched collaboration with the multimillion-celled nausea-machine, that Christ-killer of the ages—television.

HEMINGWAY

As you managed to surmise decades ago, there's no cheating life, even through television.

MAILER

Just as there is no escaping all the disease-inspiring habits of your bad blood, the vast wastes of your dullness, and the thwarting and abuse of others—the very souls of others.

HEMINGWAY

Plenty of that before television.

MAILER

Television is the apotheosis.

HEMINGWAY

No question it made wastefulness a lot more convenient.

MAILER

And the growth of the corporate cancer and the death of democracy more convenient.

HEMINGWAY

You once thought I might intercept the acceleration of democracy's death by writing about Castro's Cuba. Throw my weight behind a meeting between Castro and Kennedy. You thought Americans would listen to me, and the new President. You were always a man of considerable idealism, Norman. Your idealism was the source of your rage.

MAILER

Say I hated to see America ruined, finally. So I wrote that open letter to Fidel Castro in his earliest years, asking him to invite you back to see for yourself and tell us the truth of what you saw, after the Batista tyranny we had supported so long. Before Fidel went over to the Soviets precisely because of our lack of contact. By then the landscape of our psyche had been bleak, gutted, scorched by fifteen years of mindless government, all nerves withered by the management of men who were moral poltroons. .

HEMINGWAY

Why do you think I was an expatriate in Cuba almost two decades? When I finally came back to Damerica it was to a country I too loved and hated. I had by then learned the failures of all the systems. Whatever I might have

said traveling around Cuba anywhere, as you put it, unmolested, unob-
structed, unindoctrinated, would not have made any difference to Americans by then.

MAILER

You were underestimating yourself, Ernest. A paragraph, a line, a poem,
a statement, whatever you said as a Nobel winner could not have been
ignored.

HEMINGWAY

Anyone could have ignored it and probably would have. The President
would have ignored it.

MAILER

Kennedy couldn't have ignored you, as Castro agreed with me during a
conversation I had with him in Cuba in 1989. If Kennedy turned out to be
a conventional leader of the party, there was still a particular magic about
him; all sorts of subtle but exciting changes were occurring in the culture
that he opened the way for, whether he wished to or not. He had taken
the lid off and with his death the lid would eventually be clamped on tight
again. My only question about Kennedy at the time was whether he had a
mind deep enough to comprehend the size of the disaster he had inherited
(not unlike President Obama . . .). I think he might have come to recognize
that if a man of Hemingway's age was willing to give up some important
moment of his time to write new words about Cuba, that the culture of the
world—that culture existing in every cultivated mind—would be judging
Kennedy if he did not respond or react to Hemingway's view (whatever it
might be) of Cuba under the revolutionary regime.

HEMINGWAY

Even if Kennedy did react, would it have made any difference by then? He
was a man of courage, and I admit that watching his inauguration on tele-

vision when we had to turn down his invitation to attend, Mary and I felt a strange kind of hope once again. But you learn to stay out of politics with the very limited time left to you. I never mixed in Cuban politics, nor gave an interview then to American papers, but took the long view of Castro's revolution. And anyway, I was incapacitated.

MAILER

It was more than just politics, it was war, future wars. Our missteps with Cuba from the first, letting the Soviets gain their foothold in our absence, nearly brought the world to an end. Our fears, our misgivings and misunderstandings, our profiteering at the expense of all other considerations. Even now we still repeat the pattern elsewhere. I wrote more than one book about that pattern. It's like some scandalous ritual Americans are bound to repeat over and again. A cycle some rue but no one can break.

HEMINGWAY

So, Norman, you too discovered the failure of political systems? That discovery either defeats you or you dig in and live your life. I moved on as we Americans had always moved on. It's easier to keep well in a good country by taking simple precautions than to pretend that a country which is finished is still good. A country wears out quickly and the earth gets tired of being exploited. Nothing left but gas stations and subdivisions where we once hunted snipe on the prairie, and all the rest of that tired story. America had been a good country and we made a bloody mess of it. Our people had seen it at its best and fought for it when it was well worth fighting for.

MAILER

You can move on or hide out only until the current system oppresses you outright, or your children and grandchildren? I have nine children and plenty of grandchildren facing a future hardly full of joy in the twenty-first century.

HEMINGWAY

Yes, of course, sometimes you do have to stand and fight. Fascism was worth defeating. Best, happiest time I ever had in my life was with the 4th Infantry Division, even wished I'd been a soldier rather than a chickenshit writer. But I wouldn't write any of that flag-waving syndicated patriotism.

MAILER

Near my end the Flag Patriots and the nominal Christians, the Fundamentalists, were the worst threat, the tools of a dangerous empire. Jesus and Marx meet in the understanding that money leaches out all other values. Democracy is always under attack.

HEMINGWAY

I wished they'd summoned me to Congress to ask whether I was a subversive. I'd have said to the committee chairman: "You cocksucker, when did you come to this country and where were your people in 1776–79, 1861–65, 1914–18, and 1941–45? That was when we all lost our health and fortunes. What did your miserable chickenshit grandfather do in those times? He was probably hiring himself a substitute and calling hogs." But it's not outright fascism anymore.

MAILER

No. It's not Hitler or Mussolini-fascism with the jackboots and death camps. But, as Mussolini saw, fascism is the eventual merger of the corporation and the state, the ever more perfect union. But because of its technologies and genius of infiltration, instead of brown shirts, it's both more subtle and insidious, more like totalitarianism for a new century.

HEMINGWAY

I doubted capitalism, but before it was over I doubted most everything. When I was a boy someone told me we had to eat a ton of it in our lives so it was better to eat it fast and get it over. So I ate it fast but then I found you were expected to eat it all your life. But sometimes I reacted a little and said, "I am very sorry, gentlemen, but I am not hungry today." Confirmed, or patriotic, shit eaters never forgive this deviation. You are alone, finally, and create your own test of virtue.

MAILER

I no longer think it's capitalism per se. It's corporate capitalism killing us all, extorting us spiritually and denying the opportunity to find our true growth. Small business, honest competition—or mostly honest—isn't the clear and present danger; it's another sort of capitalism we've used to betray democracy by a vast obeisance to the corporation and its self-perpetuating powers. It's what Islam fears, that empire of the corporation, devouring other nations' economies, infiltrating them, a cultural invasion ultimately backed up by military invasion. And it's nationalism—America's phony patriotism-become-religion.

Listen, Ernest, a poll taken by the European edition of *Time* in 2003 asked what country poses the greatest danger to the world: The United States gets 84 percent, Iraq 8 percent, North Korea 7 percent, and so on. We're too arrogant to see ourselves as others see us. We haven't the humility to consider our own flaws, to see our own stables are overflowing.

HEMINGWAY

Of course the wealthy, the powerful, are never going to change a world they control and benefit from. My sympathies have always been with the exploited working people, never the absentee landlords. I never followed fashions or orthodoxies in politics, letters, religion, or anything. If the boys swing to the left in literature, you may make a small bet the next swing will be to the right and some of the same yellow bastards will swing both ways.

MAILER

Well, I considered myself a left-conservative. So fuck off, Jack. But in fact I always seemed to be swinging in the opposite direction from the pendulum.

HEMINGWAY

There is no left and no right in writing. There is only good and bad writing. And characters in fiction have to be people, people, people; never symbols. Would as soon machine-gun left, right, or center any political bastards who do not work for a living—anybody who makes a living by politics or not working.

MAILER

But a writer can still go down fighting. In America the problem is that serious writers are so marginalized, so endangered, they can weed out the cant and bullshit with impunity. And the prosperous are wonderfully creative in their self-exculpations. They find more ways to forgive what they're doing than we can count. Also as true in the Islamic world as it was in the old Soviet Union.

HEMINGWAY

We were all communists in the early 1920s, but communism turned out to be tripe and tyranny, as did fascism. Hitler proved that war is the health of the fascist state, which must have war or threat of war to keep the state going. When a church becomes a state or a state a church you get the tyranny of all combines. But everybody has to go through some political or religious faith sooner or later.

MAILER

As I always say, "Once a philosopher. . . ."

HEMINGWAY

You can speak out against it all, but don't expect to make any difference.

MAILER

Not anymore. The CEO will listen and be polite, but he's laughing at you. He's enjoying his yacht, his airplane, his wine cellar, his private golf instruction. Meanwhile you talk or write yourself blue. If we writers had the public's attention, they'd probably line us up and shoot us.

HEMINGWAY

That's why the serious novel finally *is* dead. But every phase of the whole racket has always been so disgusting you feel like vomiting. Publishers are writers' natural enemies. So how do you like it now, gentlemen?

MAILER

Still, the work alone keeps you alive and moving. Serious fiction, if anybody would read it, raises for writer and reader not facts or final answers but questions, better questions that are harder to answer, but that you pursue in the hope the questions lead to richer insights, and in turn bring forth sharper questions.

But no one cares, even if a rare serious novelist this century might sell more copies of his than, say, you or Faulkner, the novelist is not revered; he or she no longer has that prodigious impact and influence on the young. So, as well, the language deteriorates, becomes less eloquent, less metaphorical, less salient, less poignant, and a curious deadening of the human spirit comes seeping in. And the most interesting and subtle moral questions—the questions for that time and place—go unasked, uncontemplated. The serious novel's antipathy to corporate capitalism is eviscerated, rendered impotent, and our minds grow dull and unable to withstand the onslaughts and blandishments of the Corpstate.

HEMINGWAY

But you wrote till the end. As I did. I had to write to be happy whether I got paid for it or not. But it is a hell of a disease to be born with. I liked to do it. That made it from a disease into a vice. Then I wanted to do it better than anybody had ever done it, which made it into an obsession. An obsession is terrible, but to work was the thing, the one thing that always made you feel good. You don't know how it will come out, but you also know only some of those who practiced the arts are alive long after a country is gone. One thousand years makes economics and politics silly, but art endures. Yet it is very difficult to do and now it is not fashionable, and must never be fashionable art anyway. But working you get that sense of well-being that is so much more pleasant to have than to hear about.

I wrote even when I couldn't write anymore. I had nothing left. I cracked up, and still I scribbled, however inane and formless the scribbling, until I couldn't even inanely scribble anymore. All who manage somehow to survive look forward to death by defeat, our bodies gone, our world destroyed.

MAILER

Your doctors were jerks, and you abused your brain and body even more than I did, Ernest. Which is saying something considerable! Decades of alcoholism, and you add to that your repeated brain trauma, reserpine, followed finally by shock therapy.

HEMINGWAY

I don't have any excuses anymore, and I no longer need them. We all have our demons. I'm not alone in that. I fought all my life and never defeated them, just holding the bastards at bay. Every damned thing is your own fault if you're any good. Listen, I'm all right with my conscience. I know just what kind of a son of a bitch I am, or was, but I know what I did well and did badly.

MAILER

I didn't suffer depression and dementia as you did, even as I grew more and more pessimistic. My only way to beat the devil was to work with a vengeance, still trying yet again for the big trilogy, as you had tried.

———

HEMINGWAY

I never finished the big trilogy either, but I had to have the confidence of a champion to try for it. Trilogies are the big thing: like Father, Son, and Holy Ghost.

MAILER

My lesser books appeared along the way. But I finally learned to lay certain things to rest. Working, I grew more composed, more settled, but more whole with augmented authorial ambition.

HEMINGWAY

Maybe because you were such a psycho, Norman, you exorcised many of your demons.

MAILER

So my rants on paper and on screen served a purpose? Wouldn't it be nice to think so.

HEMINGWAY

Maybe that's one way to survive. Open the sluices for more serious work to follow. In that you were often distracted but more fortunate than I was. Doesn't fucking make you Mr. Tolstoy.

MAILER

Merely a surviving truth-teller, as I saw it, stirring up a murmur of dissent here and there. In my time such a murmur was the best anyone could hope for.

HEMINGWAY

So make your peace with it, Norman. Be at rest. The world goes on, and we are beyond it. Take solace in that. Like me, you've earned solace. Those whose lives we messed up while we were messing up our own have their own bills to pay, as we do. When I couldn't even compose a few lines after Kennedy's inauguration for a collection of tributes, I began to put it all behind me and welcome death, finally. I turned at that pass to Milton and found solace and my courage, saying with Samson in the *Agonistes:*

My hopes fall flat: Nature within me seems
In all her functions weary of herself;
My race of glory run, and race of shame,
And I shall shortly be with them that rest.

> *A boat under a large single square sail—the simian gargoyle hanging from the bow like a figurehead—looms through the river fog (breaking up now) like an image on a screen. The Greyhound returns and stands on the river's edge looking intently at the boat. Both men stand up.*
>
> *Fade out to darkness.*

9

MAILER AND JOSEPH ELLIS

Unsettling Dialogues on Democracy

Nothing but integrity in private and justice in public bodies can preserve
a republic. If calamities are necessary to teach us wisdom and virtue, I
wish God would rain down showers of them upon us.
—BENJAMIN RUSH to John Adams, January 17, 1778

uring the final four years of his life Norman Mailer (1923–
2007) wanted to clarify his ideas regarding two of his central
concerns as a writer and public intellectual. To do so he opened
three dialogues. His book *On God: An Uncommon Conversation*
(2007) was a conversation with his archivist and authorized biographer J.
Michael Lennon on Mailer's metaphysical and philosophical speculations
as they had evolved since the 1950s. He also published two other nonfiction
books, both on American politics and democracy—*Why Are We at War?*
(2003) and *The Big Empty* (2006). The books on democracy opened a final dialogue with his compatriots, including the younger generations. In
the former, Mailer was in conversation with his friend Dotson Rader in
part 1, speaking with members of The Commonwealth Club in San Francisco in part 2, and in conversation with *The American Conservative* magazine about "Why I am a left conservative" in part 3 . In the case of *The
Big Empty,* he engaged in a dialogue particularly with the generation then
coming into full adulthood because the book is composed of conversations
between Mailer and his youngest child, John Buffalo Mailer, who was not
quite thirty when the book was published. "Because the younger genera-

tions are more attuned to learning from film, television, and the Internet," John writes in his introduction to *The Big Empty*, "our understanding of the past is more easily manipulated by the increasingly sophisticated political and media marketing techniques used by those who hold power today. This is why it is so important that we have these conversations with the older generations" (Mailer and Mailer x).

The political books offer Mailer's thoughts on democracy in the twentieth-first century based on a lifetime of writing about American democracy and participating in it. In articles and books, he had been covering presidential primaries and conventions since the early 1960s. He ran for mayor of New York City on the Democratic ticket in 1969, once campaigning vociferously beneath the statue of George Washington at Federal Hall on Wall Street and Nassau, where Washington took his oath of office. (Mailer had hoped that a Left-Right city coalition might "make a dent in the entrenched power . . . of the corporate center"). He was one of the earliest activists against the Vietnam War. And as a member of the "Greatest Generation" who fought as an infantryman in the Philippines during World War II, one can say that he also fought for democracy against the juggernaut of global fascism. It is striking how Mailer returns in these late nonfiction books to many of the questions the founding fathers and mothers faced in the eighteenth century. To Mailer, having the *dialogue* itself was the necessary thing, as it was to the Founders as well.

By 2018 we American citizens (left, right, and center) had come to believe that our democracy was in crisis, that we might be living, once again, in "times that try men's souls." Into our arguments over the nature and fate of our democracy, renowned historian Joseph Ellis inserted his new book examining the original debates among the Founders and extended their dialogue to us as well, *American Dialogue: The Founders and Us*. Ellis's book served as a crash course in the processes, compromises, hopes, failings, and fears of the Founders. Through a technique of alternating chapter sections between *then* and *now,* Ellis reestablishes the relevance of the founding dialogues for our own time.

Mailer in his two books was performing a similar service for his fellow citizens, though he was not as explicit in that purpose as Ellis is. But it is remarkable how much similar territory all three books cover as they awaken us to our democratic fundamentals in the opening decades of the new century. For both Mailer and Ellis, reopening our dialogue on democracy is the key to reclaiming a vital democracy. (It is perhaps fortuitous for our democracy that the National Archives recently created a digitized version of the more extensive founding dialogues—even beyond the debates that ended in the Declaration and the Constitution, beyond the better-known correspondence between Jefferson and Adams, and beyond the Federalist Papers—among six major founding correspondents in "The Founders On-line" project, available at https://Founders.archives.gov).

Three topics both Mailer and Ellis consider (as did the Founders) are among the most significant—our fragile democracy, our economic inequality, and our foreign policy. These three political concerns are, of course, mutually interactive.

The fragility of democracy (especially as it is susceptible to fascistic temptations) is a sort of undercurrent through much of Mailer's work, starting with *The Naked and the Dead* (1948) and ending with *The Castle in the Forest* (2006), but for our purposes I want to look at Mailer's straightforward reflections as he approached the end of his life. In 2003, Mailer argued that compulsive, self-serving patriotism was odious. "When you have a great country it's your duty to be critical of it so it can become even greater." He believed, however, that we were becoming more arrogant and vainer, both "culturally and emotionally."

> When America began, it was the first time in the history of civilization that a nation dared to make an enormous bet founded on this daring notion—that there is more good than bad in people. . . . Now we have to keep reminding ourselves that just because we've been a democracy, it doesn't guarantee we're going to continue to be one. Democracy is existential. . . . It changes all the time. That's one reason I detest promiscuous patriotism. You don't take democracy for granted. It is always in peril. (*Why Are We at War?* 15–16)

He saw our promiscuous flag-waving as one way of taking democracy for granted: "You take a monarchy for granted, or a fascist state. You have to" (17). Compulsive flag-waving is no better than "compulsive adoration of our leaders," which adoration Mailer calls "poison" for democracies (85). Likewise, if you love your country indiscriminately, "critical distinctions begin to go. And democracy depends on those distinctions" (108). You can be patriotic, you can love your country, you can put your life at risk defending it, and you can still be critical of it. It is precisely because democracy is "beautiful" and "noble" that it is always endangered, always "perishable." Mailer writes: "I think the natural government for most people, given the uglier depths of human nature, is fascism. . . . Democracy is a state of grace attained only by those countries that have a host of individuals not only ready to enjoy freedom but to undergo the heavy labor of maintaining it" (70–71). One of the greatest threats to our democracy is the "mega-corporation," ever doing its "best to appropriate our thwarted dreams with their elephantiastical conceits" (75). This threat is a reference to what Mailer has been identifying since the mid-sixties as "corporate totalitarianism."

The fragility theme is also central to Mailer's dialogues with his son John in *The Big Empty*. Again, fascism is a palpable danger, but, if it does come to America, it will not be comparable to what happened in Germany during the 1930s as, much to Mailer's annoyance, people keep suggesting. It will, instead, approach slowly, won't be called fascism, won't have party men in uniform. And we will allow it to develop here ourselves, whether we are Left or Right, if we keep acting stupidly (100–101). We seem too ready not to investigate the difficult questions but search for quick answers, and patriotism "gobbled up, sentimentalized, and thereby abased is one of the most powerful single forces to proliferate stupidity" (98). We have already made the shift from a country in love with "freedom and creativity (in constant altercation with those other Americans who want rule and order) into a country that's now much more interested in power" (123). He sees ominous signs in the collaborations of church (fundamentalism), state, and corporation. Capitalism per se is not the problem. Small businesses can be creative, useful, and don't seek vast power. It is the marriage of the state with corporate capitalism or finance capitalism that poses the threat (211–12). And corporations and their greed in turn are handmaidens to empire.

It was John Adams, perhaps America's first "left-conservative" (followed by Thoreau and, closer to Mailer's generation, Edward Abbey and Christopher Hitchens, for example), who was most attuned among the Founders, as Joseph Ellis points out, to the fragility of the democracy they were struggling to create. "In every society known to man," Adams wrote in *A Defence of the Constitutions of the United States* in 1787, "an aristocracy has risen up in the course of time, consisting of a few rich and honorable families who have united with each other against both the people and the first magistrate." As he would write that same year to Thomas Jefferson, who had a sunnier, European Enlightenment view of human nature, "You are afraid of the one, I, of the few" (Ellis 87). It was not a monarchy citizens of the new republic should fear most; it was oligarchy.

Ellis points out that Adams questioned certain beliefs of the French Enlightenment: belief in the preternatural wisdom of the people, the assumption that human beings are inherently rational creatures, the assumption that America was immune to class distinctions so common in Europe. No less a patriot than Jefferson, Adams nonetheless wanted as much as possible a healthy skepticism built into the constitution that would spark the vigilance of future generations as they adapted to maintain the best ideals of a living document. No threats were greater than the ruthless amassing of fortunes and the human passion for adulation or fame. In his 2018 book *Rush*, Stephen Fried juxtaposes correspondence among John and Abigail Adams and Benjamin Rush between 1790 and 1801 that demonstrates their sense that a "system of influence bordering on corruption," as Rush put it, was *already* creeping into their new republic (327, 411).

Adams seems to have retained a residual fondness for the Platonic/ Socratic Guardians of the state, whose philosophically *disinterested* leadership is only for the good of the state and its citizenry. But upon reflection, Adams must have come to suspect that such higher polity was nowhere, never was, and never would be. For without attainable recourse to Platonic Aristos (with their "better and more complete education" and "minds that are awake" and who would never *seek* political office), Adams's default became republican democracy. Democracy with protections against the excesses of the citizenry itself as well as their political leaders: three branches of government, a bicameral and representational Congress, a free press, etc. On the other hand, Adams's fears better reflect Plato's more realistic fears, as expressed in his Socratic dialogues: the treacheries of either tyranny (authoritarian rule above or in defiance of the law by one man's brutal self-interest) or oligarchy (see American democracy, circa 2020).

Madison, the first author of the constitution as the Founders were moving away from a confederacy toward a nation, also saw that only a federal government might have the strength and courage to restrain economic elites, as well as inadequately informed but passionate majorities, from controlling power for their own purposes. George Washington agreed, sovereignty needed to shift from state to federal level. Jefferson acknowledged that only federal sovereignty might suffice, but he insisted that the Bill of Rights and the framing of the constitution assured what government could *not* do by way of restricting basic freedoms. In fact, history would demonstrate that the final documents have led to a dialectical exchange on many fronts between the two levels of government, but as Ellis points out, the Founders believed they were creating a living Constitution, adaptable (with difficulty) over time, not an inflexible, dead document (141–42, 154–59). Ellis's chapter on "Immaculate Misconceptions" is a masterpiece of historical reasoning that demonstrates the corruptions that have impinged on the Supreme Court by special interests who use the misnamed "originalist" justices for their own purposes and against ideas embodied in the Framers' founding documents and dialogues (see 151–70). In *The Three Lives of James Madison* (2017) Noah Feldman also looks at Madison's view, through a process of philosophical struggles of his own and with his peers, of a "living constitution" balancing federal sovereignty with certain rights of the states.

———————

E conomic inequality, then, the Founders saw as one of the chief dangers to our democracy. Both Mailer and Ellis develop this theme at considerable length. Mailer in *Why Are We at War?* focuses on the conflict between our egalitarian ideals and the corporate takeover of America.

Nobody ever said . . . that a democracy should be a place where the richest people . . . earn a thousand times more than the poorest. . . . The people who feel this lack of balance probably make up two thirds of the country, but they don't want to think about it. They can't do a damn thing about it. We don't run our country. Corporate power is running this country now. . . . If we have a depression or fall into desperate economic times, I don't know what's going to hold the country together.

———

There's too much anger here, too much ruptured vanity, too much shock, too much identity crisis. And worst of all too much patriotism. (104–5)

If Mailer was right, we dodged an asteroid when we climbed out of the 2008–9 Wall Street meltdown, but he foresaw some of the angry forces behind the 2016 election.

The Big Empty takes this theme further. Mailer sounds the note early in this book, reminding us that democracy is the greatest of all experiments, and as such must improve or get worse. Capitalism may be stronger than socialism due to capitalism's creativity, but the "foreseeable price" is that "greed becomes paramount." For all its potential creativity, capitalism also tends to dumb down the populace, making us less civilized, less cultivated (10–11). Mailer echoes here a theme in a lifetime of work by historians Charles and Mary Beard: the history of America is the history of the struggle between capitalism and democracy. Mailer describes this struggle as a war between liberals and conservatives. And the left is losing because they are only beginning to figure out that "they can't beat the right with intelligent argument. They need punch phrases that get to the heart of the average American." The right would like nothing more than to see protests and anarchy in the streets as self-justification for the right to advance its causes (7, 16–17).

Mailer argues that true conservatives, as opposed to "Flag Conservatives," feel in accord with the left concerning the corporate stifling of our lives economically, aesthetically, culturally, and spiritually. Corporations *are* The Big Empty, but they have "massive complacency about their own corporate virtues," and our politicians have become their handmaidens and bodyguards (53–54). The struggle against the corporation is profound, and it would take at least fifty years to prevail in such a revolution, Mailer says. We will first have to release ourselves from the economic, political, and spiritual brainwashing that is far superior and more subtle than that of the crude old Soviets. He then quotes Hermann Goering on the ease with which leaders can manipulate a population toward any policy—all you have to do is convince the people they are under attack, that the pacifists and naysayers are unpatriotic, and the people will follow, in Goering's words, "whether it is a democracy, or a fascist government, or a parliament, or a communist dictatorship" (60).

The capitalism of small businesses, however, may be a resource in the battle against corporate power, Mailer suggests. The men and women running small businesses are always taking their chances, leading an existential life, gambling with their wit, energy, and ideas for what will work in the marketplace. The small business owner "may be a sonofabitch, but at least he is out there in the middle of life" (55–57). Small business owners are not corporate executives ensconced in a political protection racket, coddled in their shimmering Xanadus. At one point in the dialogue, Mailer's son John asks whether corporate CEOs and their peers can really be untouched by the economic and environmental crises they enable. After all, they too have children and grandchildren. Mailer responds, "You're not old enough yet to know how various and creative are the self-exculpations in the mentality of the prosperous. They find more ways of forgiving what they're doing than you can take account of" (109). During those last four years of his life Mailer did of course go beyond *Why Are We at War?* and *The Big Empty* to further express his concerns publicly. One example, a sort of companion piece, is a long essay, "Immodest Proposals," originally appearing in *Playboy Magazine's* 50th anniversary issue (2004). (That old issue of the magazine is less accessible by now than Professor Phillip Sipiora's edited collection of Mailer's essays, *Mind of an Outlaw* [2013], where Sipiora excerpts the key passages of the longer essay, now titled "The Welfare of the Rich.") Here Mailer expands the ideas presented in his two final political books, a sort of definitive statement on economic inequity:

> Perhaps the time has come for Americans to stop worrying about the welfare of the rich. For the last two decades, the assumption has grown more powerful each year that unless the very well-to-do are encouraged to become wealthier, our economy will falter. Well, we have allowed them to get wealthier and wealthier and then even wealthier, and the economy is faltering. Apparently, the economic lust of the 1990s has unbalanced the springs. Might it not be unnatural, even a little peculiar, to concern ourselves so much about the needs of the rich. . . . They know how to make money. They do not need incentives. Making money is not only their gift but their vital need. That is their vision of spiritual reward. Not only is their measure of self attached directly to the volume of their gains, but the majority of them know how to stay rich. They are

highly qualified to take care of themselves in any society, be it socialist, fascist, banana republic, or chaotic. Whether they live in a corporate economy relatively free of government or with a larger government presence, they will prosper. They can withstand an American safety net. And they may even sleep better. (Mailer, *Mind of an Outlaw*, 558-59)

Ellis takes up the topic of enormous economic inequality chiefly in his "then" chapter on John Adams and the subsequent "now" chapter entitled "Our Gilded Age." Adams was one Founder who saw inequality as embedded in American society. Unlike Jefferson who thought an agrarian, decentralized polity was America's future, Adams was both more prescient and more skeptical about human nature. (If Jefferson provided our democratic ideals; Adams tempered our ideals by pushing our noses closer to harsh historical realities.) Adams agreed with Locke that political power derives from the people, but he was less reverential than Jefferson about popular sovereignty—despotism could arise from many sources, popular, oligarchic, or monarchical. Our passions control us more than our reason; they insinuate themselves into our conscience and our understanding (71, 75-79). Adams, so to speak, takes Mailer's formulation a step further: we are all capable of dangerous self-exculpations. But to Adams, essentially, it was the "relentless pressure toward oligarchy," as Ellis puts it, that "needed constant attention from all branches of government." That, to Adams, was "the central problem of political science" (85, 88).

A Yankee Federalist who had participated in the debate over Hamilton's proposal for a national bank, Adams saw the serpent in Jefferson's American Eden of the 1780s as finance capitalism, a capitalism Adams viewed as establishing an emerging "commercial republic." Adams looked upon banks as "engines of inequality" and bankers as reapers of immoral profits, as "an Aristocracy as fatal as the Feudal barons." Banks, Adams believed, ought to be public institutions within each state yet under the control of Congress. Our Left-Conservative Founder was anticipating our Federal Reserve Board and New Deal banking regulations, as Ellis puts it, by arguing that the "invisible hand of the marketplace required the visible hand of government to regulate its inevitable excesses" (90-91). Financial aristocracies, like all aristocracies, would use their power to control political institutions for their own agendas, resulting in political oligarchy. Adams anticipated

Thorstein Veblen by locating the financial driver of human vanity as the desire to be seen as exceptional, the *emotional* imperative to display wealth as indicator of elite status, "because riches attract the attention, consideration, and congratulation of mankind" (94–97). If one agrees with Adams (and Veblen), might one reasonably ask whether three million years of primate evolution has culminated in human admiration of alpha-hierarchical status through displays of wealth? Isn't display of wealth one engine of contemporary celebrity?

Ellis's "then" chapter on "Our Gilded Age" is one of his most convincing, cogently presented, and data-driven. Ellis makes fine comparisons and distinctions between our time and the first Gilded Age (to use Mark Twain's 1873 terminology). Not only in light of the evidence Ellis marshals but in light of the testimony of our own senses, a reader would have to perform ingenious mental contortions of self-exculpation to come to believe we have not created a second Gilded Age through the very forces that Adams foresaw and that Mailer uncovers in his dialogues with fellow citizens. Let me add that the most convincing book I've come across uncovering the historical chain of oligarchs, their ideological enablers, and their financial and institutional mechanisms that led from John Calhoun through Nobel economist James McGill Buchanan to the Koch brothers et al. is Nancy MacLean's 2018 *Democracy in Chains: The Deep History of The Radical Right's Stealth Plan for America* (made all the more credible by Professor MacLean's eighty pages of densely packed notes and bibliography to document her historical findings). Ellis in his "now" section of "Our Gilded Age" makes it clear that "the last thing the thirty-nine signers of the Constitution wanted was for the Supreme Court to become supreme. . . . that status belonged to Congress," a *representative* body. But the "originalists" have fallen prey to fully financed campaigns and institutions to wrest control of government through judicial activism masked by verbal contortions as "originalism." Indeed, Ellis reminds us, on the contrary, "The seminal source for a 'Living Constitution' is none other than Jefferson himself" (154–55). Ellis's analysis of how the Supreme Court has abetted the emergence of our second Gilded Age and distorted true original intent on a number of crucial issues is worthy of any reader's close attention. (Mailer had predicted in *The Big Empty* that if Kerry lost to Bush, it would make little difference in restraining corporate hegemony, but Kerry's loss might nonetheless prove on many issues that the real "price we'll pay with the Supreme Court will prove too large" [83–84].) Ellis might not convince those in ideological mind-lock, but those who come to him with a hint of open mind will at the very least be given pause. And if Ellis were to be widely read and discussed, his analysis might have the potential to alter how we perceive our behavior in the voting booth when regularly reconstituting our *representative* bodies in Congress.

<hr>

The third central topic Mailer addresses is American foreign policy. Those entangling alliances and imperial impulses that the Founders also debated. Mailer sees the imperial impulses as taking several forms: cultural invasions with commercial roots, military invasions, and political invasions, the latter instigated by the corporatization of international politics and emboldened by Christian fundamentalism. None of the three types are mutually exclusive, and they all arise from similar hubris. But as expected in a book entitled *Why Are We at War?* the military aspects of the latter two impulses toward imperialism get the sharper focus.

Our cultural invasions, first, "have this tendency to take over large parts of the economies of other countries," Mailer writes. "Often we are the next thing to cultural barbarians. We don't always pay attention to what we are trampling." But what intensifies the anger against us is "how often we are successful in these commercial invasions" (24). His first example is his own experience of McDonald's in Moscow and how Russian students were excited and proud when Mailer told them their Mickey D's were better than our own. But older Russians were upset by Moscow's McDonald's because we had a role in bankrupting the old Soviet Union, communism had betrayed them, and they felt culturally invaded by "our money-grubbing notions of food." Still, it is our cultural invasion of Islam that is by 2003 more significant to us. Muslims feel endangered by our modern technology and corporate capitalism. Our culture, our Western values, seem to them to be eroding theirs. Although Mailer understands that fundamentalism and human nature can distort Islam as much as it distorts Christianity, he believes that we nonetheless blundered in without understanding that many Muslims feel devoted to and directly related to God: "Their Islamic culture is the most meaningful experience of their lives, and their culture is being infiltrated" (25–27).

In part 2 of *Why Are We at War?*, which repeats the book's title, Mailer tries to understand the "logic" of post-9/11 military invasions during the Bush administration's first term. How we ended up going from Afghanistan to Iraq as the principal enemy. It is a complicated tale, as Mailer describes it, but the most conspicuous element is a lack of evidence for the originally announced purpose for invasion—weapons of mass destruction. Mailer reminds us that while the world was reacting in horror of the Bush agenda for war, a *Time* magazine poll (European edition) revealed people's feelings across Europe. Which country poses the greatest danger to the world in 2003? Of the 318,000 European votes cast, the USA came in first, at 84 percent. North Korea came at 7 percent, Iraq at 8 percent (35–43). When our "evidence" for war was revealed to be fraudulent, both Democrats and Republicans by a majority started to believe we could bring democracy to Iraq by invasion. An ancillary benefit might be the expansion of our Christian values into the region, even if our own acts for decades smacked less of Christ's teachings than of piling up earthly wealth. The old isolationist conservatives weren't with Bush, but the new conservatives, flag conservatives, and fundamentalists looked to our striving for world empire as the solution to our own moral dissolutions at home, Mailer argues. We had become, after all, a full-fledged empire, a planetary policeman, a hyperpower whose military expenditures were about to equal those of the next fifteen most powerful states combined. I'm giving the mere outlines of Mailer's investigation of the topic, but readers are welcome to examine it in detail for themselves to assess its credibility (see 35–75).

By 2006, Mailer's dialogues with his son John in *The Big Empty* now had the benefit of some hindsight on how our adventures in the Middle East were turning out. Our "unholy urge to purvey democracy to all countries of the world was not working out." Nor was our empire-building, because "global capitalism does not speak of a free market but of a controlled globe." In the post-Cold War world of the 1990s, the political—and economic and military—"exceptionalists" felt the "need for America to become a Roman power in contrast to other nations who will serve as our hardworking Greeks. . . ." (41, 150). To a large extent, George W. Bush was their man. (See esp. pages 71–77 for an extended analysis of Bush and his administration for some of the root causes of our twenty-first-century adventures in imperialism.) George W. Bush had something to prove, in relation to his father, in relation to his own vacuous military service, in relation to his corporate and fundamentalist enablers. In one of several moments in both books of what we can now see as prescience, Mailer asks, "How clear will it be in the awareness of Middle America that Kerry was a combat hero and Bush was a National Guard flight suit? It will be interesting to see how the Republicans will look to tarnish Kerry's war record" (47). Mailer hoped that our failures to expand Pax Americana into the Middle East and elsewhere during and since the Cold War might make for a chastened view of our "exceptional" status and powers, might dampen our willingness to expend blood and treasure for the foreseeable future. Certainly, one element of the rise of Left and Right populism is populism's isolationist tendencies that could be bearing Mailer's hopes out, but as yet we are still enmeshed in (if struggling to end) decades of our miscalculations in the Middle East.

In his "Abroad" section of chapter 4, Ellis considers the founding roots of our Americans' isolationist preferences. Preferences that should temper our opposing compulsion toward global empire-building. I would summarize it this way: Between them, George Washington and John Adams developed a theory of isolationism abroad and imperial expansionism at home. Adams wanted "commercial relations with all foreign nations but diplomatic relations with none," as Ellis puts it. Adams feared involvement with the convulsions and controversies of Europe, and Washington, agreeing, wanted the new republic to focus on expansion into the western frontier. Both wanted to avoid entanglements—and especially wars—abroad. Maintaining neutrality during the war between Great Britain and France in 1793 was the first example, despite our agreements with France in the Franco-American Treaty of 1778, a treaty resulting from France's crucial help during our own revolution (192–93).

But how can democracy function as an imperial power? It can't on a global level; expansion westward, however, would enhance the building of our own nation. That was Washington's conclusion. The western domain and its natural resources were to be the economically depleted new nation's post-revolution prize and the source of its independence. The prize also would provide a spacious welcome to European refugees escaping war, poverty, and the oppressions of monarchy. Immigration was desirable. Immigrants in the western territories would become citizens. Such would be Jefferson's argument also for the Louisiana Purchase—a way to extend his agrarian ideals. Jefferson would be asked to chair the committee preparing a temporary government for the western territories, "where neither slavery nor hereditary titles would be permitted" (175–81).

Of course, human fallibility being what it is, political problems arose early and late: The conflicts over whether slavery could be expanded westward; the moral debates over "conquest theory" in the taking of Native American lands; the lurking dangers of European powers who had certain claims to the West. Washington and General Henry Knox struggled to maximize Native American rights. The Treaty of New York (1790) with the Creeks seemed to be a model moral and political breakthrough. (Ellis points out that Abigail Adams, who had been made an honorary Creek and given the name Mammea, looked over the treaty proceedings from the gallery of Federal Hall). But politics being politics, the terms broke down almost immediately when the Georgia legislature defied federal jurisdiction and allowed settlers to pour over the sanctioned border (185–91). And the coming generations of the nineteenth century would violate Native American rights more horrifically than the founding generation.

Ellis boldly takes on the contradictions of American freedom and slavery and of Native American conquest. These are complicated issues, and I recommend that readers turn to Ellis to understand the nuances and political complexities, the conflicting human follies and nobilities at play. For our purposes, we might say that the horrors perpetrated by subsequent generations in the conquest of western territories over the next century were inexcusable, even if given the troubling history of human nature we might find them unsurprising. There were those Founders who fought for greater rights for slaves and native peoples; there were those who fought against them. There were those who were living contradictions of both positions.

But it is hard for us in the twenty-first century to remember that our nation's Founders (flawed human beings like ourselves) were emerging in their corner of the Western Enlightenment from a five-thousand-year *global history* of normalized warfare, conquest, captivity, enslavement, torture, and slaughter of innocents practiced across many racial, ethnic, tribal, and geopolitical lines. Founders such as the active abolitionist

Dr. Benjamin Rush were of course exceptional but not alone in 1780s and '90s America. For example, Stephen Fried points out in *Rush: Revolution, Madness and the Visionary Doctor Who Became a Founding Father* that Benjamin Franklin and John Dickinson joined with Rush in their early abolitionism. Rush not only fought for the emancipation of slaves but for the formal education of African Americans, women, and immigrants; he was also instrumental with Jefferson in passage of Article VI of the Constitution furthering religious freedom in the new democracy. Rush also wrote the first book in America on mental illness and addiction, against the horrific incarceration and treatment of the mentally ill common at the time.

That the Founders as an assembly were able to do only so little in their moment to solve such an historical train of abuses of what we now call human rights—that their best instincts were crushed by the politics and compromise of their worst—we can hold against them. That they began the political processes and the debates that would expand human rights for future generations perhaps we can conditionally credit them. Some progress has been made, but it's not as if the generations that followed the Founders, right into our own in the twenty-first century, have resolved what feel like eternal problems of racism and greed. Let alone the problems of looming economic and environmental crises we are leaving for the generations who follow us. Nonetheless, we should learn from the Founders' skepticisms, built into their debates and founding documents, that global imperialism, the sort of American empire-building begun in the nineteenth century and accelerating since the Second World War, would place our own homeland security and sovereignty in danger.

Washington's "Farewell Address," as Ellis points out, is the key document here. The Jay Treaty (1796) had negotiated the removal of British troops (who were inciting Indian wars) from the frontier and paying off America's debts to Britain. But the political imbroglio that accompanied the treaty's passage shook Washington deeply. He now saw the enormous, baleful potential for demagoguery in domestic politics, especially over foreign policy, that could threaten the new republic. "The great rule of conduct for us in regard to foreign relations," Washington said in farewell, "is in extending our commercial relations, to have them with as little political connection as possible. . . . 'Tis our policy to steer clear of permanent Alliances with any portion of the foreign world" (199–201). Of course, that was then; this is now. But might one be forgiven for making the case that twenty-first-century "originalists" and "conservatives" are the last people who should be thumping our founding documents in support of conducting preemptive wars or invasions to transplant democracy or extend American empire abroad?

It is our global empire-building since the Cold War that Ellis examines in the final portion of his book, "At Peace with War," the "now" to the eighteenth-century "then." Like Mailer, Ellis views with jaundiced eye America's hegemonic role, the assumption that we can now create, in President George H. W. Bush's phrase in 1991 after the fall of the Soviet Union and the defeat of Saddam Hussein, "a new world order" that would remake the world in our image. The consequence has been an improvisational foreign policy rather than a comprehensive foreign strategy. That improvisational quality of the policy made us easier prey, so to speak, for demagogues. And after September 11, 2001, we found a new Evil Empire (to use Ronald Reagan's old 1983 formulation) to rationalize the expansion of defense and security budgets, executive powers, and foreign invasion. An all-voluntary military made it easier to sustain a "fully militarized foreign policy" (208–12, 215). Andrew Bacevich, a former career military officer and professor emeritus at Boston University, has also written extensively about our militarization of foreign policy. See, for example, *American Empire: The Realities and Consequences of U.S. Diplomacy* and *Washington Rules: America's Path to Permanent War.* And even Benjamin Rush foretold such skewed militarism in a democracy when in 1793 he wrote a satirical piece advocating a Peace-Office as counterpoise to the Department of War, recommending demilitarization and even gun control (see Fried 343).

Ellis points out that the founding generation left a legacy of American exceptionalism that means the opposite of what that term has come to mean. Jefferson believed, idealistically, that our unique democratic principles would be destined to be spread *by living example* throughout the world. In the next generation John Quincy Adams agreed we could become a role model, but he was clear in a Fourth of July speech that we shouldn't import our ideals and institutions by force: "America goes not abroad in search of monsters to destroy." On the contrary, the Founders looked to Tacitus on the Roman Empire and to Britain's colonial policies as examples of the cyclical demise of empires—chiefly by the overextension of economic and military resources into vast foreign holdings. Ellis summarizes:

These voices from the past . . . constitute a chorus in sounding three clear notes. First, the United States has committed the predictable mistakes of a novice superpower most rooted in overconfidence bordering on arrogance; second, wars have become routinized because foreign policy has become militarized at the same time as the middle class has been immunized from military service; and third, the creedal conviction that American values are transplantable to all regions of the world is highly suspect and likely to draw the United states into nation-building projects beyond its will or capacity to complete. (215–16)

Is it possible that thinking American citizens would have found a living dialogue between Mailer and Ellis on the publication of Ellis's book in 2018 of great interest? Mailer's death in 2007 closed that possibility of a final dialogue between a member of "the Greatest Generation" and a historian who came of age in the 1960s, one generation later. Both men have devoted much of their lives to writing about democracy in America. And as we had seemed to arrive at a state of national political crisis by 2018 when Ellis published his book, the dialogue between the two writers might have helped stimulate a hard look at where we've allowed ourselves to be at this moment in our national destiny. We had to settle, instead, for the charged political season of the 2020 presidential campaign. Maybe Mailer's and Ellis's published dialogues could have some small effect on future debate, but would anyone put money on it?

Isn't a serious, unfrenzied citizens' dialogue on our democracy, nonetheless, the important thing in our historical moment? We would first have to struggle to put aside our ideological litmus tests and our political correctness on the left *and* the right. Mailer suggested this idea when he told his son John: "Political correctness is not a satisfying activity when you get down to it. People may just get tired of mouthing it all the time. It's a boring way to live and a shaky method for shoring up one's psyche" (*The Big Empty* 162). We would have to try to suspend whatever cherished dogmas or delusions we've allowed to close our minds while we ensconced ourselves in comforting ideological enclaves. We would have to give up our cartoons of Enlightenment founding figures as either nothing but bourgeois oppressors creating new forms of subjugation, or as nothing but divinely inspired Paragons of Reason who created inflexible documents that are not intended to help us adapt to prodigious changes over centuries and epochs. We would have to get back to documented factual analysis and to the best science available. We would have to ask a lot more of ourselves than we have for a long time.

And we might have to acknowledge the Founders' courage in rebelling against the colonial system of capitalist empire. Their families, their fortunes, and their very lives were on the line. The Declaration of Independence is arguably the most treasonous document in the history of the British empire. Had the revolution failed, the Founders would have been lucky to be shot or hanged. As an example against future armed revolutionaries, they might have suffered the agonizing demise for "high treason" that John Thelwall, friend of Wordsworth and Coleridge, and other British radicals faced in the 1790s merely for "seditious" writings and speeches arguing for parliamentary and constitutional reform: they were to be taken to a place of execution to be hanged, cut down alive, their "privy parts" removed, disemboweled, and their bodies quartered. Their body parts could then be displayed or disposed of in any way at the King's pleasure. Thelwall ultimately was acquitted by jury, but it's worth recalling in this context that during Thelwall's trial the prosecution held up Thomas Paine's writings (especially *The Rights of Man*) as the epitome of treasonous intent. And we might recall as well that both Founder Richard Stockton and General Hugh Mercer, seen as traitorous revolutionaries, were tortured on the battlefield without trial immediately upon being captured. Mailer said in *The Big Empty* that "courage is transcendence . . . we are obliged to go beyond ourselves, to transcend ourselves, if we wish to rise so high as courage itself." When son John then asks Mailer if courage is a virtue, Mailer responds, "Absolutely a virtue—Make it *the* virtue" (144–45). If we are able to recognize the Founders' courage, it might be a little easier for us to suppress our smug condescension toward them for their shortcomings and failures (for their imperfect humanity) and perhaps a little easier to learn from what wisdom they possessed in their time.

Mailer's words in his two books have been conversational and informal. Ellis's have been more measured, formal, and deeply sourced, if still styled for a general audience. But both men agree that there seems to be a conversation, an evidence-based dialogue, that we Americans have been avoiding, perhaps at our peril. And during any forthcoming American dialogue our raising of difficult, discomfiting questions would be more important to us at this point than answers, certainly more important than easy answers. As Founder Benjamin Rush put it, "Serious men ought not to flinch from dangerous questions" (Fried 425). Might it still be possible for us to start at least by doing the hard work of framing essential questions? At the end of *The Big Empty*, Mailer puts it this way: "Let us be ready to argue it both ways. No authorities exist who have certain knowledge. . . . Often I believe we are here to leave the world with better questions than the ones with which we came in. . . ." (218). These words valuing questions above answers—and valuing further questions to allow for improving our provisional answers—remind me of what Mailer wrote regarding his own anxieties in 1971 (during another period of national crisis) near the end of *Of a Fire on the Moon*.

If brooding over unanswered questions was the root of the mad . . . and sanity was the settling of dilemmas, then with how many questions could one live? He would answer that it was better to live with too many than with too few. Rave on, he would. He would rave on. (458)

WORKS CITED

Adams, Laura. *Existential Battles: The Growth of Norman Mailer.* Ohio University Press, 1976.

Als, Hilton. "Joan Didion: The Art of Nonfiction." *Conversations with Joan Didion,* edited by Scott F. Parker, UP of Mississippi, 2018.

Anderson, Chris. *Style as Argument: Contemporary American Nonfiction.* Southern Illinois UP, 1987.

Bacevich, Andrew. *American Empire: The Realities and Consequences of U.S. Diplomacy.* Harvard UP, 2002.

———. *Washington Rules: America's Path to Permanent War.* Henry Holt, 2010.

Begiebing, Robert J. *Acts of Regeneration: Allegory and Archetype in the Work of Norman Mailer.* U of Missouri Press, 1980.

———. "Twelfth Round," *Harvard Magazine,* Mar.–Apr. 1983, pp. 40–50.

Cowen, Michael. "The Quest for Empowering Roots: Mailer and the American Literary Tradition." *Critical Essays on Norman Mailer,* edited by J. Michael Lennon, G. K. Hall, 1986, pp. 156–74.

Didion, Joan, "I Want to Go Ahead and Do It." *New York Times Book Review,* 7 Oct. 1979, pp. 1, 26–27. Reprinted in *Critical Essays on Norman Mailer,* edited by J. Michael Lennon, G. K. Hall, 1986.

———. "Last Words." *Let Me Tell You What I Mean.* Knopf, 2021, pp. 99-122.

———. *Salvador.* Washington Square Press, 1983.

———. "A Social Eye," *The National Review,* 20 Apr. 1965, pp. 329–30.

———. *The White Album.* 1979. Farrar, Straus, and Giroux, 2009.

Edmonson, Mark. "Romantic Self-Creations: Mailer and Gilmore in *The Executioner's Song.*" *Contemporary Literature* 4, 1990, pp. 434–47.

Ellis, Joseph. *American Dialogue: The Founders and Us.* Knopf, 2018.

Emerson, Ralph Waldo. *Selections from Ralph Waldo Emerson.* Edited by Stephen E. Whicher, Riverside Press, 1960.

Feldman, Noah. *The Three Lives of James Madison.* Random House, 2017.

"The Founders Online." Founders.archives.gov.

Fried, Stephen. *Rush: Revolution, Madness and the Visionary Doctor Who Became a Founding Father.* Crown, 2018.

Geist, Stanley. *Herman Melville: The Tragic Vision and the Heroic Ideal.* Octagon Books, 1939.

Griffin, Peter. *Along with Youth: Hemingway, the Early Years.* Oxford UP, 1985.

Hemingway, Ernest. *Death in the Afternoon.* Scribner's, 1932.

———. *A Farewell to Arms.* Scribner's, 1929.

———. "Introduction," *A Treasury for the Free World.* ARCO, 1946.

———. *The Letters of Ernest Hemingway.* Edited by Sandra Spanier, Cambridge UP, 2011–2020. 5 vols.

———. *Men at War.* Crown, 1942.

Income, Poverty, and Health Insurance Coverage in 2009. US Census Bureau, http://www.census.gov/prod/2010pubs/p60–238.pdf.

Jung, C. G. *Memories, Dreams, Reflections.* Edited by Aniela Jaffee, Pantheon Books, 1963.

———. *The Red Book: Liber Novus, A Readers' Edition.* Edited by Sonu Shamdasani, Norton, 2009.

———. *The Spirit in Man, Art, and Literature.* Translated by R. F. C. Hull, vol. 15, Princeton UP, 1966.

———. *Two Essays on Analytical Psychology.* Translated by R. F. C. Hull, vol. 7, Princeton UP, 1966.

Kateb, George. *Emerson and Self-Reliance.* Vol. 8, Sage, 1995.

Lee, Michael. "Norman Mailer Invokes the Devil, to Take on Hitler." *Cape Cod's Literary Voice,* 18 Jan. 2007, pp. 4–5, 19–22.

Leeds, Barry. *The Enduring Vision of Norman Mailer.* Pleasure Boat Studio, 2002.

Lennon, J. Michael. "A Conversation with Norman Mailer," *New England Review* 20, no. 3, Summer 1999, pp. 138–48.

———. E-mail to the author. 21 Mar. 2021.

———. E-mail to the author. 2 Dec. 2019.

———. *Norman Mailer: A Double Life.* Simon & Schuster, 2013.

Levitas, Louise. "The Naked Are Fanatics and the Dead Don't Care." *Conversations with Norman Mailer,* edited by J. Michael Lennon, UP of Mississippi, 1988, pp. 3–11.

Lounsberry, Barbara. *The Art of Fact: Contemporary Artists of Nonfiction.* Greenwood Press, 1990.

MacLean, Nancy. *Democracy in Chains: The Deep History of the Radical Right's Stealth Plan for America.* Viking Penguin, 2018.

Macdonald, Dwight. "Politics." *Esquire*, May 1968, p. 42.

Mailer, Norman. *Advertisements for Myself.* 1959. Harvard UP, 1992.

———. *An American Dream.* Dial, 1965.

———. *The Armies of the Night.* New American Library, 1968.

———. *Cannibals and Christians.* Dial, 1966.

———. *Deaths for the Ladies (and Other Disasters).* 1962. New American Library, 1971.

———. *The Deer Park.* G. P. Putnam's Sons, 1955.

———. "For Whom the Will Tolls." *Boston Globe*, 14 Mar. 2002, A14.

———. *The Gospel According to the Son.* Random House. 1997.

———. *Lipton's Journal.* Edited by J. Michael Lennon, Susan Mailer, and Gerald R. Lucas. projectmailer.net/pm/Lipton's_Journal.

———. *Lipton's Journal/Correspondence of Robert Lindner and Normal Mailer.* Edited by J. Michael Lennon, Susan Mailer, and Gerald R. Lucas. projectmailer.net/pm/Lipton's_ Journal/Correspondence_of_Robert_Lindner_and_Norman_Mailer.

———. *Mind of an Outlaw.* Edited by Phillip Sipiora. Random House, 2013.

———. *The Naked and the Dead.* The Modern Library, 1948; Henry Holt 50th Anniversary edition, 1998.

———. *Of a Fire on the Moon.* Little Brown & Co, 1970.

———. *Pieces and Pontifications.* Edited by J. Michael Lennon, Little Brown, 1982.

———. *The Prisoner of Sex.* Signet/New American Library, 1971.

———. *Selected Letters of Norman Mailer.* Edited by J. Michael Lennon, Random House, 2014.

———. *The Spooky Art: Some Thoughts on Writing.* Edited by J. Michael Lennon, Random House, 2003.

———. *Why Are We in Vietnam?* Putnam's, 1967.

Mailer, Norman, and J. Michael Lennon. *On God.* Random House, 2007.

Mailer, Norman, and John Buffalo Mailer. *The Big Empty.* Nation Books, 2006.

Mailer, Norman and John Buffalo Mailer. *Why Are We at War?* Random House, 2003.

Matthiessen, F. O. *The American Renaissance: Art and Expression in the Age of Emerson and Whitman.* Oxford UP, 1941.

McCarthy, Todd. "Mailer Gives Film Another Fling with 'Guys.'" *Variety*, 4 May 1987, pp. 2, 13, 14.

Merrill, Robert. *Norman Mailer Revisited.* Twayne, 1992.

Meyers, Jeffrey. *Hemingway: A Biography.* Da Capo Press, 1999.

Middlebrook, Jonathan. *Mailer and the Times of His Time.* Bay Books, 1976.

Millett, Kate. *Sexual Politics.* 1969. Columbia UP, 2016.

Mosser, Jason. *The Participatory Journalism of Michael Herr, Norman Mailer, Hunter S. Thompson, and Joan Didion.* Edwin Mellen Press, 2012.

Nakjavani, Erik, "A Visionary Hermeneutic Appropriation: Meditations on Hemingway's Influence on Mailer." *The Mailer Review,* vol. 4, 2010, pp. 162–93.

Owett, Trudy. "Three Interviews: Joan Didion," *New York,* 15 Mar. 1971, p. 41.

Pagels, Elaine. *Why Religion?* HarperCollins, 2018.

Plimpton, George. "Ernest Hemingway," *Writers at Work (Second Series),* Penguin Books, 1977.

Reinholz, Mary. "A Word with Kate Millett, Activist, Artist, and Bowery Pioneer." *Local East Village,* June 2012, localeastvillage.com/2012/06/06/35371/.

Reynolds, Michael. *Hemingway's First War.* Basil Blackwell, 1987.

Singer, June. *The Boundaries of the Soul.* Doubleday, 1972.

Storr, Anthony. *Solitude: A Return to the Self.* The Free Press, 1988.

Trilling, Diana. *We Must March My Darlings: A Critical Decade.* Harcourt, Brace, Jovanovich, 1977.

Villard, Henry, and James Nagel. *Hemingway in Love and War: The Lost Diary of Agnes von Kurowsky.* Hyperion, 1989.

Vonnegut, Kurt. *Slaughterhouse-Five.* Delacorte Press, 1969.

Welsford, Enid. *The Fool.* Farrar and Rinehart, 1935.

Werge, Thomas. "An Apocalyptic Voyage: God and Satan, and the American Tradition of Norman Mailer's *Of a Fire on the Moon.*" *Review of Politics* 34, Oct. 1972, pp. 108–28.

World Economic Forum, "Global Gender Gap Report 2014." weforum.org/reports/global-gender-gap-report-2014.

INDEX